Kaddishel

A LIFE REBORN

AHARON GOLUB

with

Bennett W. Golub

DEVORA
PUBLISHING
JERUSALEM ◆ NEW YORK

Kaddishel is based upon extensive interviews with Aharon Golub, with additional material from other interviews and research. We hope that there are no instances where we have misquoted or failed to properly credit a source, and respect all of them. *Kaddishel* makes use of subjective personal memories and opinions. We apologize for any statement interpreted as unfair, injurious, or inaccurate.

KADDISHEL: A LIFE REBORN

Published by DEVORA PUBLISHING COMPANY

Text Copyright © 2005 by Aharon Golub with Bennett W. Golub
Cover and Inside Design: David Yaphe
Editor: Kitty Axelson-Berry, Modern Memoirs, Inc., 34 Main Street, #6, Amherst, MA 01002-2356, (413) 253-2353, kitty@modernmemoirs.com, www.modernmemoirs.com
Editor: Fern Levitt, Devora Publishing Company

Author Credits
Gilbert, Sir Martin, Routledge *Atlas of the Arab Israeli Conflict*, Thomson. p.38

Hoffman, Eva, *Shtetl: The Life and Death of a Small Town and the World of Polish Jews*, New York, © 1997 Mariner Books, Houghton Mifflin Co.

Sachar, Howard M., *A History of Israel* © 1976 Alfred A. Knopf, Random House, Inc.

Segev, Tom, *1949: The First Israelis*, © 1986 New York The Free Press, Palgrave Macmillan Inc.

Van Creveld, *The Sword and the Olive: A Critical History of the Israel Defense Force*, New York, © 1998 Perseus Book Group

Yahil, Leni, *The Holocaust: The Fate of European Jewry*, translated from the Hebrew by Ina Friedman and Haya Galai. © 1990 Oxford: Oxford University Press

Library of Congress Control Number: 2004112406

Cloth ISBN: 1-932687-47-5

Email: publisher@devorapublishing.com
Web Site: www.devorapublishing.com

Printed in Israel

To the members of my family, of blessed memory,
who were murdered by the Nazis and their
Ukrainian collaborators:

Baruch Golub, my father,
Gittel Yanoshifker Golub, my mother,
Chava and Esther Golub, my sisters.

And to my beloved wife,
Ruth Silverstein Golub,
without whose dedication and active participation
this book could not have been written.

וְהִגַּדְתָּ לְבִנְךָ בַּיּוֹם הַהוּא לֵאמֹר, בַּעֲבוּר זֶה עָשָׂה הי לִי בְּצֵאתִי מִמִּצְרָיִם.

"And thou shalt relate to thy son on that day saying, 'This is on account of what the Eternal did for me when I went forth from Egypt.'"

וְהִיא שֶׁעָמְדָה לַאֲבוֹתֵינוּ וְלָנוּ. שֶׁלֹּא אֶחָד בִּלְבָד עָמַד עָלֵינוּ לְכַלּוֹתֵינוּ. אֶלָּא שֶׁבְּכָל דּוֹר וָדוֹר עוֹמְדִים עָלֵינוּ לְכַלּוֹתֵינוּ. וְהַקָּדוֹשׁ בָּרוּךְ הוּא מַצִּילֵנוּ מִיָּדָם.

"...for not only one has risen up against us, but in every generation some have arisen against us to annihilate us, but the Most Holy, blessed be He, always delivered us out of their hands."

— PASSOVER HAGGADAH

Table of Contents

Foreword

A haron Golub's life is a consistent story of coherence and convergence: his happy childhood that ended in mutilation and endless pain; his adolescence and journey from the darkness of the Diaspora to the light of the State of Israel; and finally, happiness and a family of his own in the United States. Divided into four parts, this book by Aharon Golub depicts a satisfying life in a shtetl that prided itself not only in the usual synagogues but also in its Tarbut School that nourished Judaism and Zionism, and finally the disintegration of Ludvipol into a cruel inferno during the Holocaust.

Although Arieh (as Aharon was called) Golub's narrative is autobiographic, anyone who went to the Tarbut School and experienced the intransigence of the Ukrainians will be compelled to recognize himself in this story and reflect on his own past. Readers who never lived in Ludvipol and associate the Holocaust mainly with Auschwitz and its cruelty can hardly imagine Ukrainian bestiality. If you compare and "measure" atrocities committed by various groups, you will find that the Ukrainians were crueler than all others.

Arieh Golub makes a skillful transition from the liberation from the yoke of the tormenters to national resurrection. It seems as if the Holocaust had been the labor preceding redemption by the Messiah. Although this is a rather "vague" claim, it is quite obvious to anyone from Ludvipol because the *meshuganer* of the town, known as Dovidl Meshiakh, used to announce this kind of redemption all the time. Another miracle was that Arieh Golub, a child from a loving family, now exposed to permanent persecution, managed to escape his persecutors through the forests on mutilated legs.

The first place of rest he found on his long journey was a kibbutz in the newly founded State of Israel. It seems that the adolescent devoted all the love that had built up inside him to this kibbutz. Although he had to overcome many problems, the proficiency in Hebrew he had acquired at the Ludvipol Tarbut School provided a solid foundation for his integration into his new environment. Everything he had missed during his life among the partisans in the forests, all the suffering his frozen limbs had caused him was now repaid to him with joy and friendship. Although Aharon's narrative and his suffering seem to be similar to what we, the other survivors, particularly the former Tarbut students, went through, his suffering was different and he experienced it as such. The establishment of the State, the transition from the damp and dark forests to sunny Israel was something holy, something truly Messianic, for Arieh. If America became the Golden Land for him, Israel remained the Promised Land to which he is strongly emotionally attached. His is the kind of attachment that Chaim Nachman Bialik described in *"El Hatzipor"* ("To the Bird"). It is also, however, a kind of love that no one else from Ludvipol has managed to give to their children yet. Arieh succeeds in passing this almost Messianic attachment on to his children and grandchildren as their heritage. Having started to read this book because I had to and becoming more and more enthralled as I read on, I can only wonder how this boy from my former school could muster so much strength and love.

I was also wondering whether Arieh, who is younger than I and finished neither the *cheder* nor the Tarbut School, would appreciate all that in the same way I did. Would Arieh reserve the same place in his life for our school as we, the graduates, did? Arieh Golub has managed to remember the Tarbut School in his American life in the same way as I do in my Viennese life as a professor. Arieh is a miracle to me, as is his book, so *yasher koach*, Arieh!

Professor Dr. Jacob Allerhand
University of Vienna, Vienna, Austria
Graduate, Tarbut School, Ludvipol

Preface

Only as you mature and gain perspective on life do you realize what was unique and different about your childhood. Being Aharon Golub's son, my life was necessarily impacted by my father's life history. As I was growing up, I realized that in certain respects, my experiences were different from those of my friends. Some differences were superficial. For example, as a young child, I came to realize that sports played only a small part in our family life. My father did not know or care about the primary pastimes of American boys, baseball and football, which I attributed to his growing up in Poland and then living in Israel. Also, his feet caused him a lot of pain, so though he was quite a good bicycle rider, he did not participate in other sports. When he went swimming, he always wore sneakers.

Our home was filled with the sounds of many languages. My dad would speak in English if all of us were to be included in a conversation, Yiddish if my mother was to be included but not my sister or me, and Hebrew if even my mother was not part of it. On rare occasions, he spoke in Russian or Polish. Although I never heard it myself, people told me my father spoke English with an accent. They sometimes tell me that I do as well.

Visitors frequently stayed in our house for extended periods of time. My father's cousins from Montreal and California would often visit. His Argentinean cousins would come for weeks as they sought out the latest in New York fashion to bring home to their customers. I remember watching with fascination as they sipped maté out of a gourd. Often visitors from Israel stayed with us. My father's friend Ezra, from Haifa, would live with us for weeks at a time as he learned about America. In fact, when he eventually moved his family to the United States, they lived only two blocks from us for the first few years.

Other differences were more profound. I learned that there were two kinds of people in the world: Jews and *goyim* (non-Jews). There were good and bad Jews and good and bad goyim. Bad goyim, the Nazis and Ukrainians, had murdered my father's family and had almost killed him, leaving him with severely frostbitten feet. Good goyim had helped my father stay alive by bringing him milk to drink when he was abandoned to his fate because some bad Jews would not risk taking a crippled child along with them.

My father's personal experience, as well as the holidays of Purim and Passover, taught me that bad non-Jews repeatedly set out to murder Jews on a collective basis. Their most recent attempt to annihilate Jews had almost been successful and had created major gaps in our family. My father's parents and his two sisters were murdered for no other reason than that they were Jews. While other kids read about the Holocaust and understood it in an interested but emotionally detached manner, for me it was very real in the most visceral sense; I saw the damage to my father's feet, and was haunted by old photographs.

In his desk, my father kept a worn gray leather billfold filled with those old photographs of people I never knew. Every so often, he would show me these black and white photos and tell me about the people in them. They were, for me, ghosts of a life and world beyond my grasp and comprehension. My father also had (and still has) a large rifle, a British Enfield 303, and a large jar of bullets. I remember the rifle from the time I was as tall as it was. My father told me that he had sworn to himself that he would always have a gun to protect his family, and if anyone came to hurt us, he would make sure that they would die before we would be taken away. He encouraged me to handle the rifle. His father had not had a rifle, he said; Jews always needed to have guns. Today I own both a rifle and a shotgun.

All things having to do with Israel were a passion for my father and our family. I remember the tension leading up to the Six Day War, when I was ten, and our exuberance after Israel survived this threat to its existence. My dad had many close friends in Israel, and he spoke to them on the phone and visited them, or they came to visit us. While I do not remember a lot of discussions about U.S. politics in our house, I do remember an intense focus on what was going on in Israel.

My father would often talk about what a distinguished and respected man was his father, Baruch Golub, after whom I was named. He would describe in great detail his father's businesses and his active support of the Tarbut School, the Zionist Jewish day school my father attended in Ludvipol, where he was raised. He told us with pride that my grandfather was one of the most prominent citizens of Ludvipol. Sometimes, we teased my father about being from the "aristocracy of Ludvipol," caricaturing it as a primitive little town. Yet it left an impression on me when I heard two old women at a get-together of Ludvipol landtzmen refer to my father with respect as "Golub's son." More recently, my father was seated in a place of honor at a meeting of landtzmen that we attended in Israel. This intrigued me.

My father was, and remains, a gifted storyteller. Somehow, whatever he described became interesting and exciting. This had two impacts. First, it made the world of Ludvipol, the shtetl he was born in, come alive for me. His reminiscences made other stories, like *Fiddler on the Roof*, very meaningful, beyond the fact that he does an excellent rendition of Zero Mostel's song, "If I Were a Rich Man." His stories fascinated me and always made me want to know more. But they also brought it home that in some respects, my father was born to a world of two centuries ago, a world very different from that of my contemporaries' parents.

Learning as much as I could about my father's past became one of my major interests. My dad says he had trouble talking about his past, but I do not remember it that way. Perhaps he felt more comfortable talking to me than to other people. Or perhaps on those occasions when he talked about the past, his words were engraved in my mind and became an integral part of me. Part of my life journey has involved trying to understand his journey.

The summer after I graduated from college, I attended an *ulpan* (an intensive Hebrew language course) at the Hebrew University in Jerusalem. I have always felt that my limited knowledge of Hebrew is a great personal inadequacy. That summer, I had the opportunity to spend time with some of my father's Israeli friends, which made me feel closer to him. At the end of the summer, I almost stayed on for a year to work for the Israeli government.

In 1988, ten years later, I made contact with a distant relative, Samuel Tiktin, who lived in Rovno, a city close to Ludvipol, and who fortunately spoke fluent English. After corresponding with him, I decided to "return" to Ludvipol and see it with my own eyes. My new and accommodating wife Cindy and I went off in search of my roots. The trip was memorable for many reasons, but when I went to Sosnovoye, as Ludvipol had been renamed, instead of feeling a sense of fulfillment or triumph in the knowledge that our family had survived, a tremendous sense of emptiness set in. Ludvipol felt like the far side of the moon, devoid of any personal connection or of anything Jewish, and I realized that whatever I was looking for was not there.

In 1998, for his seventieth birthday, my father and I traveled to Israel. This was the first time we had been there together. We visited Kibbutz Yagur and met with many of his friends, both his Ludvipol landtzmen and the group of orphans he had lived with when he arrived in Israel, who had become his extended family. Along with one of those friends, Moshe Trosman, we threw a surprise seventieth birthday party with over eighty guests. This was a very special evening for my father and for me, and it helped me understand where to find the roots for which I had been searching.

The Book

After hearing about my father's life, whether directly from him or indirectly from me, many people have suggested that he write down his story for future generations. To his credit, my father had already gone through the painful process of giving interviews on video-tape to Steven Spielberg's Survivors of the Shoah Visual History Foundation. But a serious, comprehensive book would lend rigor to the process, as well as incorporate the positive aspects of my father's life before and after the War. His life has been defined by many other forces besides the Nazi atrocities. I also wanted to re-ally understand his story, perhaps because a son has an intense need to understand his father; I have always judged myself rela-tive to him and, in view of the sheer amount of life he has lived, always felt somehow shallow. Such a book would also give my father some degree of immortality which, I think, every son desires for his father.

I am now a father myself, with three young children. But I was born and raised in America. I knew that I would never be able to convey to my children the richness of Jewish history that my father could. He has lived through three important historical eras — tra-ditional Jewish life in a town in Poland on the verge of modernity; the mindless horrors of Nazi mass murders; and the rebirth of a Jewish nation in the land promised to our forefathers. I felt a direct visceral connection to these events, but part of me felt like an im-postor or voyeur, talking passionately about things I had not per-sonally experienced. I believed that I could accomplish many goals at once by systematically documenting my father's personal his-tory: demonstrating that his memories were objectively accurate, juxtaposing his with the intersecting stories of his contemporaries, and identifying the historical context of Eastern Poland, Ukrainian atrocities, and the excitement and challenges of reestablishing a Jewish presence in the land of Israel. I knew that I would learn a lot from this process, and that my father could give future generations the ability to understand these periods in a personal way.

Convincing my father to undertake this project was no simple matter. Clearly, some of his memories are extremely painful. Also, the work would be time-consuming and considerable. There would be interviews, edits, questions, and interactions with friends, especially around contradictory recollections or unflattering memories; all of these would be draining. For quite a while, serious medical problems prevented my father from feeling up to the task. Fortunately, after a series of major medical procedures and operations, all of which turned out successfully, my father was ready to proceed.

I was fortunate to come into contact with Kitty Axelson-Berry from Modern Memoirs, which is specifically in the business of writing and publishing commissioned personal memoirs. Although the project I had in mind was of a different scale and scope than those the company had undertaken before, she enthusiastically agreed to work with my father and me. While I certainly wanted to capture my father's personal story in his own words, my goal was to create a document involving a high level of research and scholarship. Personal recollections, particularly after sixty years, can fade, and my father's perspective of pre-war Ludvipol was primarily that of a ten- to thirteen-year-old boy. As the father of two ten-year-olds, I had a sense of how he must have perceived his daily life at that age. I also wanted to be sensitive to the innocence and poignancy of his retelling of his childhood, given how tragically things turned out for his family.

Therefore, extensive interviews with my father's contemporaries on three continents were conducted in a variety of languages. Historical archives were researched to capture the context of the places and periods. All of these materials were then compared to clarify what actually happened or, where facts could not be established, to describe the range of possibilities. In that process, many facts were clarified and old memories were revived, resulting in a richer, deeper, and more accurate story.

This book is notable for what it does not contain. Readers who know Aharon Golub might not be aware that throughout his life, he has had to endure constant pain and limitations on his lifestyle due to the injuries he sustained during the War. By the dictionary definition, he is severely crippled. But other than to state some of the facts surrounding what happened to him, his narrative is silent of any sense that he sees himself as different from others. I believe that this speaks to the fact that despite his damaged feet, my father never assimilated into his psyche the concept that he was less worthy or able than anyone else, or that he needed or deserved sympathy.

What is also missing from this book, and not as a result of zealous editing, are expressions of anger, rage, or hatred. One would not begrudge a person a fair amount of anger for having lived through the kind of suffering he did, seeing his own mother shot as she tried to save his life. Even sixty years later, such anger would be understandable. Instead, we hear clearly the positive conclusion my father has reached: that the Jewish people need to be a normal people with their own state, Israel, and have the power to protect Jewish interests across the world.

This story, I believe, matters. Clearly, it matters to all family members and friends of Aharon Golub. But also, since it describes in a very human way a world that no longer exists, a series of purposeless horrors, and a sense of what personal rebirth is all about, the story of his life and times may be of importance to many others. For example, catching a glimpse of Ludvipol raises some intriguing questions. The strong pull of Zionism in places like Ludvipol makes us consider an alternative history, one in which the return of the Jews to Zion might have occurred, had the Holocaust not intervened. The desire and energies of the people of Eastern Europe were greater than the stereotypes often evoked of Tevye or of sheep being led to the slaughter. Tragically, we will, of course, never know.

Through these pages, visit, through the eyes of a young boy, a world that is no more. Admire those few people who lived through unimaginable horrors, and then understand those survivors who went on to create a new homeland for the Jewish people. In the process, meet someone I am proud to call my father.

Bennett W. Golub
August 2004

Acknowledgements

I want to thank and acknowledge my son, Ben Golub, who inspired me to write this book as an obligation on my part to my grandchildren and future generations to inform them of the atrocities committed against the Jewish people in Europe. This knowledge should help them prevent future disasters against our people. It should also encourage them to support the State of Israel, our most reliable protector. My daughter-in-law, Cindy Golub, supported my son in this endeavor, which took so much precious time away from his family. My daughter, Elizabeth, provided important moral support to me during the stressful period during which this project was completed.

My landtzmen from Ludvipol greatly contributed to the creation of this book. I would like to thank those who contributed to the creation of the Yizkor book, many of whom are no longer alive, which was an important reference. Their farsighted actions have helped keep the memory of Ludvipol alive. In addition, I would like to thank Moshe Furshpan, Itzak Gurfinkel, Leibel (Arje) Katz, Pesach Kleinman, Shmuel Shafir, Abraham Shapira, and Yona Tuchman for agreeing to be interviewed for the book. My cousin Boris Edelman, whose courageous actions helped keep me alive during the war, contributed a chapter to this book telling his own story, including how our two paths crossed. I also want to thank Professor Dr. Jacob Allerhand for agreeing to read the manuscript and for contributing a beautiful foreword.

Many of the Dror children, who became my new family at Kibbutz Yagur, also agreed to be interviewed for this book. I would like to thank Hannah Haklay, Arie Medlinger, Shmuel Peleg, Leon Rubinstein, Ezra Sherman, Moshe Trosman, and Behira Zakay for their valuable memories and lifelong friendship.

Finally, I would like to thank Kitty Axelson-Berry for her invaluable help in collecting, assembling, and reviewing all of this material, and for her sensitive handling of the emotions and challenges of this project. She and her team helped make this book both a deeply personal story and a reference source on three of the historical periods through which I have lived. Also thanks to Fern Levitt who did an excellent and timely job preparing the text for publication, both in improving the text and in restructuring it to improve its flow.

The title of my book, Kaddishel, is perhaps mysterious to those not familiar with Jewish customs. *Kaddishel* refers to a son who will, when one or both of his parents die, recite the prayer for the dead on their behalf; the prayer is said daily for eleven months and then every year on the *yahrzeit* (anniversary) of the parent's death. As the only boy in our family, my mother used to call me her *kaddishel*, the one who would say Kaddish for her. It was a term of endearment. I did not want to call my book Kaddishel at first because every time I hear that word I am reminded of my parents' death, but I realized that it is a good, short title that might help people understand our traditions as well as what I went through.

Aharon Golub

Editor's Note to Readers

Readers will notice that Kaddishel utilizes two distinct "voices." Aharon's first-person narrative is based on my audio-taped interviews with him, the transcripts of which were edited, reorganized, and reasonably augmented. The background sections, located in the Historical Background and Interviews, are based on interviews with individuals whose lives intersected with Aharon's life before, during, and after the Holocaust, supplemented by extensive archival research in Poland and Germany and previously published reports. These two "voices" speak back and forth, but appear in separate sections. The background sections located in the Historical Background and Interviews provide additional details or corroboration to Aharon's first-person story. Through this device, the reader can access useful historical information and contextualize Aharon's personal experiences. The statements by his contemporaries enrich Aharon's story and, we hope, provide perspective.

When Ben Golub first approached me to interview his father and produce his as-told-to memoirs, with additional research to fact-check and add context to the story, I little realized how deeply involved I would become in all aspects of Aharon's story and the history of Poland, the Holocaust, and Israel. Nor did I foresee how much I would come to admire Aharon, his wife Ruth, and Ben himself. It was, perhaps, *basherte* (meant to be) that facilitating this book coincided with my becoming an adult bat mitzvah.

It is my sincere hope that Aharon Golub's story will not only keep the memory of his family alive, but will so enlarge our understanding of history as individuals that we never feign ignorance and allow another Holocaust to take place, and never callously dismiss the complex challenges Israel faces in its struggle to survive and honor the needs of its diverse people.

I would like to warmly acknowledge the following individuals for their participation in this project. Aharon has proven himself to be a veritable library of information and a delight to work with, indefatigable in his review of drafts, and always willing to delve further into his memories. Ben has been the impetus, catalyst, and enabler of Kaddishel in its entirety. He provided invaluable insights and ideas, as well as unstinting attention to a myriad of details, including research, editing, and reviews of drafts. He involved himself to good effect at every step.

Also to be acknowledged are the individuals on the team referred to earlier by Aharon. They include journalist Stephanie Kraft for Polish translations, research, and reporting for the Polish section of the book; Hadas Ragolsky for Hebrew translations, research, and reporting; Pnina Ragolsky and Bluma Aloni for Yiddish translations; Laurie Salame for fact-checking and other services as needed; Laurie McClain for transcriptions; Susan Rosenberg for web-based research; Shaul Ferraro from Yad Vashem for encouragement and relevant documents; Sherry Hyman and Misha Mitsel of the American Jewish Joint Distribution Committee archives in New York for relevant documents; Susan Elbow for establishing communication with Zentrale Stelle der Landesjustizverwaltungen archive, Dr. Borgert of that institution for relevant documents; Roger Stenlund, as well as Erkan Emre and Alex Paige for German translations; Shmuel Bolozky and Tal Even for correspondence in Hebrew; Joel Zoss and Jocelyn Axelson, as well as David Perkins, David Quinn, Art McLean, and Steve Diamond for helping copy edit drafts; Art McLean, as well as Michael Burke for proofreading; Jess Meyers for assistance with footnotes; Audrey Markarian for typing; Lynne Adams for complete design and formatting prior to the association with Simcha Publishing Company; cartographer Mike Kirchoff for map preparation; and Michael Berenbaum, Andrew Krull, Elliot Rabin, Jim Wald, and others for reading drafts and suggesting helpful changes.

And last, but not least, the many survivors in both the United States and Israel who so willingly opened their hearts, minds, and memories to us.

Kitty Axelson-Berry
Modern Memoirs, Inc.
34 Main Street, #6
Amherst, MA 01002-2356
(413) 253-2353
kitty@modernmemoirs.com
www.modernmemoirs.com

GOLUB AND YANOSHIFKER FAMILY GENEALOGY CHART

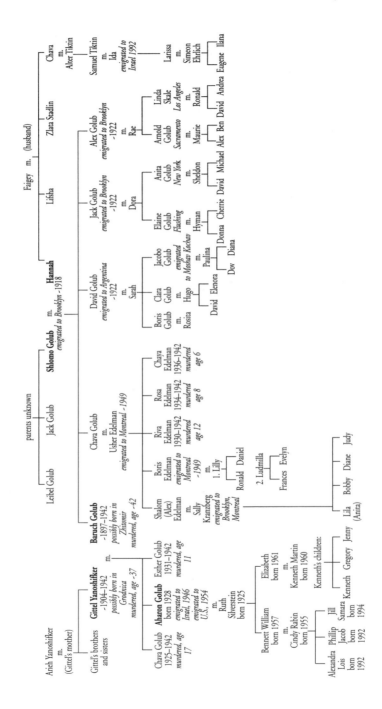

EASTERN EUROPE (1999)

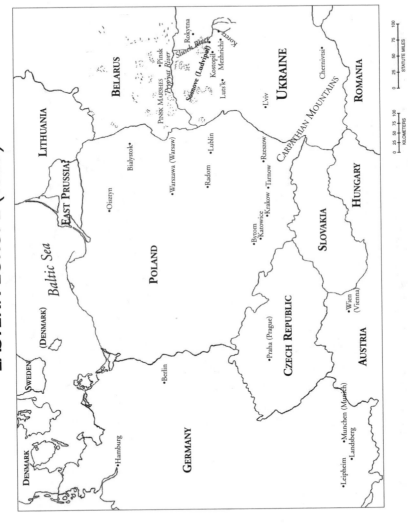

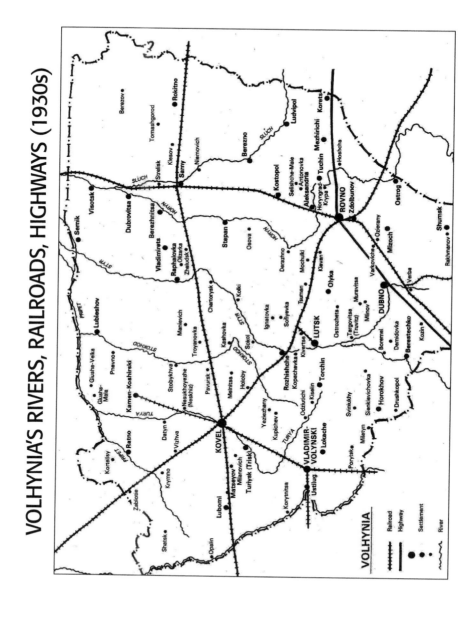

VOLHYNIA'S RIVERS, RAILROADS, HIGHWAYS (1930s)

I

Ludvipol:
A Modern
Shtetl

LUDVIPOL (1930s)

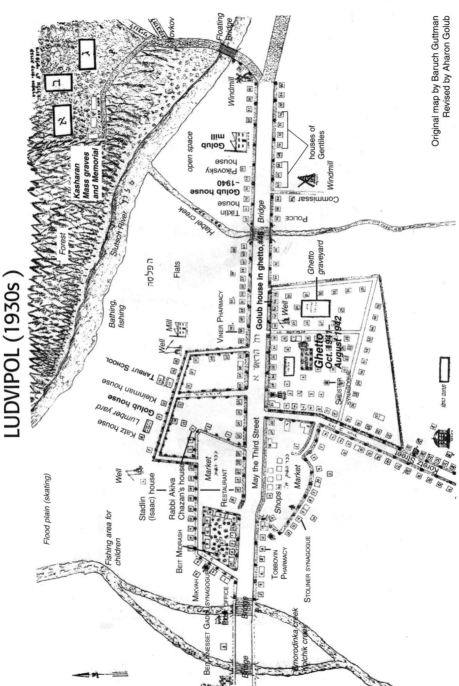

Original map by Baruch Guttman
Revised by Aharon Golub

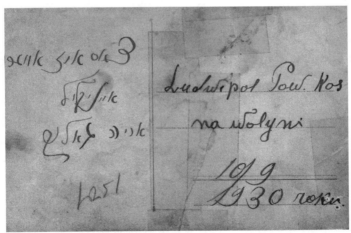

"This is your grandchild, Arieh Golub, age two. Ludvipol, Municipality of Kostopol, Province of Volyn. Year, 1930." Baruch Golub wrote these words on the back of the photo (above) that he sent to his father in Brooklyn. The information was later used to help establish Aharon's correct age.

27

A Happy Childhood

Iwas born in 1928 on the second day of the Jewish holiday Shavuot, which fell that year on May 26. Jews often had names in more than one language; my parents named me Leibel, but everyone called me Arieh. Leibel is Yiddish for lion, and Arieh is lion in Hebrew. Later in life, my name appeared on documents as Aharon, but to this day, the people from my hometown call me Arieh.

My father, Baruch (Baruch in Yiddish and Hebrew, Boris in Polish) was a handsome young man, a modern thinker for those days and a successful businessman who had a thriving lumber mill and granary.[1]

My mother, Gittel (Gittel in Yiddish, Genia in Polish) used to tell me that when my father came by on horseback, all the girls would flirt with him. When she met my father, my mother was already a graduate of a two-year Russian college in a town called Gorodnisa, where she was born and grew up. This was an unusually distinguished education for a woman. She was an intellectual, sophisticated lady and a skilled photographer who ran her own studio. My parents married in 1924 when she was about twenty years old and my father was twenty-seven. My father promised my mother that she could continue to work in her profession, though the family did not need her income, and she always maintained her photography studio. She was a progressive career woman, both a housewife and a photographer.

My father was the eldest of five children. To my sorrow, I did not know my paternal grandparents because they had already emigrated to the United States by the time I was born. Most of my father's family had left Poland, his parents in 1918 and his three younger brothers sometime between 1922 and 1925. It had been a difficult time in this part of Poland, and my grandfather had set out to find a better life for his family. But my father and his sister, my aunt Chava, remained. Chava was married to a successful businessman and my father also had a thriving business; there was no motivation for them to seek a better life at the time.

I know even less about my mother's family. My mother's parents were dead. I know that my mother had brothers and sisters, that her maiden name was Yanoshifker, and that her father's name was Arieh. I believe I was named after him.

Before the war, we were comfortable and we had a good, happy life. We lived in a small, old Jewish town in Poland named Ludvipol. Today, this town is in the Ukraine and is called Sosnovoye. Ludvipol was surrounded by Ukrainian and Polish villages, but most of the people were Ukrainians because this section of Poland was almost a Ukrainian province near the Russian border. In our town, there were approximately two thousand inhabitants, including some 150 non-Jews, mostly Polish and some Ukrainian.

The Ukrainians had been trying for generations to gain their independence. After the First World War, new borders had been established and the Ukraine was split, with half given to Russia and the other half, where we lived, annexed to Poland. The Ukrainians were frustrated to be part of Poland and were hostile to the Polish government.

Meanwhile, Poland was anxious to control the area and bring Polish settlers, *osadnikie*, there. To strengthen its foothold, the government encouraged Poles from as far away as Warsaw to resettle in our area, Volhynia, and gave them subsidies and excellent farming land. Poland needed its own settlements to gain control over the province. As a result, 10 to 15 percent of the farmers were Poles, and there were entirely Polish villages in strategic locations near crossroads or rivers. It was before my time, but I do not believe that any Ukrainians ever moved farther east into the Ukraine, where good land was available. In those days people did not repatriate easily. When I was born, only eighteen or twenty of the villages in our area were Polish and the rest were Ukrainian. We got along better with the Polish people than the Ukrainians, if only because both the Jews and the Poles were minorities; we were friends by necessity.

I loved growing up in Ludvipol. The Jewish community, which consisted mostly of craftsmen, professionals, and shopkeepers, was very friendly and many people were related to each other. Life there was pleasant and the town was beautiful. Wooden boxes full of flowers bordered the sidewalks along the main street. There were lovely areas of grass with benches.

Ours was a small town, but it was a commercial center with numerous businesses. Every Monday was farmers' market day. The farmers lined up their wagons, horses, and oxen near the big square. Each wagon was like a market stand. You could barely pass through the streets crowded with hundreds of farmers who had come to sell their produce: berries, fresh butter, sour cream, sweet cream, and everything else you could imagine. There was a brisk trade in horses and a major cattle market, where the Jewish dealers bought hundreds of cattle from the farmers, mostly for meat. Herds of cows would be taken to nearby towns and put onto trains to be transported to other parts of Poland or to slaughterhouses.

Ludvipol was a modern and cosmopolitan little town, unlike the *shtetl* portrayed in *Fiddler on the Roof*. People dressed in suits; the town had many stores and well-designed buildings, some quite elegant. After farmers sold their produce, they bought supplies. They would go to a hardware store to buy shovels or picks, or to one of the stores that sold horse gear for harnesses or saddles, or to a dry goods store to buy fabric.

Stores did not sell ready-made clothes, other than lingerie for women. A friend of ours, Leah Gandelman, owned a large and beautiful dry goods store, well-stocked with silk fabric and other fine merchandise. People would choose and buy their fabric, then take it to a tailor or seamstress to be made up. The tailor took their measurements, and they would come back to try on and fit the garment a couple of times. If you wanted a pair of shoes or boots, the shoemaker made them for you to measure, although ready-made children's shoes were available in stores. Our winter boots were made from thick, heavy pressed felt with durable leather soles to protect us from the deep snow.

A bus passed through town twice a week and occasionally someone would arrive in a private automobile, which was exciting, but people usually traveled by horse and wagon. Only a few people owned their own horse or wagon; the rest would hire a rig from a local business when needed or they would hitch a ride with someone already driving to or through their destination. My father owned a fine carriage with two horses and had a driver on call.

Everyone in Ludvipol knew each other, and many had lived in the town and known each other's families for generations. They shared life's triumphs and defeats. The entire town celebrated at weddings and mourned at funerals. They helped each other during financial crises and were especially generous to people making *aliyah* (immigration to the land of Israel). The community donated generously to local charities, such as the no-interest loan association, and to international Jewish charities such as the KKL (*Keren Kayemeth L'Yisrael*, the Jewish National Fund for Israel).

The Jewish people got along well with each other. We shared a common environment, surrounded by Ukrainians and a few Poles. Everyone could speak Ukrainian, although the government was Polish and we lived in Poland. There was great respect for parents; one did not do things to hurt one's parents, nor to drastically challenge tradition. Our town was slowly emerging from the nineteenth century without abandoning its Jewish roots and traditions.

In Europe, your position in society was based on your profession and economic status. Social status was very important in our town and everyone knew his place. The poorest in town were shoemakers, tailors, and other artisans, while the wealthiest were the owners of stores and mills.

Since my father was a successful businessman, my family was well-to-do and respected throughout the community. My parents offered a helping hand to anyone who needed it. When community members were sick, a relative would come to our house and my mother would send me down to the cellar to bring up preserves. She would send a jar along because she felt sick people needed a little special treatment and nourishment. After the war, in Israel, when people from Ludvipol would invite me to dinner, the hostess would say to former neighbors, "Do you know who this boy is? He's Golub's son!" This was a sign of distinction, a *yiches*, the Yiddish term for a prominent family background or pedigree.

We lived in a beautiful house. It was distinguished by its shiny zinc roof, which few houses had. On every corner of the house there were elaborate leaders, topped by a decorative little rider sitting on a horse, and drainpipes for rainwater runoff. There was open space around the house and a big side yard. Our garden, which we shared with our neighbor, was behind our house, as was the out-house. Adjacent to our yard was a fenced-in lumberyard, owned by a local businessman named Mr. Guttman, where he stored cut lumber from our mill for people who wanted to purchase small quantities.

Our house had six rooms, but we were required by the government to rent three of the rooms to a Polish officer during much of my early childhood. We used one big bedroom, where my parents, my older sister Chava and I slept. My sister Esther, three years younger than I, slept in the large living room. It was furnished with a credenza holding books on one side and nice dishes, platters, silverware and household items on the other, a serving buffet, a large dining table and chairs and a couch. Our kitchen was huge. Large windows lit the house by day, and after dusk elaborate kerosene lamps provided enough light even to read music. I do not remember specific family heirlooms, but I know we had valuable articles of sterling silver because we buried them in the ground when the Russians came later to Ludvipol.

We lived near the border with the USSR and there was a big Polish army base nearby in the place where the Nazis later murdered all the Jews of Ludvipol, except the few who escaped. The commander of the Polish cavalry in our region chose our lovely house as a suitable place to live. The officer had a separate entrance and a front balcony in addition to his three rooms. After he moved in, we were crowded and our overnight guests had to sleep on the couch in the living room. We were not happy, but we had no choice.

Attached to the house was my mother's photography studio, which had a glass roof for light. There was no electricity. When you were inside, it felt as if you were in a glass house. There were curtains you could draw when it was too sunny. The studio building had its own entrance from street level. My mother kept her photography supplies in one of the unheated storage rooms, and geese in the other. A hallway led to the steps of the cellar, where we stored preserves. A big shed provided additional space.

We had a radio that ran on batteries in our house. Installing a radio in those days involved putting up a huge antenna, built from two tall poles with a wire stretched between them and running down into a drum of coal. Inside the house, we had a switch on the wall. As soon as a lightning storm would start, though we had lightning rods on our roof, we ran to disconnect the antenna so that it wouldn't attract lightning.

Our housekeeper was a Polish girl who helped with the cooking, cleaning, and other housework. She slept in the kitchen above the big brick oven, twice the size of a kitchen table, with a sleeping platform on top. She lit the stove every day. We also had a kitchen fireplace with a long chimney that zigzagged behind the walls through the rest of the house; each room had a brick wall that was warm and radiated heat. The fire did not have to be burning all the time for the house to stay warm. The bricks held the heat well, sometimes all night. We would light a fire for a few hours in the morning and then again in the afternoon when the bricks had cooled.

Another woman brought water every day to fill the big water tank. There were several wells in town. Next to our house was an old-fashioned well, with a big pole that was split on top, and a long stick balanced across it and anchored with a pin. A heavy metal weight hung from one end of the stick to weigh it down, and a pail hung from the other end. You would grab it and drop the pail down into the well. Pushing it down was hard, but bringing it up was easy because of the counterweight. Metal bars across the pail prevented horses from drinking directly from it. The well probably was not very deep, perhaps only six or eight feet. A more modern well had a bucket with a chain or rope that you could let down and bring up. There was a well with a pump in the center of town.

A woman used to come and take the laundry to the river for washing. After she dried the laundry, she would put the towels and some of the linens through a mangle, which was three or four feet long and very heavy. She would lay the towel down on the table and roll the roller over it, then it would be pressed by going through the rollers. Finally, she folded it. Fine linens, like pillowcases, were ironed with a metal iron; the top of the iron could be opened and a hot coal placed inside. It worked quite well.

We always raised large geese that provided lots of feathers. After they were slaughtered, a woman used to pluck them. She would sit outside and handle each individual feather to separate the goose down from the hard central quill, which she discarded. Then she would take the down to her home and stuff the pillowcases she sewed from fabric and zippers my mother provided. Every year, we had five or six new big square pillows. These pillows were part of the dowry when a daughter married, and were the finest that money could buy. When I came to America, I could not get over the fact that people here slept on such little pillows. I was used to pillows in Poland of at least double the size.

I, of course, had to help out with chores. For big jobs, like picking beans from the vines, my mother paid me. Our vines were trained to climb up long stakes, which my father brought from our lumber mill, making it easier to pick the beans off the plant. We stored these stakes in the shed during the winter. Sometimes my mother asked me to bring one or two friends to help pick beans and she paid all of us, which gave us an incentive to work. We played in the process and had a lot of fun.

I performed other chores for my mother, buying what she needed from the store, looking after my younger sister, Esther, and making my bed. Sometimes I resisted interrupting my games with my friends and refused her request. My mother's calm reply to me was always, "It's your choice: you can obey me or deal with your father." I always preferred to obey my mother's request. I would say, "Okay, okay. I'll go and do it," because dealing with my father was not the preferable option. I only got a few lashes a couple of times in my childhood — but just the reminder that this could happen was enough to get me moving. I would sometimes get a few smacks on the behind, mostly for show. If I did something bad, I knew my father would hear about it, and I wanted to avoid that humiliation. Generally, the extent of my punishment was a severe reproach and docking of some privileges.

I remember one time when I was physically punished. My friend's father was a clerk for the government and worked with a Polish tax collector. If you owed taxes but did not pay on time, they came and confiscated belongings from your house. The tax collector had confiscated merchandise, including cigarettes, from a shopkeeper who had not paid his tax bill. One day, we were playing hide-and-seek at my friend's house and we saw big boxes of Polish cigarettes with elaborate filters stored in the attic. It was tempting to experiment with them, so my friend brought a box of the cigarettes to school and all the kids tried smoking them. Word got out, of course, and this was considered a heinous crime by the school administration. We all admitted to taking puffs and were punished with detention. The school would not discharge us until our parents came to take us home, but it took time to notify the parents, and we were waiting for a long time; it seemed like all night. I ran away to the rabbi's house because it was on a hill with a good view of my house. I saw my father come out and look for me, and wave to me to come home. I had to drop my pants and lie down across his knee. I got two lashes with his belt on my bare behind.

Most of the time, I enjoyed special treatment because I was the only boy in the family. In Jewish tradition, when a parent dies, the son says Kaddish every day for the first year and thereafter on the anniversary of the death. Saying Kaddish is a way for a child to add merit to the soul of his parent, so that it can go to a higher level in heaven. People used to be petrified of dying and having no one to say Kaddish for them, but they felt safe if they had a son. Many times, when my mother spoke to me affectionately, she would call me *Kaddishel*, the one who would say Kaddish for her. This was not meant in a morbid way; rather, it was in recognition of this deeply ingrained tradition.

Being plump was an obsession with the townspeople, who believed that chubbiness in children and babies was a sign of good health. To them it was meant that you were well-nourished and amply provided for. Because I was not plump, my mother was always terribly concerned that I was not eating properly. As we lived right next-door to my school, many times she would bring a glass of cocoa to me during class. She discovered that I was so embarrassed by her presence that as soon as she showed up, I gulped it down quickly, whereas at home I probably would have refused to drink it at all.

When I was sick, my mother used another incentive to get me to take my medicine: for every spoonful of medicine I took, she gave me a *zloty* (a Polish coin). By the time I was better, perhaps a week later, I had a whole pile of coins. Of course, she always took it back. After all, what was I going to do with it? I had nothing to spend it on. She probably told me she would save it for me until I grew up.

I used to have to take all types of cures and terrible-tasting medications like cod liver oil. Since people were always concerned about children getting worms, we used to eat something like sauerkraut as a remedy. It was like straw, finely chopped, and it stuck in your throat. My mother used to mix it with jam to try to make it more palatable. I hated those cures like poison.

In our town we had a *felsher*, a folk doctor who prescribed medicine; for more serious problems, the townspeople would bring Jewish doctors from Mezhirichi, a larger town than Ludvipol, and from Rovno, about sixty kilometers away. Their names were Dr. Segal and Dr. Tzitel. Midwives delivered babies. We had two drugstores in our town.

I used to get sore throats quite often, and the local doctor thought my tonsils should be removed. My father decided to take me to Rovno, which had at least twenty-five thousand Jewish inhabitants, about half its population.

We traveled by horse and wagon to Koretz, and from there we took a bus to Rovno, which was a big city with electricity. We stayed in a hotel overnight. My father promised that if I was a good boy and cooperated, he would buy me all the ice cream and other treats I wanted. He took me to the doctor's office to be examined, where they put me in a chair and strapped down my hands so that I could not interfere with the examination. The doctor looked down my throat and poked his finger in as well. I was uncomfortable, gagging, and so unhappy that I screamed and yelled afterwards. But it took only a few minutes for him to decide that there was nothing wrong with my tonsils. He explained that the tonsils help the body fight infection and guard against the spread of illness through it, although in the process they themselves can become infected. He advised against removing my tonsils.

My father then took me into the center of Rovno by trolley car. It was like night and day as compared to our town. I had never been in such a place before. We walked around and went into the stores, where I saw ready-made garments. We walked into an ice cream parlor, the first I had ever been in, with flashing red and blue lights in the windows. A beautiful girl, elegantly dressed, recited the list of available flavors. Even today, I remember how she chanted, *"Seetree nova, malee nova, chekoladova,"* meaning lemon, raspberry, and chocolate. She named so many flavors that I became confused. Eventually, we managed to order something, and my father and I sat at a table and ate our ice cream.

That trip to Rovno, to the big city, was a real adventure. When I came home, all my friends were waiting to hear what it was like, especially the electricity. I remember that when I told them about the ice cream, they licked their lips just hearing about it. We brought back presents to hand out.

The most positive outcome of this great adventure was that the doctor in Rovno told my father, "Don't torture the boy with fish oil and all the rest." He prescribed an expensive, cherry-flavored syrup called *jaleeza* (iron). It came in an elaborate bottle with a little glass measure. Even today, if something comes in a tiny, beautiful bottle, I say, "In my town, no one would ever throw out a bottle like this. They would use it as an ornament." The syrup tasted so good that I used to ask for it. From then on, I no longer had to take fish oil. That was a major act of liberation.

We had our own ice cream in Ludvipol, which we would go to buy on Saturdays after dinner. This was always a big deal. My father would give my sisters and me some money and say, "If you lose the money, you lose the ice cream." I used to squeeze the coin so tightly that the lady had to practically scoop it out of the skin of my hand.

The ice cream lady made the ice cream by hand. She bought a chunk of ice and mixed the ingredients in a big metal container, which she placed inside a wooden pail with the ice around it, and then manually turned the metal container in the ice. We were so anxious for our ice cream that as soon as we finished eating dinner, we ran over. We would line up and watch her turning the metal container, and every so often she would peer inside and say, "It's not ready yet." When it was finally ready she would lay a flat wafer in a measure, spread on a layer of ice cream, and top it with another wafer. We watched to make sure she filled the whole measure to the top. Then she would squeeze it and give it to us. She had two containers and, although she might have had other flavors sometimes, I remember the vanilla and chocolate. We licked the ice cream all around. That ice cream was delicious.

One day, a major technological innovation was introduced to the ice cream manufacturing process. Picture a mechanical carpenter's hand drill. The ice cream lady attached a similar contraption to the handle of the canister, which gave her leverage. With this improvement, instead of standing and turning the entire container, which was tiring and slow, she could sit down and turn a little handle, holding her other hand on top to keep it steady. This was less tiring and much faster. To us, this innovation was a major breakthrough, on a par with the invention of the atom bomb.

During the summer, I used to visit my uncle Usher and aunt Chava, (my father's sister), and my first cousins, Shalom (Alex), Boris, Riva, Rosa, and Chaya. They lived in the Ukrainian village of Bistricht, about ten miles from Ludvipol. My uncle would drive me there and back in his horse-drawn wagon, which took about an hour each way. Boris was a few years older than me, and remembers walking or bicycling between their home and ours.

Bistricht was a big village with three or four hundred families. My uncle and aunt's house was beautiful. Every morning, my aunt, who was young and as quick as a gazelle, would run out to her garden and come back ten minutes later with her apron full of vegetables, scallions, and radishes for a spring salad. They had some land of their own on which they grew their own potatoes and vegetables. They kept chickens and four or five cows, so they had their own cream, butter, and cheese. Their dog was a large German shepherd who was tough; I could never get near him. At night, he was chained to a wire that crossed from one edge of the property to the other, and he could run back and forth across it on his chain. Nobody could cross the property without encountering him.

My uncle was well known and quite well-to-do by all standards. Like my father, he had a big flour mill with many employees. Farmers who lived closer to his village went to my uncle's mill.

I remember some of my father's friends and associates. Mr. and Mrs. Goldman, for instance, were of the upper class of our town. Mr. Goldman, a prosperous lumber dealer, was respected throughout the community. He was a tall, handsome man, always well dressed, polite, and articulate. His wife had come from a large city and always wore a beautiful hat and fine clothes. Their house was quite elegant and modern, with indoor bathrooms, which were a rarity at the time.

My mother was always nervous when the Goldmans were invited to our house for a special occasion. She used our finest china and linens, and wore her finest clothes and jewelry. I suppose she wanted to be on a social par with Mrs. Goldman. In another way, however, I think that my mother felt luckier than Mrs. Goldman. Our family had three lovely children, while the Goldmans were, unfortunately, childless.

My father's business partner, Abraham Pikovsky, a distinguished local businessman, lived in a large house near the mill outside of town. At some point, he had owned the business and the land it stood on. My father bought into the business when it was still small, and it developed steadily after he came on board. Pikovsky had two children, a son named Josef (Yonie) and a younger daughter, and many relatives in Ludvipol.

We had a good relationship with our rabbi, Rabbi Akiva Chazan. He and his family lived atop a hill near us, looking down at our place. We would pass his house on the way to the market square. In the summer, they kept all of their windows and doors open, so we occasionally had a chance to chat with him as we passed. His wife, the *rebbitsin*, sold baking yeast from her house to supplement the rabbi's income, and though we did most of our shopping in a grocery store, we bought our yeast from her.

On Fridays, we always brought our pot of *cholent*, a one-pot Shabbes meal of meat, potatoes, beans, and other ingredients, to the rebbitsin to be baked in her oven.

I am sure that my father found a dignified way to help the rabbi financially; he had a large family with many children who needed food and clothing. Perhaps the rebbitsin was paid for baking the whole town's cholent, or perhaps the town's support of the rabbi and his family included such essential services as this.

I spent a lot of time at the home my best friend, Eli Kleinman, the youngest child and only son of Yeshua Kleinman. Eli and I were close and attended the Tarbut School together. The Kleinman house was in the center of town, facing Main Street. Mr. Kleinman was a hard-working man who bought cattle from the farmers and sold them to dealers for shipping to big cities for slaughter. Between these transactions, the livestock was kept in a fenced area of his backyard. Eli's mother was a fine, hard-working woman who devoted all of her time to the care of her family. She was a good cook and always offered me her famous cookies when I came to visit. There were six children in the Kleinman family: five girls and Eli. The girls helped at home every day after school. Our families were closely connected: Eli's oldest sister, Tibel, worked in my mother's photo studio. His grandfather was our next-door neighbor.

Our neighbors on the other side were the Katz family. Pincus Katz was engaged in commerce. He bought hog bristles, dried mushrooms, and other items from the farmers and resold them to wholesale dealers for export, so he was constantly traveling from village to village on his horse and wagon to conduct his business. Pincus and his wife Razel had two girls, Tzivia and Batya, and a son, Arje. I was in class with the younger daughter, Batya. We often did our homework and played together. The family owned a few cows, and the neighborhood children used to go to their house in the evenings to drink the fresh warm milk, which was considered therapeutic for children.

Another family I recall was the Stadlins, our relatives. Zlata Stadlin was my grandmother Hannah Golub's sister. They were prominent businesspeople in our town. This large family was involved in cattle trading and the meat business. Isaac Stadlin owned a good-sized butcher store where his son Zelig worked. I was afraid of Isaac, a tough-looking fellow, because he wore a white apron splattered with blood and often wielded a large cleaver in his hand. When I went to his butcher shop with my mother on Thursdays to buy meat for the Sabbath, he always made an effort to win me over with a smile. My mother was a preferred customer at his shop, and he always sold us brisket with lots of fat, a valuable and scarce commodity in our town.

I was also related to Alter Tiktin and his wife, Chava, who, like Zlata Stadlin, was one of my grandmother Hannah Golub's sisters. Alter Tiktin was an important man in Ludvipol. He was the Jewish mayor, representing the Jewish community, which was 95 percent of the population (there was also a Polish mayor). Alter was an employee of the Polish government, which gave him high status; our relationship to the Tiktins raised our family's prestige. They had one son, Samuel (Shmuel), approximately five years my elder. They built a home facing the main street on the edge of town near our mill, past the Habel creek, which flowed into the Slusch River. Chava owned and operated a general store in the house. When I visited my father's mill, I always stopped at the Tiktins' house and was treated to chocolates and candy. Our families were friendly and got together on holidays and other happy occasions. Since I had no grandparents nearby, I thought of *Tante* (Yiddish for Aunt) Chava's mother, Faigey, as my surrogate grandmother. I loved her very much and visited her often.

I enjoyed sports as a child. Soccer was our favorite game, but we also played basketball, and I was a good ice skater. We skated on the river about a mile from town and on a big, low-lying pasture that filled with water and froze over in the winter. There were three square miles of ice. After a heavy snow, when the ice was covered, all the townspeople would come out with shovels and brooms to clear and sweep it away.

We used to fashion our own skates from wood. We carved a piece of wood into a triangular shape, then made a groove along the bottom angle or edge, where two of the sides met, and ran a heavy piece of wire in the groove. We drilled two holes in the opposite "platform" flat side of the wood and threaded a piece of rope through them; we then tied the skate to our shoe by means of the rope.

My father once went to Rovno and bought me and my sister Chava real metal skates. We were the envy of the town. Only a few other well-to-do kids had metal skates. Some even had rounded blades on their skates, which worked better when there was snow on the ice. The skates came with metal plates for the shoemaker to nail to our shoes to attach them securely to the skates. To attach a metal skate to a shoe, they drilled a hole in the heel of the shoe and attached a metal plate with a diamond-shaped hole in the center. On the skate was a diamond-shaped knob that locked into the hole in the plate. Two brackets on the sides of the skate held the shoe in place. You loosened and tightened the brackets, opening them to put your shoe in and then tightening them with a wrench. A strap went across your foot for additional stability.

We did not have team sports on the ice — our play was not that sophisticated — but I was already almost twelve years old, so I used to hold hands with a girl and skate in pairs. This was the beginning of adolescent romance.

One time, I was wearing my metal skates and saw one of my uncles, Alter Tiktin, come along on his fancy big sleigh. I grabbed hold of the edge of my uncle's sleigh hoping to be pulled along for a ride, as children often did when a farmer came into town on a sleigh. The farmers did not like this at all. My uncle's driver, not recognizing me, tried to get me to let go, but I hung on. When he used his whip on me, it somehow wrapped itself around my neck. I was not badly hurt, but afterwards I sported a big welt.

It was customary for every household to have a garden. We had a big piece of land with a vegetable garden. The soil was dark and rich even without fertilizer. The garden was divided into sections separated by walkways. There was a big section for beans, and others for radishes, scallions, tomatoes, cucumbers, and carrots. We also had beets, string beans, cabbages, peas, and pumpkins, which we grew for the seeds. We grew a kind of squash that was twelve to eighteen inches long, from which we made pancakes on Sundays. We also grew herbs, including dill and parsley for soups.

We raised two kinds of beans. We ate green beans, like the kind you see in the store, every day. You could open them up and take out the beans, like peas. They tasted wonderful when we ate them raw. In most of the bean section, though, we let the beans ripen on the vine. Picking the pods off the vines was a big job because they grew so plentifully. We all used to sit for days after picking to open the pods and take out the beans. We let them dry out even more and then stored them in containers. The beans lasted the whole year, although we bought additional beans from farmers.

We also grew potatoes. Because we liked to eat them when they were young, we used to take one or two potatoes from each plant, and a few days later new ones would be ready for us to dig up. I remember that we grew a certain kind of scallion, from which we took the green shoots off the top and left the bulb in the soil until the end of the season. We bought onions in braided bundles from the farmers; they, too, lasted the whole winter.

In the spring, my father would send people from our mill to dig up the garden, make the sections and walkways, rake it, and prepare it for planting. Then, under my mother's supervision, we would plant the seeds and maintain the garden. We all worked in the garden, and it was a labor of love. This garden was for vegetables; we did not grow flowers in it, but flowers grew around the house.

Before the end of each summer, we would buy apples and pears to cut into sections and dry in the sun. These, too, would last through the winter. Among my favorite fruits were the plums, dried whole into prunes. Besides buying apples we also picked apples, although we did not have our own orchard, and put them into drums and made delicious pickled apples. I have never seen that type of pickled apples in the United States.

We grew other things, like strawberries that were sweet as sugar. The farmers used to come around selling blueberries, strawberries, and all types of fruit; some of them were picked in the woods, where they grew wild.

We did not have a cow, so every morning we bought milk and butter from a woman who came to our house. You had to provide your own container into which she would measure the milk out and charge accordingly; we usually bought two or three measures. Butter was bought ready-made from the farmers, wrapped in green leaves since they had no paper. You would buy a kilo of butter wrapped in two huge leaves. And you did not get plain butter: when you opened it up, it was an artistic creation. The farmers used spoons to carve wonderful designs, such as flowers, on the top of each slab of butter. I know they did not use a stamp or press because I once saw a woman etching the design with a spoon. They were expert artists. We used to go and buy the butter in the cool morning because it got too warm later in the day.

Even though we could have afforded to buy anything, there were some things that were simply not available for purchase. We made our own cream and farmer's cheese, for instance. We used to let milk sit in a ceramic container that was narrow on the bottom and wide at the top. In a few days, the sweet cream rose to the top. After we skimmed off the sweet cream, we put the remaining milk into the oven to curdle. The curds were transferred into a heavy triangular cotton bag, which was securely tied and pressed under a heavy stone. After the liquid had drained, the curds became farmer's cheese.

We bought fresh dairy products every two or three days since we had no refrigeration except for the cold cellar under the house. It was dug in the ground and its wooden walls and supporting planks prevented it from caving in. Two hatches allowed us to walk down the staircase into the cellar. Inside were many well-stocked shelves. We had preserves dating back many years, mostly fruits sweetened into jams and jellies, but also pickled vegetables and fruits. We kept dried fruits in the cellar and a barrel of sour pickled cucumbers and tomatoes. We bought raisins; grapes did not grow in our corner of the world. Before I left Poland, I had eaten grapes only twice in all my life and they had been brought from the city, imported from abroad. But we had a number of fruits that you do not see in the United States. Some of them I cannot even describe. We made liquer from enormous cherries, called *karsh*, that were dark, sweet, and juicy.

We made delicious *schav* (sorrel soup) from greens similar to spinach leaves. Some people cooked it with meat and served it hot, but we drank it cold. Another drink that enhanced the appetite was called *salata*. It was made from lettuce leaves, romaine or endive or some other variety, mixed with dill, garlic, spices, and lemon or vinegar.

For certain special occasions, my mother hired a cook who prepared doughnuts and fancy pastries. Ducks and geese would be roasted and all kinds of delicacies prepared when we invited the principal of the Hebrew school and a teacher or two, a speaker or other visiting dignitary to the town, or my father's business partner.

We made wine at home, and the wine served at those dinners was usually homemade. I remember the light shining through the bottles on the window sills as the wine fermented. We also made *vishniak*, a liqueur from prunes and cherries. Every house had some store-bought vodka; its production was government controlled so this was something we could not make at home.

The big tavern and liquor store in town was owned by a Jewish man, but because a Jew could not get a permit to run a liquor store, the formal owner, in whose name the permit was issued, was a Polish partner. The partner, who was inactive, was probably compensated in whiskey for allowing the use of his name on the permit.

The Polish government had a strict monopoly, as well, on all other liquors, tobacco, matches, and sugar. A woman was once arrested in town for possession of saccharin. I thought saccharin was some kind of a poison; all I knew was the sinister name and that anyone who came near saccharin was risking arrest. Possession of saccharin was a serious crime because Poland was a major exporter of beet sugar, with which saccharin competed. Likewise, when farmers were arrested, it was more often for the crime of growing tobacco than for killing or injuring someone.

I loved kielbasa, a popular food in Poland, though poor people could not afford it. Today kielbasa is made of turkey and, although I am careful with food, once in a blue moon I buy some, strictly for memories of the old days. When I later suffered from hunger during the war, I dreamed that one day, when I would be rich, I would hang hundreds of salamis the entire length of my house. Even today, when I disappear from my wife's side in the supermarket, she knows she can find me standing by the glass case displaying bologna, salami, and sausages. I stare longingly at them. Here they are by the hundreds, even kosher ones, right in plain view. It makes my mouth water.

Most people baked their own bread at home and each house had a baking oven. My family, though, had bread delivered daily. A woman came to our home with a big basket, so big that it took both her arms to hold it. She bought breads and rolls of all types from one of the town's two bakeries and delivered them to her regular customers. She charged seven pennies for delivering an item she bought at the bakery for five pennies; she earned her living by providing this delivery service.

A woman who worked for us bought live chickens at the market, directly from the farmers, and brought them to the *shochet* (Jewish ritual slaughterer) for slaughter. The chickens were brought home, plucked, singed, salted, and soaked to *kasher* them. Only then were they ready for cooking. I remember many times seeing the woman separate the feathers on the bird and then blow on them, showing my mother that the chicken in question had a good layer of fat under its skin. Polish chickens were "free-range" birds, so few of them had fat on their bodies. Fat was considered a delicacy, unlike in the United States today where we remove all the fat for health reasons. In those days, when chicken fat was not commonly available, it was fashionable to leave it when it floated to the top of the pot of soup, and not to skim it off. If you were really lucky, there was enough fat to render into *shmaltz*, a particular delicacy made of chicken fat with fried onions.

There were two types of oil, the regular quality and a better quality filtered oil favored by the well-to-do. Our family used *baimel*, a pure, highly-filtered poppyseed oil. We also had sunflower and cottonseed oil, but not olive oil, as olives did not grow in our climate. The farmers brought their seeds to my father's mill to be pressed into oil. Massive machinery pushed the seeds into the system and then crushed and squeezed them. Prime, fresh oil would pour out of the spigot into buckets. The seeds were squeezed under tremendous pressure, so after the oil was drawn off, a hard, rocklike rectangular cake was left. This was called *makecha* and was valued as cattle feed.

In our backyard, we raised about a dozen geese at a time in cages in a little shed. Because fat was so prized, something only rich people could afford, we made a special effort to fatten up the geese we raised. We fed them well for four to six weeks. Part of my father's mill was a granary where flour — mostly wheat and rye — was ground for the farmers in the area; we also ground buckwheat into *kasha* (buckwheat groats). A machine separated the raw wheat kernel from the chaff. Since we owned the granary, we were able to feed the geese a higher quality of grain than many people could afford to eat themselves. Our maid cooked potatoes for the geese and force-fed them, stuffing the potatoes directly into their mouths; they also ate the grain. When it came time to slaughter them, the geese were so heavy from their thick layer of fat that they could hardly walk.

Removing the fat and making goose shmaltz was a big project. When the fat was rendered, the crisp skin became the *greivenes* (cracklings). We stored the fat and greivenes in big ceramic pots where it would last for the whole year. I had a special fondness for greivenes, so my mother would scrape the bottom of the pan, where the greivenes and some fried onions had settled, into a special pot that was designated for me alone. Even today, certain restaurants in New York serve mashed potatoes with greivenes. It may be high in cholesterol, but once a year, this wonderful treat is worth the price.

For some reason, we never raised ducks. People used to hunt or buy wild ducks, but of course they would have to be slaughtered by a *shochet* to be kosher.

My family was a good customer of the kosher meat markets in our town. Since we were related to the butcher, Isaac Stadlin, we had the privilege of buying the breast, which was a big deal since it had a lot of fat. People used to render the fat from the cow; it hardened up like tallow. To flavor soup, one would break off a piece of fat with a hammer and fry onions in it. This was considered a great luxury.

Later, when I came to the United States, my uncle Jack Golub was a butcher and shared his store with a produce stand. The first day I arrived in America, I went to his store and saw a woman come in and order rib steaks. After she gave my uncle her order, she left his counter for the vegetable stand. I watched my uncle trim off all the fat from the steaks and throw it in a pail. Distressed,

I thought he was cheating the woman of this valuable commodity while her back was turned. After she left, I questioned him about it. He pulled out a drum and showed me an immense quantity of trimmed fat; he told me that in America it was almost worthless. It would be picked up and sold for two or three cents a pound and melted down. In the United States, this fat was used to make soap or candles. This was one of my first lessons in the many differences between my new country and my old.

Slusch River near Ludvipol (1988)

---

1. Evidence suggests that he was born in Zhitomir and attended secondary school in Warsaw at the Hoehere Schule.

Business associates and friends of the Golub family in Ludvipol. *Back, left to right,* (Mr. Pikovsky's daughter), Abraham Goldman, Rosa Gandelman, Josef (Yonie) Pikovsky and Fruma Gandelman Pikovsky, (unknown), Mr. Cherepipchnick, Mrs. Leah Gandelman, Shneier Tolbin. *Middle,* Yitzak Gandelman, Gittel Golub, Mrs. Goldman, Mrs. Pikovsky, Mr. Abraham Pikovsky, Aaron Gandelman. *Front,* Grisha Tolbin, Itzhak Gandelman, Chava, Esther, and Aharon Golub, and the daughter of David Pildish (1936)

Rabbi Akiva Chazan (middle row, second from right) and his family (Yizkor book)

51

Back, Gittel and Baruch Golub. *Front*, Aharon, Esther, and Chava Golub, in Gittel's photography studio (1938)

Chava Golub, age three (1928)

Chava Golub, kneeling, with her violin (*lower right*), with her Tarbut School classmates and teacher Genya Shnepper (Shavuot 1934)

Chava and Baruch Golub in Gittel's photography studio (1938)

Chava and Gittel Golub (about 1938)

Back, Gittel Golub, Zlata Stadlin (Aharon Golub's great-aunt), Baruch Golub. *Middle*, Chava Edelman, Chava Golub, and Chava Tiktin (Aharon Golub's great-aunt). *Front*, Lifshe Shapiro (about 1926)

Chava Golub (left), with Chaia Verner behind her and Channah Golda next to her. None of these girls survived. (about 1936).

Chava Golub and Yona Tuchman (Tibel Kleinman)
(about 1938)

The Family Business

My father's primary business was a mill about a mile from our house that performed a variety of functions. It was a large establishment in our town, with two huge steam generators, similar to the steam engines you see on trains in old cowboy movies. The engines powered upper wheels that had huge belts going to a series of smaller transmission wheels. By attaching equipment to those wheels, all sorts of work could be done.

When I was a small child, the generators burned wood to produce steam; coal was not available. A few years before the war, my father bought a more modern unit that was half the size of the old one and consumed much less wood. There was great excitement the day it came off the railway, and it was brought in on a special platform. A dozen horses pulled it, and the whole town came out to see. It was a big improvement for the business.

The major part of my father's business was grinding different grains. The mill had a sophisticated setup. Sifters removed the husks from the grains, and we were able to produce all types of cereals, grits, kasha — I do not even know some of their names in English — as well as a variety of flours, such as pumpernickel and white flour for challah and white bread. The farmers usually paid for the grinding of their grain into flour with a standard-sized scoop of grain. The scoop would be dipped out of each fifty-kilogram bag. Because of this, we had large silos full of grain for ourselves, and when the season was over, we ground some of it into flour to sell.

We also had contracts to supply grain to the Polish army, which took pride in its elegant cavalry and had thousands of beautiful horses, which needed to be maintained on feed grain.

Harvest time in July and August was the most active period. The farmers did not have telephones to schedule appointments for their turns at the mill, so they just came with their oxen and wagons, hoping that they would not have to wait longer than two weeks in line. When they arrived, they would get a number and would wait their turn, with their entire harvest in sacks on their wagons. Rain soaked the farmers, wagons, oxen, and grain, and the hot sun broiled them, so my father built a big structure with a metal roof to provide free shelter from the weather. The structure accommodated up to twenty wagons with their horses and oxen, and the farmers would sleep on their wagons until their number was called. They brought their own food and we supplied water.

The farmers used to sing beautiful songs accompanied by a concertina or guitar, especially at night. My father would hear them singing when he worked late. I still remember many of the Ukrainian songs they used to sing. Though I dislike the Ukrainians for what they did to the Jews, their music is a part of my heritage. I still like to hear the music and watch the fantastic Polish and Ukrainian dancers in their colorful costumes and red boots.

The "wagon hotel" provided us another source of income. By the time the season was over, a huge amount of valuable manure had accumulated. The metal roof was approximately fifteen feet off the ground at the perimeter and twenty feet at the center posts. Towards the end of the season, the last farmers to arrive had to climb up a hill of manure inside, until they practically touched the roof! We used to sell the manure back to farmers, who paid a good price to haul it away.

Farmers fed their cows with the straw left over after wheat threshing. Poor farmers would use hatchets to chop it up by hand, but those who could afford to would bring their straw to the mill and have it chopped by our machines; they would go home with huge bags of chopped straw.

Electricity was generated in our plant; it was the only estab-

Luboml WOJEWÓDZTWO WOŁYŃSKIE Ludwipol 2181

Fotograficzne zakłady (photographes): Golub R.

Młyny (moulins): Gurfinkiel E. (par) — Pikowski A. i Handelman L. (par).

Page from the Polish Business Directory (1929) for Ludvipol showing the listings for the Golub photography studio and the mill which was owned in 1929 by Abraham Pikowsky, Baruch Golub's future partner.

lishment in town with electricity. The mill and the lumberyard were lit brightly with electric bulbs burning all over the place. Eventually, when the Russians came to our town, they installed electric power lines and used my father's facility to electrify the whole town.

Telephones and radios used a type of low-voltage battery called an accumulator, and we recharged these batteries for everyone in the area. The accumulator was made of glass — you could see the liquid inside — and was mounted inside a wooden case with a rubber strap. The factory charging area was impressive, maybe thirty feet long, with benches and shelves. People would exchange their empty batteries for charged ones. The charging of batteries was a big business in and of itself, even by American standards.

Lumber was also cut at the mill. The region had tremendous forests and numerous merchants shipped lumber by river to the major port cities of Poland. During the summer, people would lease portions of the forest for logging, and would cut the trees and pile the logs up on the other side of the river. They would wait until winter before bringing them across the river.

When the river froze, farmers, who could not farm in the winter, would be hired to transport the logs across the river on sleds to our mill, where they would be stored in huge stacks for cutting. The lumber merchant would specify how the logs should be cut. Usually the widest center part of the trunk would be cut into beams about four inches thick. Then the rest of the log would be sawed into boards approximately one inch thick. The bark was removed by a circular saw to square off the boards. They would be stacked to dry, with strips between them to let air pass through. There were two or three acres full of stacks of cut lumber in our lumberyard. Then, when the weather warmed up, the lumber merchants would ship the boards to their destinations by river.

My father also bought logs during the winter and when he had idle time left on the machinery between contract work, he cut standard boards to sell. Nothing went to waste — he used the bark and other scrap wood trimmed from the logs to fire the mill's furnaces. A whole row of workers chopped the pieces to size, and fed the furnaces that powered the steam engines. Extra scrap was sold for kindling. All the heating in our town was done with wood, and Ludvipol had many poor people who could not afford properly dried wood. They had to use "green" wood, which did not light easily, and stoves required pieces of kindling of about a foot long. All day another row of workers stood with hatchets and as the edges fell down from squaring off the boards, they chopped them up and laid the pieces out by sizes for kindling. Since the lumber was brought in during the winter and cut all summer, the kindling would dry by the time it was sold.

In the process of cutting boards, tons of sawdust accumulated and had to be removed so it would not clog up the works. My father and his mechanic, Masik, dug a basement with an exit ramp under the cutting floor so that the sawdust could be removed. When lumber was cut, the sawdust fell down into this basement by the truckload. They designed a metal container that they attached to the steam engines, and burned the sawdust for fuel for our furnaces.

Sawdust was also sold for use in storing ice. There were quite a few icehouses in town, dug deep in the ground with a structure put up on top. During the winter, the farmers went to the river and cut huge blocks of ice and brought them into the icehouses. When the ice was insulated with sawdust, it would not melt for a whole year, even during the summer. Ice was used to bring down fevers, to make ice cream, to keep food chilled, and for many other things. The ice vendors needed a lot of sawdust. So everything had its use; even the sawdust could be sold.

My father had many employees and was a very progressive employer. He provided a medical plan for all his workers, similar to Blue Cross, called Kasa Chora (sick fund in Polish). Occasionally, while chopping wood, a worker would chop off a finger or have some other mishap. The employee's medical treatment was covered at no cost to him by the insurance plan.

One of my uncles, Alter Tiktin, owned a floating toll bridge, which he put in place over the Slusch River from April to October. He charged a zloty to cross with a wagon; pedestrians could go free. The bridge was not strong enough to support wagons with huge loads of lumber. It floated on empty barrels, and sometimes when you got to the center, it would sink slightly and water would come up over the edge, although not above the rims of the wheels. Every year, it was removed before the river froze solid so the ice would not damage the bridge and the drums. Besides, who would pay to cross on a bridge when they could ride across the ice for free?

About a year before the war, in 1938, changes occurred near the border. The Polish army decided that certain sections of the country were vulnerable and, as a result, the entire population in our area was required to get new documents. My mother's photo studio was given the contract to provide most of the photographs for these documents. The job involved traveling with the Polish officials from village to village to take pictures of the farmers. She did not want to do the traveling herself, but the contract was so lucrative that my father freed himself from his own business affairs to supervise and handle this enterprise. They hired people to help with the photography.

That summer, when I was ten years old, my father took me along with him for two or three weeks, traveling with a government-provided horse and wagon to the villages to take photographs. We spent a couple of days in each village. Three or four Polish officials were sent with us with their list of all the inhabitants, against which they verified their documents. The villagers were supposed to sign their names to the papers, but most of them could not write so they signed with a thumbprint. Then they were sent to us to be photographed for identification on their documents. The photographs were not developed immediately, but eventually each photograph was identified and wound up on the proper document.

There were many villages with hundreds of people each, so it was a big job. The Polish government paid my father a fixed sum per photo, and every person needed two photos. My father came up with some very clever ways to handle the volume. In those days, most pictures were exposed onto glass plates coated with an emulsion. We traveled with many boxes of expensive glass. My father developed a frame that enabled him to expose one side of the glass, then turn it over and expose the other side, which saved a lot of time and materials. My father had just purchased a Leica camera, which was considered a great innovation because, for the first time, motion could be photographed. But for this job, the older system was used.

Every village mayor provided us with housing, food, and everything else we needed. We were welcomed in each village to accommodations equipped with clean towels and linen. The hostess would prepare us fried eggs and potatoes for breakfast. Bacon and eggs was popular with the villagers and the Polish officials. The farmers had huge frying pans that held twenty eggs and a pound of bacon. We avoided food like bacon, although we did eat on the farmers' non-kosher plates on which *treif* had been served. I believe we ate meat in the evenings.

I found this experience very exciting. I saw firsthand how such a major enterprise was handled. We met many people, and we were wined and dined in villages which I had never even visited. Everybody showed us respect because we were with the Polish officials. The family business prospered.

Jewish Life

L udvipol was a secular town with deep Jewish traditions. Most people were not particularly religiously observant by the standards of Eastern Europe, but they lived fully Jewish lives. Everyone Jewish in Ludvipol followed the Jewish faith, the Jewish holidays, and Jewish customs. People consulted the rabbi when they had a problem.

My family was modern, yet traditional. A mezuzah hung at the entrance to every room in our house. My father occasionally used to pray in the morning, and wrap the leather *tefillin* (phylacteries) on his arms. Naturally, we all went to synagogue on Shabbat because this was our way of life. Our house was kosher and so was everybody else's, but sometimes we children ate non-kosher foods outside the house. Our Christian maid probably lit the lamps on Shabbat, but we did not cook on Saturday.

People observed and followed the rules, but were not ultra-Orthodox. Our town had no Hasidic population. Certainly, no one dressed like a Hasid, except for the rabbi, the shochet, and maybe one or two others who wore the hats or other clothes that the Hasidim wore. Married women did not cut their hair and wear wigs. Men did not have *payess* (ear locks). People wore *yarmulkas* (skullcaps) when they went to shul, of course, but this was not a community where everybody dressed alike.

Ludvipol had all the usual Jewish institutions. We had five synagogues, which were divided by social status and economic class. Everybody went to synagogue, especially on the holidays. There was the *Beit Knesset Gadol* (the Big Synagogue, the *Shneiders'*

(Tailors') Synagogue, the *Shusters'* (Shoemakers') Shul, the Beit Midrash, and the Stoliner synagogue.

My father belonged to the Stoliner synagogue, which was the most elite, although it was not the biggest or fanciest, nor built of brick. Rabbi Akiva Chazan was the whole town's rabbi, but he always prayed in the Stoliner synagogue. Synagogue members held assigned seats, so a person generally attended only the synagogue to which he belonged.

To the best of my knowledge, there was never a conversion to Christianity nor an intermarriage in our town; that would have been considered sacrilegious. In a sense, everyone in Ludvipol was "Orthodox" because there was no other option; there was no such thing as Reform or Conservative Judaism. All the synagogues performed the same services and prayers, and followed the same rituals. Women and girls were not treated as the equals of men and boys in the religious arena. Women went to synagogue but sat separately from the men on a balcony or the other side of a *mechitza* (divider). During the 1930s, Rabbi Akiva Chazan was the official rabbi of Ludvipol, with other out-of-town rabbis, such as Rabbi Iztkel from Brezno, visiting sometimes, which was always a cause for celebration.

In school, we learned about religion, but it was taught as a Jewish study, not in a religious way. Every Jewish child needed to know the five books of the Torah. We read prayers, but did not chant them. There was some leeway in people's level of observance.

On Friday afternoons, the men bathed in the mill pond and then rushed off to Kabbalat Shabbat to celebrate the entrance of Shabbat. Almost every Shabbat, the rabbi sent a stranger to have dinner with my family after shul. My mother was always able to accommodate spontaneous guests. Whenever someone came to town, sometimes from far away, and needed a place to eat, the rabbi would tell my father, "I'm sending somebody over for dinner." We fed these strangers in our home, then they went to sleep at a guest house or local inn.

Jewish law prohibits cooking on Shabbat, so people did not cook on Saturday, even in our house. Every Friday, many people brought their pots of cholent over to the rebbitsin's big oven. It was left in the hot oven overnight. Saturday morning at around 11:30, my sister Chava or I was sent with a towel to bring back the hot pot — and we had a hot meal without having to cook. At noon, when my father came home from shul, the cholent was our delicious lunch. The potatoes had turned soft and brown, and the long slow cooking gave the cholent a special taste. The whole town ate cholent on Shabbat.

Often on Shabbat and holidays, Rabbi Akiva had a *kiddush* (a festive glass of wine and a meal) at his home in the afternoon after shul, and the rebbitsin served cholent and cakes with wine. Everybody sang *zmirot* (Sabbath songs). Rabbi Akiva would take his portion first and then everyone else would fill their plates. The children often stood behind their fathers, who slipped them pieces of meat and chicken.

Not everyone went to synagogue on Shabbat, but no one would dare profane the day. No one traveled, nor did they do anything offensive or improper in public on the Sabbath. On Shabbat afternoons, after the big family lunch together, fathers would often nap. In the spring, they would nap under the blossoming apple and pear trees. In the evening, people gathered to stroll through town from one bridge to the other.

Most people, including my mother, would also prepare something that could be eaten cold, like egg salad or borscht. Another dish we used to prepare that did not require cooking on the Sabbath was *chalodetz*, a stew made from the leg of a steer or a cow, eaten hot or cold. Before cooking, the foot was singed, cleaned, and chopped. There was a lot of marrow in the big bones, and egg yolk, garlic, and other spices were added. You could dunk challah into the hot stew and eat the meat, or you could let it cool and gel into a solid. We called this cold-foot, and it is very delicious. I think you can still buy cold-foot in New York.

The only day of the week I got up early without being prodded was on Friday mornings, when my mother baked challah from the dough that had been set to rise the night before. Especially for me, she would take some of the dough, flatten it into a circle, put it into a frying pan, and bake it in the oven. After it was baked, I dunked it into freshly rendered chicken fat with a lot of greivenes (cracklings) and crisp fried onion. This was my favorite treat.

Every household used to bake its own challah for Friday night and, at the same time, challah dough pastries. Flour was put in a wooden tub, much like the kind of tub used for bathing a child, and divided into two piles. I remember vividly that one pile was for the challah, and certain ingredients were added to it. The other flour, for the pastries, was mixed with oil, butter, cinnamon, and sugar.

My mother also made pastries from plain dough. The plain pastries came out of the oven lighter in color than the fancy dark cinnamon and sugar pastries. Being a bit of a fussy eater, I liked the plain ones better. My mother would tease, "What's wrong with this boy? He prefers plain pastries!"

Every Friday, some extra pastries and challot were baked for the poor and for one or two households who needed a hand.

All the Jewish holidays were celebrated scrupulously in Ludvipol. My family spent holidays together. We went to synagogue together, although the women sat separately. Pesach (Passover), Rosh Ha'Shana (the Jewish New Year), and Yom Kippur were considered the three major holidays. Houses were painted and thoroughly cleaned for these holidays.

We children most liked Pesach and Rosh Ha'Shana because we always got new clothing. Since our family was well-off, we gave our clothes to the needy, rather than passing them down within the family. We played games with walnuts or filberts, and the winner would go home with a pile of nuts.

During Elul, the month before the Jewish New Year, both adults and children reflected upon their actions and thoughts during the past year and tried to make amends with their fellow townspeople. At Rosh Ha'Shana, people did *m'chila*, apologizing to each other for the actions they regretted and doing their best to make up, increasing the sense of *sholem* (peace), wholeness, and well-being in the community. Of course, there were some exceptions, but most people tried to make peace with all of their neighbors, Jew and non-Jew alike. That is how we lived. For the Rosh Ha'Shana *Tashlich* ceremony, groups walked from our synagogue to the Slusch River or the smaller Kolchik Creek and threw in bread crumbs to symbolize cleansing and casting away of our sins.

Between Rosh Ha'Shana and Yom Kippur, people traveled to the graves of their relatives, even if they were far away. On Yom Kippur, huge yahrzeit candles that burned for twenty-four hours or more were set in boxes of sand within the synagogues in memory of deceased loved ones. Everyone, of course, fasted.

On the major holiday of Sukkot, we ate our meals in our *sukkah*, the temporary dwelling we built to commemorate the transient lifestyle of the early Israelites traveling out of Egypt. It was cold, but we thatched the roof with greenery from a far part of the meadow behind the house, the same area that used to get flooded in the winter and was used for ice skating. We would invite many friends to eat with us in the sukkah. My father carried his *lulav* (bundled palm fronds and other branches) and *esrog* (citron) into the sukkah in keeping with the tradition of the holiday.

On Simchat Torah, the people of Ludvipol walked with torches from the various synagogues to Rabbi Akiva's house, where he made Kiddush over vodka and honey cakes. The children carried flags topped with an apple stuck onto the stick and a candle stuck into the apple. On that day, in addition to reading from the Torah, we danced around the shul with the Torah scrolls. Little children who began to learn Hebrew at that time of year licked honey off of Hebrew letters as a symbol that it is sweet and good to learn, and we all dipped apples in honey for a sweet new year.

On Hanukkah, we exchanged small presents and played *dreidl* (a game of tops), betting small amounts of money, like pennies and Hanukkah *gelt* (Yiddish for money). Jelly doughnuts were our traditional Hanukkah fare.

Purim was a very happy holiday, with special cakes and cookies, just like today. Kids ran around with decorative paper flags and made a racket with wooden *groggers*. People commonly drank wine at Purim, but not to the point of true drunkenness.

For Passover, we had three seders, one on the first day, one on the second, and one on the last. The town had its own Passover bakery, where everybody bought their matzah. My Uncle Usher was part-owner of this operation, a sophisticated one for a small town. There were tools to mix the dough and special roller wheels to prick the little holes. The matzahs were round and six or seven inches in diameter. Each one was put into and taken out of the oven by hand.

We also used to bake our own Passover kugels from vegetables or potatoes. We baked individual potato kugels in a pan with six little cups, like a muffin tin, and they came out like big muffins. We also made kugels from matzah meal. You could not go and buy ready-made matzah flour in a store, so we had to pound the matzah in a wooden mortar until it turned into flour. Then it was sifted. This flour was used for Passover, when regular flour could not be used. All kinds of things were baked from it, including cakes and pastries.

I remember the bonfires we lit to celebrate Lag b'Omer and how people danced around them until late into the night.

Other traditional holidays and events we celebrated included the night of the New Moon, when people would come out of shul and look up at the moon and recite the *Kiddush Levanah* (sanctification of the moon, also called the *Birchat HaLevanah*, blessing of the moon). After that, they would say, *"Shalom aleichem,"* peace be unto you, to each other.

The local Klezmer band played at weddings and other celebrations. Bilinke was the short, stocky violinist, the tall trumpet player was named Shlaifer, and a young drummer, and sometimes people on saxophone, clarinet, or accordion, played along. Jewish entertainers from Rovno who toured small towns performed in Ludvipol as well.

The town had a few *mikvahs* (Jewish ritual baths). I do not recall my mother going, but the rabbi would not perform a wedding ceremony unless the bride had visited the mikvah. Some people did all their bathing at a mikvah, if they did not have bathing facilities at home.

I imagine that in the big cities of Poland, when I was a young boy, Jewish people were more "European" than they were in our town, with young people trying to assimilate to some degree into the culture of the country without abandoning Jewish life in their homes. The Jewish Bund organization had already been established and a lot of Jews wanted to free themselves from what they perceived as the "Jewish yoke." They wanted to be equal to other people, at least in the outside world. They learned to speak Polish and became professionals, and to do so they had to fall in line with the majority of the population.

The Zionist Dream

The cornerstone of Ludvipol's Tarbut School (Hebrew for culture) was laid in 1930 with an impressive ceremony in the newer part of town. Everyone volunteered time or money, and the school quickly became the jewel of Ludvipol, even though it had seemed like an impossible dream at first. Some people had opposed the school because it would weaken the influence of religious education, but my father, a vice president of the school and a major contributor, was excited about it. He was a strong supporter of education and saw the school as a jumping board to the fulfillment of the Zionist dream in Israel.

Chava, Esther, and I attended the Tarbut School, which was located just on the other side of the home of our neighbors, the Kleinmans. Living so close to school was very convenient. We would get up in the morning, have breakfast, and then rush to school. Two of my cousins, Boris and Riva, stayed with a family in Ludvipol so that they, too, could attend the school.

Tarbut was a Jewish school, and therefore received no financial support from the Polish government. All costs were borne by the community. Tuition was set according to a sliding scale based on family income.

A small percentage of Ludvipol's Jewish children still attended the government-supported school in Selishtch, about two miles away. They underwent ordeals that we at Tarbut did not have to face, sometimes coming home with torn, dirty clothes and broken bones. Students at the Tarbut School perceived those kids as tough. Maybe they had to be tough!

The school was similar in approach to today's Solomon Schechter schools, both humanist and traditional. Two buildings housed about six hundred students, age six to seventeen or eighteen, with twenty to twenty-five students in a class. It was not at all like the traditional *cheder* (traditional one-room religious elementary school).

Tarbut was a very good school with high standards, strict about students' behavior and schoolwork. Grades were important; when we earned good grades, my parents were very proud, but they and our teachers always encouraged us to do better. We had tremendous respect and admiration for our teachers, who were dedicated to excellence. Our uniforms had to be clean, and the teachers inspected our ears, hands, and nails for cleanliness as well. If students did not behave, a note was sent to their parents.

In 1937, with the deteriorating economic situation, people thought it prudent for young people to learn more about the trades, and the second building was built, followed by a vocational school. Building and administering the vocational school required additional generous contributions of time and money from the community. A fund was established to pay tuition for needy orphans, and the vocational school quickly filled with students.

Zionism was the mainstay of Ludvipol, and the Zionist spirit was an important element of the Tarbut School. Many of its graduates who survived went on to hold high positions in the government of the State of Israel. All subjects, even arithmetic, were taught in Hebrew, which the students learned to speak fluently. Polish was taught as a second language. Even today, after almost fifty years away from Israel, Hebrew is my strongest language.

We memorized Hebrew poems, some of which I can still recite. The poetry of Chaim Nachman Bialik, who was born not far from Ludvipol, still resonates for me. Bialik had a significant influence on the creation of Jewish self-defense units in Russia, as well as on worldwide Jewish support for Zionism and the Second Aliyah to Palestine. In one beautiful poem, "To the Bird," he talks to a bird that is leaving for warmer climates. He says to the bird, "If you fly to Israel, please bring my love to my friends who are so far and yet so close to me."

We studied history, mainly Jewish history — we followed what went on in Eretz Yisrael — but also Polish history. We studied the Bible as history and stories of Jewish leaders like King Saul and King David. I remember the Bible stories better now than I used to because I have told them to my grandchildren so many times.

The school was secular, with no religion or prayers, but we celebrated all of the Jewish holidays. For instance, every Tu b'Shevat, the fifteenth day of the Jewish month of Shevat — planting season in Israel — the whole school used to go outside and plant trees.

The school was strong in extra-curricular activities. My sister Chava, who took private music lessons from the age of five, played the violin in the school orchestra with the older kids and performed at concerts and shows. She also acted in a play about Purim, *Esther HaMalka* (Esther the Queen). Most of the plays had Biblical themes, but not all. I remember how the girls danced like swans in one play. I was in the school choir; we mostly sang Hebrew songs such as *HaShkedia Porachat* (the Almond Tree Blossoms), or traditional songs like *Hinei Ma Tov*. We also had a good physical education program and a soccer team.

The Tarbut School was an important and happy part of our lives. I was bright and a good student. I did not need any help with my homework and never had problems with schoolwork. I had many good friends, and we spent a great deal of time together and slept over at each other's houses. Most of my friends from early childhood were later killed by the Nazis, but Itzak Gurfinkel, from my kindergarten class, is still alive.

The language of instruction had particular political significance. For two years after the Russians took control of Ludvipol in 1939, we were not allowed to study Hebrew or Polish. We were only allowed to read and write in Yiddish and Russian. My early life made me and my friends quite multi-lingual. I have learned five languages well — Hebrew, Yiddish, Polish, Russian, and English — and can speak and understand Ukrainian, although not as well as I once could. I also understand German.

Ludvipol's thinking about the future of Israel was modern. As a result, we had many Zionist organizations, mostly for young people. My sister Chava and I belonged to a Zionist youth group, and most of our friends belonged to Zionist organizations. In fact, all the Jewish organizations in Ludvipol at that time were Zionist. They were very important in lifting the morale of the Jews because we lived in fear of anti-Semitic Ukrainians mistreating and beating us. The Jewish organizations brought spirit into the town by teaching self-assurance and self-defense.

We knew that Judaism originates from Zion. It is said, *"Ki m'Zion tetzay Torah ud'var Adonay m'Yerushalayim,"* which means, "From Zion will come knowledge and God's word from Jerusalem." We took this very much to heart.

Hebrew was very important to us. We had an organization called *B'nai Yehudah* (Children of Judah), founded by Eliezer Ben Yehuda, the chief figure in the revival of Hebrew as a spoken language. Like almost everyone at the Tarbut School, my sister Chava and I belonged to B'nai Yehudah. Someone had heard that Arabs spoke Hebrew to the Jewish merchants in Tel Aviv, so the students in Ludvipol pledged to speak in Hebrew all the time, even in the marketplace, at home and in the community, to their parents, the farmers, and everyone else. Even if you went to a Polish store, and had to explain yourself with hand movements, you tried to speak only Hebrew. There was a big chart of our names displayed in the main lobby of the school. If someone broke the rule by not speaking Hebrew, a minus mark was placed next to his name.

Adults were also involved in Zionist activities. They established *kibbutzim* (collective villages) in Poland for training purposes. Young people used to leave town for a kibbutz, where they learned agriculture and self-sufficiency in preparation for making *aliyah* (immigration of a Jew to Israel). "Aliyah" means to ascend in Hebrew. When someone goes to Israel, they go up, ascend; if they leave Israel, they *yored,* or come down. The young woman who worked for us in my mother's photography studio, Tibel Kleinman, later Yona Tuchman, spent a year or two at a kibbutz in Poland before she married.

One of the most pronounced memories I have from Ludvipol involves Zionism. In about 1936, Joseph Schwartzman, the son of our *shochet* (ritual slaughterer) Mottel — a prominent man, very well liked and respected — who had already immigrated to Palestine, arranged for his entire family to join him. Joseph had left his children, Shlomo and Chaia, behind with Mottel and now they all were to join him. Their departure for Palestine was a major event and the cause of a great celebration.

The day they left, all of the stores in our town closed and all of the students of the Tarbut School, dressed in our uniforms, marched alongside their wagon waving flags. The Schwartzmans rode by horse and wagon to the railway station in the next town, and everyone in Ludvipol marched out to the farthest bridge to bid them farewell. Horsemen rode in formation, as if they were the Polish cavalry. These rough, simple men were so poor that they did not even own saddles, but used blankets and robes to try to look like cavalry. Each one carried a Jewish flag, blue and white with the Star of David. It was an impressive spectacle that demonstrated the deep Zionist sentiment of the entire town at that time.

Everybody was envious that the Schwartzmans were on their way to Palestine. In those days, our people's big wish was that when they died, they would be buried in Palestine and become part of the soil of Israel. I assume that this was one of the motivations of the shochet, who was a pious elderly gentleman, to go and live with his son. He probably wanted to die in Palestine.

My father's parents would not have considered moving to Palestine back in 1918, when they went to the United States. For one thing, the Zionist organizations that helped people emigrate to Palestine for ideological reasons barely existed then. For another, they left Poland for economic, not ideological, reasons. People went to the U.S., not to Palestine, when they wanted a more comfortable life for themselves.

Palestine in the 1930s was under the British Mandate and there were approximately 300,000 Jews living there. Among the Zionist organizations in Palestine, also represented in Ludvipol, were *HaShomer HaTzair* (the Young Guard), *Dror HeChalutz* (Pioneer's Freedom), Gordonia, and Beitar, which represented the Zionist right wing.

The big tavern and liquor store in town was always full of Ukrainians drinking, and many got very drunk, very often. Drunk Ukrainians looked for trouble. If they ran across a Jewish man, they would often beat him up. Jews tried to avoid the area of the tavern at night so as not to run into trouble. I do not recall the police doing anything about these incidents.

The Zionist organizations emphasized self-defense and brought a spirit of strength to the Jews of the town. This was the particular emphasis of Beitar, the youth group led by Ze'ev (Vladimir) Jabotinsky that would become Menachem Begin's political party. Beitar was by nature a political and militarist organization whose ideology was "only in blood and in fire can you conquer a land." They felt that Jews could not afford to be passive, and that sooner or later, they would need to fight and make sacrifices for their independence. In fact, Beitar adopted a uniform that was very similar to both police and Nazi uniforms: brown, with belts similar to those worn by police officers, one around the waist and one strapped diagonally from the shoulder to the waist. They also wore hats that were similar to police hats. In our town and all over Poland, Beitar created tough Jewish groups that could defend themselves. They trained people with sticks and taught them judo, karate, and marching in the streets. When they marched in a parade, they looked like a paramilitary group.

For the Jews of Poland, who lived in fear of police and drunk

Tarbut School class in Ludvipol. *Bottom row, second from right* is Riva Edelman, Usher and Chava Edelman's daughter; Boris attended the Tarbut School too. Riva and Boris boarded with friends in town during the school week. (*Yizkor* book, 1936)

Tarbut School students (*Yizkor* book, about 1936)

farmers, this was inspiring. People felt very good upon seeing our own young men walk so proudly in a parade. We felt that we were equal to other people. Our pride and confidence grew tremendously because we knew we had someone to defend us.

The Polish government, however, could not tolerate the Jews suddenly acting with chutzpah and arrogance, and at some point, they decided to suppress these groups. They outlawed the paramilitary uniforms and the appearance of military strength. They closed the Beitar office, but the members continued to meet clandestinely.

The Zionist organization my sister and I belonged to, Dror HeChalutz, had wonderful get-togethers, dances, speeches, and pep talks that we were always eager to attend. Many years later, after the war, I joined Kibbutz Yagur, which was founded by members of this organization.

Zionism taught us to have confidence in ourselves and to believe that we were equal to other people. We learned that we should not live in fear.

Our Two-Year Reprieve

We lived relatively happily until the war broke out in 1939. I was not aware of what was going on in the world, nor that things had gotten so bad for the Jews in Germany. Although the newspapers began in 1938 to print information about what was happening in Germany, we could not even imagine the extent and we were not very well-informed. We were removed from the outside world by poor communications; we lived far from a major city and so relied on the local newspaper.

By 1939, we were aware that things were deteriorating. When the war broke out between Germany and Poland, we heard about it from refugees who streamed in from distant places and told us of the terrible atrocities that the Germans were committing.

The Germans rapidly overran Poland. Because Hitler was concerned that the Russians would declare war on Germany or interfere with his planned conquests, in August 1939 a non-aggression pact was signed by Joachim von Ribbentrop, the German foreign minister, and Vyacheslav Molotov, the Russian foreign minister.

After World War I, the Ukraine had been divided between Poland and Russia, and the part of the Ukraine we lived in became part of Poland. Now Russia and Germany essentially divided Poland in half. The area around Lvov and Ludvipol wound up on the Russian side. This was meant to satisfy the Russians' desire to unite the Ukraine as one nation under Russian control. Russia was also not ready for a war with Germany.

Refugees from the rest of Poland — those who had vision — started filtering into our area. They did not want to remain on the

German side, so they fled to our side, the Russian part of Poland. The people of our town became very concerned.

The Russians occupied our area in September 1939. We children stood in the streets to watch their arrival. We understood Russian. We were not afraid. There were rumors that they would rob and hurt us; my father remembered the chaos in the aftermath of the Russian Revolution, in about 1922, so he hid our valuable possessions, including our sterling silver. Still, we stood in the street to watch, and we did not perceive any danger to our lives.

The Russians had great military might, although nothing compared to the Germans. I remember being disappointed upon seeing the Red Army march into town. I was used to the elegant, if ineffective, Polish army. Polish soldiers wore beautiful uniforms with shiny buttons, and carried beautiful leather knapsacks. Their horses were sleek and well-fed; they fed their horses better than they fed their soldiers. But the Russian soldiers came into Ludvipol like a bunch of poor slobs. Their bayonets were very long in comparison to the bayonets used by the Polish soldiers, which made the marching Russian soldiers look small in comparison. And they were so poorly dressed — they truly looked like slobs. We said, "My God, who are these *shleppers?*" (haulers, workmen). The cannons they pulled were so big that it was difficult for them to navigate corners. We stood there and watched their attempts.

One Russian officer jumped off a jeep and came over to us. He opened up his knapsack, which looked like a *shmatta* (rag) in comparison with the Polish army's knapsacks. He pulled out a blue rock. With his bayonet, he broke off a few pieces and offered them to us, but we were afraid to take them because we did not know what it was: Russian sugar. We did not recognize it because we were accustomed to Polish beet sugar in pristine white cubes wrapped in beautiful packages; it was one of Poland's export items. All he wanted was to give us children some of his precious sugar. We hurt his feelings by turning down his gift.

The Russian soldiers could not get over how a small town like ours had so much wealth. They could not comprehend how rich we were in comparison to their villages. They really had nothing. I remember stories of how the Russians ran into the stores and bought nightgowns as dresses for their wives because they did not know the difference.

Russian occupation was, in a sense, a reprieve from the Germans because it took another two years before Germany declared war on Russia and occupied our area. However, the occupation of our town by the Russians caused major upheaval. They immediately proclaimed that the proletarians, the laborers, the workers were everything and that all other people were on the way out. They resented rich people. They had a campaign to eliminate the intelligentsia and the well-to-do. They pronounced that those people who had been "somebodies" were now "nobodies." The proletarians were now in power, and the rich people were "bloodsuckers" who had lived off the proletarians' blood.

The Russians believed that the Jewish people were underprivileged under the Polish government because the Jews were always persecuted and because there was a lot of anti-Semitism in Poland. In Russia, officially, there was no anti-Semitism — it was against the law. The official Russian policy was that everybody was equal. In Ukrainian and in Polish, a Jew was called *Zhid,* which was a derogatory term; the Russians did not allow its use. A Jew was henceforth to be called *Hevrei,* or Hebrew. This really bothered the local goyim — it ate them up alive that they could no longer call a Jew *Zhid.* Now, every time they forgot themselves, we would ask, "Do you want me to report you to the government?" They painfully replied, "No, no, no, excuse me, Hevrei," which gave us great satisfaction.

From the Russian point of view, the most reliable locals were the young Jewish men, rather than the Ukrainian village peasants, and when they created a militia, about 80 percent of it was Jewish. They had many good reasons for this. The Jews were better educated and, because of the Zionist organizations, some (especially members of Beitar) even had some military training. The Russians also considered the many poor people in our town to be under-privileged, and thus more ideologically reliable.

Under the previous Polish government, seeing a Jew walking around with a rifle or pistol had been very rare. But the Russians trained the Jews for a few days, gave them rifles, showed them how to use them, and deputized them as the temporary militia. The townspeople were very proud to see young Jewish men, armed with rifles, patrolling the streets. We felt secure and happy. The Russians pronounced that all races were equal and made no distinction between Jews and non-Jews. For a while, there was an atmosphere of euphoria.

But gradually, the Russians established themselves. They brought in their own policemen as a permanent force and the local militia was gradually phased out.

One negative aspect of the occupation was that from the instant they arrived, the Russians mandated that the Jews had to speak Yiddish, rather than Hebrew. Jews were a recognized minority in Russia. In Russia, every ethnic group had its own state — the Uzbeks, Kazakhstanis, Ukrainians, and Byelorussians all had their own republics, albeit under Russian dominance. They even tried to create a republic for the Jews called Birobidzhan, except that it did not work. The Jews did not want to be confined there. They wanted to be free birds.

Theoretically, the Russians wanted to treat the Jews as equal to other ethnic groups. But they were against Zionism and did not believe that the Jews should go to Israel, so they forbade Zionism and did not allow the speaking of Hebrew. They wanted the Jews to speak and read in Russian and Yiddish. I already knew how to speak both languages, but from 1939 to 1941, when the Russians occupied our town, we went to Russian schools and learned to read and write in Russian and Yiddish.

Officially, the Tarbut School became a Russian school where the teachers were ordered to teach us in Yiddish and Russian.

Though the Russians did not arrest anyone for disobedience, the school's entire library of Hebrew books was sent to the paper mill and destroyed. Instead of teaching about Eretz Yisrael, self-empowerment, and self-sufficiency, educators had to teach about Russia, Communism, and solidarity. Jewish cultural life, always closely connected with education, suffered.

Studying in Russian was supposed to inculcate in us Russian national values. The Russians were very proud that they had defeated Napoleon. We learned a Russian poem about how the Russians did not surrender Moscow to Napoleon, even under siege. Rather than surrender, they burned the city down and left only ashes for him. In another famous poem, a grandson says, "Tell me, Grandfather..." and the grandfather answers, "It's not for nothing that Moscow was burned down to ashes. There were very brave people in those days who sacrificed their lives to save the city. A difficult fate was bestowed on them.... Their destiny was death," and so forth. We studied another Russian poem about a prisoner who sits in jail, in a dark cellar behind metal bars, like a wounded eagle, and dreams about freedom...how he wishes he could spread his wings and fly out into freedom and be liberated.

We also studied a writer of Russian allegories named Ivan Krilov. To describe a greedy man, he wrote a famous story about a wolf and a lamb: "On a very hot day, a small lamb was standing by a tiny river drinking water. In the grass was sitting a wild wolf that had already made up his mind to kill that little lamb and eat it. But the wolf's conscience bothered him a little bit, and he walked over to the lamb and said, 'Why are you polluting my water?' The lamb, who sized up the situation, replied, 'Your Honor, look at me. I'm a little lamb, with a long neck, and I stretch my neck into the water — I am not polluting the water.' The wolf said, 'Oh, if you're not polluting, then maybe your cousin was polluting or maybe your uncle,' and ate the lamb." The moral was, "The guilty one always blames someone else."

We had to study the writings of Sholom Aleichem, Mendele

Mocher Sefarim, and other Jewish writers who wrote in Yiddish. A stop was put to all of our Zionist activities. All Zionist parties and organizations were disbanded and officially outlawed. We carried on a little, in secret, because we did not lose our sympathy for Israel on command. The Russians also prohibited most religious practices and shut down the cheders, although they looked the other way when people went to shul.

One tactic the Russians used to gain control was to get rid of the leaders and the people in the upper classes. They started to selectively harass and persecute the "aristocrats" and bourgeoisie, the people they could not trust and who were considered undesirable. My father fell into this group. Our ownership of a big factory made us, in their worldview, capitalist exploiters.

In April 1940, the Russians started to issue identity cards; anyone who refused to get an ID card was rounded up and exiled to the interior of the Soviet Union. Each ID card indicated its bearer's social standing. The intelligentsia, aristocrats, and bourgeoisie were given the number eleven. Foresters, too, were targeted because they knew how to use weapons. If your card had a number eleven, you were deemed untrustworthy and were not considered loyal to the regime. Your belongings were confiscated and your family was forced out of its home and ordered to give away its factories, mills, and properties. You were not given ration cards for food. You were subject to arrest and exile; without notice, families with number eleven were suddenly taken away during the night.

Since my father had people working for him, the Russians said that we lived on the blood of the workers and we were given the number eleven. It was irrelevant that my father had been a progressive employer.

My mother was allowed to keep her photography studio because she was not considered an exploiter — she had only one employee, which did not count for much with the Russians.

The Russians told us that we were *persona non grata* and our fate was to be deported to Siberia. Our business was confiscated and the government appointed someone else to run it. My father could not get a job. We had to let go of the help we had in our house. When the Russians established a paramilitary youth organization at school, the Pioneers, and all the children in our school joined, children like myself, whose father had the number eleven, were excluded. We could go to school and we could study, but we could not take part in the extracurricular activities.

We began to feel like outcasts. Nobody wanted us. We had almost no income. We did not go hungry, though; we used our jewelry and other valuables to buy food from the farmers. My Uncle Usher, who still lived in another village and had his own gardens, provided us with food. The Russians had entered his village, but they apparently did not bother him because his business, just a small flourmill, was much more modest than my father's. They left him alone. Every so often Uncle Usher came to visit with a wagon full of food. Our friends also stood by us.

Then the Russians decided that our house was big enough to convert into a medical clinic, so they threw us out. It was terrible. We had to leave on short notice, and there was no one to whom we could appeal. We just gathered our possessions, whatever we could carry, and left for the apartment we were assigned.

Things for us were very tense since we were considered upper class and the number eleven placed us on the undesirable list. It was essential to try to get ourselves removed from the list because it was constantly reviewed to determine who would be deported next.

I remember the nights during that time. People in our circle of friends were disappearing during the night. The Russians came and threw them into wagons and sent them off to Siberia. They were merchants or big lumber dealers, people whom the Russians felt they could not trust. During the night, any scratch or noise made us expect a knock on the door. We lived in terrible fear, not for our lives, but of exile to Siberia. We did not yet know that things would be much worse later on.

We had nothing. We, who had been somebodies, became poor nobodies. We lived in fear and were very unhappy. I could not even participate in the games at school. We felt that everybody looked at us cross-eyed. It was embarrassing.

We had to move yet again because the government needed the apartment for an official. This time we moved to a nice little house with a garden on the edge of town, which was actually more comfortable than the first one they had put us in, but because it had the straw roof of a peasant's dwelling, we felt degraded. This was a real slap in the face, to wind up living in a small farm house outside of town. Nice as it was, I am sure my father was depressed and humiliated.

Meanwhile, we were working behind the scenes to bribe someone to get the number eleven taken off our identification cards. My Uncle Usher was always a doer, a tough guy, and at one point he succeeded in making contact with the Russian commissar in charge of the town. I do not know the details because he and my father were very secretive, but one day my uncle came and announced, "Your troubles are over. You will be getting a new ID in one week and the number eleven will not be on it. You are being taken off the undesirable list." Sure enough, we got a new ID, and no longer feared deportation. Then my father was summoned to the main government office and they said, "Why is a capable man like you hanging around and doing nothing? The state needs people with brains — managers and business people who can run things," and they gave him an important job in charge of procuring lumber for the Russian state and managing a large lumberyard for the Russians.

As the economy was nationalized, Jews were integrated into the Soviet system, with its expanded public services and bureaucracy, and some Jewish professionals were employed. At first, the economic situation seemed to improve. Even though the shops were closed down, cooperatives for different trades and crafts were established. Agriculture was the only area that was not collectivized right away. They tried to establish communal farms for the farmers, called *kolhoz,* but the farmers were very reluctant to join.

The system was that everybody worked for the Russians, and everyone got paid at subsistence level. There was some job security, and there were some social benefits, such as daily food rations. Each department ran its own affairs and had its own store because food and produce were difficult to obtain. Soap, sugar, oil, and many other items were impossible to find. Rations were distributed, but they were insufficient. However, if someone worked for a government agency, they were better off because each agency took care of its workers. My father had a few hundred workers in his department, and horses and wagons. They had a big store which sold to the workers. My father was directly in charge of everything, so we had more than enough. Of course, we had ration cards and got what everyone else was getting, but on top of that were the provisions from his organization.

When the restrictions on us were removed, I was immediately called into school and notified that I could participate in all the activities. Everything returned to normal, although we did not get our house back because a clinic had already been established there. We remained in the little house, but we got used to it. The house was far from the school, but it was a nice walk.

Nobody owned anything, but our life had improved considerably. We were no longer afraid to fall sleep at night. This was the last year before the Germans came in. We felt lucky for having escaped deportation. Ironically, had we been deported to Siberia, perhaps our entire family would have survived the Holocaust, but that is in hindsight.

By then, we had heard many stories — the German atrocities were no longer a secret — from the refugees who came and settled in our town. We knew things were very bad and hoped that the agreement between the Russians and the Nazis would hold. But the Germans gained military strength and declared war on Russia, and it became obvious that the Russians would soon withdraw.

The Russians encouraged the Jews to leave with them. Many people believed that things would be better for them in Russia, especially if they had cooperated with the Russian government. Many young people who had been in the militia, had sympathized with the Russians ideologically, or had been happy during the Russian occupation felt that remaining behind would be unsafe, in fact feared for their lives. A number of people from our town left for Russia and most of them survived the war. Tibel Kleinman, who worked for us in my mother's photography studio, and her family escaped to Russia with the retreating Russian soldiers; her father had worked for the Russians and they gave him two horses. Tibel took some photographs from my mother's studio with her — only because she rescued them do I have them today.

At this time, my family was in a unique position to escape because, since my father was in charge of the lumber establishment, horses, wagons, and provisions were at our disposal. My father had the key to the store of provisions, and could have loaded whatever we needed, and extra to sell along the way. We could have driven to the railroad station and then taken a train deep into Russia.

But my father had been so hurt and humiliated by the Russians that he said to my mother and us, "After the treatment I received from the Russians, why should I run after them? I'm glad to be rid of them." He did not know what was coming next. So we remained in town.

We were not the only ones staying. Most of the town stayed because they were afraid of becoming refugees. The feeling was, "We're going to stay and whatever God is going to give, that's what we're going to take." People asked each other, "How bad could it be?" Who would ever have believed that the Germans were going to kill innocent people and burn them to death? Think of September 10, 2001: who would ever have believed that the next day someone was going to blow up the twin towers of the World Trade Center and kill three thousand innocent people? Perhaps you could believe that someone might hijack an airplane and make some sort of demand, but to use the planes as bombs, to such awful effect — who would believe that? Only the first time an unimaginable atrocity occurs do you know how bad it can be.

The Russians with whom we were in contact behaved very well toward us. A friend told me that in the town of Kostopol, Jews were given preference for boarding trains into Russia, even though wounded Russian soldiers were waiting to board. Perhaps the Russian commander was Jewish and did this on his own, and this was not Russian policy. Nevertheless, he told people that if the Jews remained, they would be killed by the Germans so they deserved first preference to board the train and escape.

Before the Russians left, as part of their general military strategy, they burned down my father's factory and most of the lumber nearby in order to prevent the Germans from benefiting from it.

I will digress a bit regarding anti-Semitism in our part of Poland. Officially, the Russians, as Communists, thought the Jews should be treated equally, but anti-Semitism was so deeply rooted in Russian society that this was impossible. Most of the hatred for the Jews stemmed from the teachings of the church, which directly and indirectly blamed the Jews for the death of Christ. The church never taught their followers that Christ himself was a Jewish rabbi, about the circumstances of those times, or that Christ did not conform to the teachings of the rabbis of that period. They only taught that Jews were guilty of Christ's crucifixion. People were ignorant. They only knew what they were told, and all they were told was that the Jews had killed their god.

For many generations, anti-Semitism has been a chronic sickness in the Ukraine involving jealousy and religious hatred. The Ukrainians and the Poles were envious of the Jews because most of the stores in town were owned by Jews; they got the impression that all Jews were wealthy and did not work hard. In fact, this was very far from the truth; most of the Jewish people in town were poor, hardworking people, struggling to provide for their families.

The Poles were also anti-Semitic and should be even more condemned than the Ukrainians for their collusion in the atrocities because they were better educated and should have known better. The Ukrainians were simple people who did not question what they were taught. Ignorant people do things out of ignorance, but informed people do things intentionally, and should be aware when their actions are morally wrong. They have a responsibility to think about what they are doing.

II

The War

On the Day of My Bar Mitzvah

We did not go to Russia. We stayed in the little house on the edge of town and things were quiet for a couple of weeks.

The date of my Bar Mitzvah was July 7, 1941, less than two weeks after the Russians left Ludvipol. Because of the uncertainty and the fear of the Germans getting closer to our area, no celebration of any kind was feasible. Nevertheless, when we went to the Stoliner synagogue for the religious service, my mother baked a cake and we took along a bottle of vodka for a Kiddush. To our surprise, there were many people present in the synagogue.

The atmosphere was somber, and there was sadness and fear on the faces of the congregants. The coming of the Germans was imminent — from the description of the refugees, there would be nothing but hard times ahead. Few people suspected, however, that this could be the last time we would assemble in our beloved synagogue as free people with civil rights.

Despite this gloomy scenario, the service was conducted with dignity and the prayers were chanted with great emotion. I handled my part of the service well, but with trepidation. Rabbi Akiva complimented me on my prayer reading, and we all wished each other "Mazel Tov."

As we were returning home from the synagogue, the Germans rolled into town on motorcycles. From that moment, everything became chaotic and very dangerous. The Germans immediately started to harass people, beat them up and make arrests. Eight people were killed immediately. Nothing in our life was ever the same.

As soon as the Germans arrived, the town's leaders met at the rabbi's house and decided to send a delegation to greet the soldiers. The nearby Ukrainian and Polish communities had already sent their leaders and priests to welcome the soldiers, and the Jewish community was afraid that it would be interpreted as a lack of respect, if they, too, did not send a delegation.

The delegation included Mottel the rabbi's son, Isaac Hersch Guttman, Shichna Shemesh, and Mottel Primak. Others remember Rabbi Akiva Chazan and Itzhak Koperband as the leaders of the delegation.

The delegation set up a table near the post office and decorated it with bread, salt, flowers, and a big rusty key to symbolize the handover of the town. The first soldiers to arrive thanked the men for the reception. But minutes later a second column of Germans arrived, smashed the table, and beat the delegates, who fled in terror along with the other Jews who were out on the streets.

My family was living in the small house just outside of town, so we ourselves were not affected immediately the way people living in the center of town were. However, within one week, we all lost our rights as citizens. We no longer had any protection. We were fair game. The German military overwhelmed the town with its presence, and everybody had to serve them, peeling potatoes, bringing them wood, and, in the process, being beaten. They raped every woman they ran into. Although this treatment did not reach us right away, we knew that whatever happened to the people in town was going to reach us sooner or later.

As more Germans came into town, they parked their trucks closer to where we lived. They knew we were Jewish immediately, and made us work for them. We were peeling potatoes and working in their kitchens, and they beat us often. It was a horrible time, and it became worse.

The German commander promptly appointed a middle-aged German teacher from the local Polish school as the new mayor of Ludvipol. Mayor Hering began by going into the town square, accompanied by German officers, and dividing the Jews into work forces to clean the town and bring water and wood for the German troops. Within a few days, the Germans had found local Ukrainians who were more than happy to serve as police officers and armed guards. Within two weeks they set up a civil police administration, called the *gendarmerie*, run by Germans and Ukrainians. Some of the German soldiers then left, continuing their advance into the Ukraine. The Jews tried to bribe Mayor Hering to protect them, but were unsuccessful.

A few months after the Germans arrived, on October 1, they issued an order for all Jews to wear the yellow Star of David to identify themselves as Jews, and they created a ghetto and started to evict people from their houses. Our town had two main streets running crosswise. They took one quarter of the town, about seventy homes, erected a ten-foot high wooden fence with barbed wire around it, and shoved in all the Jews from the entire town. The ghetto walls ran along Szewska Street from Habel Creek, starting at Isaac Kogot's house, to the corner of Koretz Street, and from Yankel Raber's house to slightly beyond Barder the baker's house, then along May the Third Street.

In a cold, driving rain on October 14, 1941, during Simchat Torah, we were forced out of our homes and into the ghetto. Those who looked physically able to handle hard labor were put in a work camp. A few craftsmen were given special certificates that allowed them to remain on the Craftsman Street, which faced out from the ghetto, because their services were needed by non-Jews. About two thousand people had to fit into this small area. There was no food and hardly any water for drinking or washing. People referred to the ghetto as Kasrilevke, from Sholom Aleichem. Ukrainian police stood guard on all sides of the ghetto.

A special commission searched each family's belongings when they entered their new residences in the ghetto. Everything of value was taken from them, and they were left with only a few blankets and the clothes on their backs. Four or five families had to live in each small house, sharing their living space with neighbors and relatives. The men were separated from the women and sent to quarters near the Tarbut School at first, but after meeting with a delegation, Mayor Hering canceled that arrangement.

We were not allowed to have any communications with the outside world. We could not gather, visit, or talk to each other. One of the synagogues was in the ghetto, but we could not hold services, although some people met secretly and conducted services elsewhere. We were not allowed to have any food other than what they gave us. A strict curfew was imposed. We were not allowed to leave the ghetto without a permit, and no permits were issued for after 6:00 PM. The only way out of the ghetto was through a gate that was heavily guarded by Ukrainians. If you were caught outside without permission, you were shot.

The rules were enforced by Ukrainian police, who patrolled the ghetto constantly. If someone was caught, he was killed. Anyone who broke the rules was killed without hesitation.

New identification cards, requiring new photographs, were constantly being issued, so the Germans gave my family one of the houses facing the main street whose entrance was not blocked off by the ghetto fence. The family of another photographer, Asreal, who had come from elsewhere six or seven years before the war and had set up in competition with my mother, lived with us in the house. The fence went between our house and the houses to each side of it, but the front of the house faced freedom. We could even slip out the front windows, albeit at great risk. I ran out on occasion and got food from people we knew, paying for it with whatever little bit of money or jewelry we had managed to sneak past the guards. We were always frightened when one of us left through the window.

Both of my parents worked at the studio, providing photographs for whomever needed them. My father also worked on a road construction project. The Germans decided to build an eighteen-mile road from Ludvipol to Brezno, the largest town in the area, for the German war machine. Every able-bodied person and child was rounded up every day at six o'clock in the morning, and guards walked us about three kilometers to work on the road construction. Small children and old people, too, were forced to go to the road construction site.

My sister Chava and I worked on the road. My job was to break large stones into pebbles. I sat on a big rock and hammered all day long to break up the stones. There were approximately twenty people of all ages, a whole row of people sitting and smashing rocks into pebbles. Once we had a pile, women would come with hand platforms, and we would shovel the pebbles onto the platforms. Then the pebbles would be brought over to the road construction site and put where the foreman wanted them.

There was a military kitchen, just a big kettle of water in which they boiled a small clump of kasha, and at noon there was a break for a half hour. Every little bit of food was precious. People made sure no crumb fell on the ground.

We used to march with our shovels over our shoulders, and one day, as I was walking, I slipped, and my shovel fell. It hit the heel of my right foot and seriously injured it, although it did not cut through all the way to the tendon. I had a lot of trouble getting better. The wound would appear to heal — a scab would form — but then it would start to ooze all over again. I could not put a shoe on that foot so I wore a sandal instead.

After working twelve- to fourteen-hour days, we were given a small portion of bread, not more than 200 grams and usually about half that much, and some watery soup. Those who could not do physical labor — small children, the sick, and the elderly — got nothing. They had to share the forced laborers' rations, but the workers were already so weak from lack of food that many of them could not continue to work. Housewives cooked meals from nothing. Infants had nothing to eat. Their mothers' milk had long since dried up, and there were no domestic animals to milk. Some ate grass and a few dared to knock on peasants' doors to ask for potatoes.

People began to starve. Children, especially, suffered. They ran around with bulging knees. They became bloated, turned blue, and began to die. Anyone who had a supplemental source or supply of food kept it secret. People traded their clothes or anything else they had for a bit to eat. Some had left their belongings with Ukrainian neighbors for safekeeping, but I do not think anyone was successful in getting them back.

Moshe Font, the tailor, was the first person to be murdered inside the ghetto. A Ukrainian officer shot him when he saw a goy give Moshe a goose in payment for sewing a pair of pants.

Life was miserable. The German commissar in charge of our town, Franz Norgall, used to come by on his horse twice a day, and anyone with whom he found fault was shot on sight. Nobody knew when the commissar would show up. When he came, he always managed to find a victim. Sometimes he humiliated people by lashing or beating them with a whip in public.

One time, he rode up on his horse and found fault with Leibel Keck's work. Leibel, who was only sixteen or seventeen years old, had the misfortune of sitting down for a moment. I was about twenty feet away and heard Norgall ask Leibel why he was not working. The boy was apparently terrified and did not answer. Norgall ordered him to lie down, then took out his pistol and shot him through the neck. This frightening scene horrified us. The workers had to bury him there and remove all traces.

Commissar Norgall and his deputy, Spiegel, were cruel. Although Kostopol was the site of the German headquarters, Norgall, Spiegel, and Glanz, who was the head of the *gendarmerie*, established themselves in Ludvipol. The night Norgall first arrived, he rushed to the ghetto and told his aides to bang on the doors of the Jews and order them to run to the square immediately to hear his speech. The speech was full of hate; he cursed the Jews and their God and said they were the enemy of the German people. To make sure we understood his intentions, he took out a pistol and fired into the crowd. Miraculously, no one was hurt. People rushed home, and later that night we were told that every piece of gold, silver, and copper in the ghetto had to be turned in to him or we would all be executed by sunset the next day. In the morning, we surrendered all the goods and valuables we still possessed to the new commissar. I remember that my mother gave up her remaining jewelry and gold Russian coins.

When the commissar noticed a good-looking girl, he would call to the foreman, point the girl out, and say, "At such and such a time, this girl is to be brought to my house." All the women lived in fear of attracting his attention. My younger sister was too young to go to work, and my mother did not have to participate in the forced labor because she ran the photography studio, but my mother was worried about Chava, who was a beautiful seventeen year old. To make Chava ugly and invisible, my mother dressed her in a long baggy dress, tied a babushka's scarf over her head, and painted dark circles under her eyes. She told her never to look up, to always look at the ground so that she would not be noticed and raped by the German commissar. This protected her, and thank God, nothing happened to her while we lived in the ghetto.

In the ghetto, we were assigned a small apartment of three rooms — a living room, bedroom, and kitchen — which we shared with a young couple and their baby. The couple had come to our town as refugees when the Germans had occupied the western part of Poland. Their names were David and Manya Zuker.

Manya Zuker was beautiful. The commissar saw her at the photography studio and ordered her to sleep with him. Someone from the Judenrat (a council of Jews organized by the Germans) told him her name. I was sent out of the room, but I remember my mother helping Manya make it look as if she had her period. But Manya had to go to the commissar a number of times, and I remember that she was always scared to death.

David was constantly planning ways to resist the commissar by force. He and Israel Dobina, who were in their early twenties, were planning a revolt together. They reasoned that, although the first few people who tried to escape might be shot, others might succeed in escaping. They apparently gathered all the weapons they could find and got ready for their action, but at the last minute, they were convinced by the community to abandon the plan. The Judenrat had gotten wind of it, and people were afraid that the Germans would retaliate and kill everyone in the ghetto. Of course, the Germans eventually killed most of us anyway.

David Zuker and Israel Dobina eventually were arrested. While being taken for interrogation to another city, they overwhelmed and killed their Ukrainian guards, then escaped into the woods to join the Russian partisans. Unfortunately, they came across a group of Ukrainian renegades instead. These groups had been formed when some nationalist Ukrainians realized that the Germans were not going to keep their promise of a Ukrainian state. They broke away from the Germans to create their own partisan, or renegade, groups. They hated the Jews, like most Ukrainians, and they killed Israel Dobina and David Zuker.

As a family, we did not discuss the possibility of armed resistance. We knew when David Zuker was arrested, because his wife was left alone with the baby in the room next to us. But the community was not organized for any kind of resistance. A revolt was just not in the cards. Only a few young people thought it was even remotely possible. We were not equipped to organize a revolt, and our people were not ready for one. No one had any weapons at all. The people who had joined the militia in 1939, when the Russians came in, had been trained to use weapons, but they had left as soon as the Germans came in, knowing that they would be the first to be persecuted because they had supported the Russian government. Most of them retreated with the Red Army into Russia.

Things were getting worse all the time. When winter came, it was cold — temperatures there could be minus thirty degrees Celsius — and there was no firewood. The snow was sometimes three feet deep. More than once, we could not open the outside door and had to climb out the window. Supplying wood to Jews was illegal, and Jews could not leave the ghetto to gather it themselves. Some villagers were willing to sell us firewood, but they demanded mercilessly high prices.

At night, the people in the ghetto would try to take apart anything in the ghetto that could be used for heat. The place became a real mess. Anything that could be was broken and burned — furniture, floorboards, fences, barns, shelving, and wood-lined walls. Getting a hot enough fire going to sterilize the filthy water was so difficult that we suffered from thirst, as well as hunger and freezing cold. The laborers would come home cold and wet, and could not get warm.

People were desperate and lived in constant fear. They used to come up with theories of why we were not being killed. For instance, we thought that the road was very important to the Germans for their war machine, and that we might be safe until the road was completed. Apparently, the Germans had different plans.

The Mass Murders and Our Escape into the Forest

One of the most terrifying tactics used by the Germans was the night roundups, when the Ukrainian police would come banging on the doors and windows of the houses in the ghetto. They would wake everyone up in the middle of the night, chase them into the square, and line them up in rows. People came out in their nightclothes or whatever else they were wearing. Sometimes they had to remain there waiting for hours, anxious about what was going to happen to them. Suddenly, the commissar would arrive on his horse and deliver a speech, usually about cleanliness. He would bellow that the ghetto was dirty and that he was going to conduct inspections.

This was a calculated strategy. The Germans feared that the Jews might rebel when the Final Solution came. They thought that the Jews, once they realized they were being taken to be killed, would cause trouble. Every couple of weeks, in order to accustom people to roundups, the Germans would pull them out of their houses in the middle of the night. Everybody in the ghetto believed that this was just one of the sufferings we had to endure. But the Germans knew that one of those nights, when they had made the decision and arrangements for the final liquidation of the ghetto, the Jews would already be used to coming out to the square. And that was exactly what happened.

During our time in the ghetto, my father wanted to spare us the humiliation of being taken out at night into the square. There was a small basement in our building and my father managed to find some old wood. He created a false floor that hid the basement hatch. As a result, when you walked into the room, you were not aware that there was a basement underneath. From the floor in the kitchen, we were able to lift up two wooden planks and slide into the basement. Every time they started banging on the shutters and chasing the entire ghetto into the square, we would slide into the basement and sit there for an hour or two, waiting until we heard the noise of the people returning. We would come out when we knew it was safe.

My father built the hiding place with Asreal, the other photographer who worked with my father and mother in the ghetto, and he and his family hid in the basement with us.

Everybody grows up quickly in times like this. Everybody knew perfectly well that we were living on borrowed time. We heard from time to time that a liquidation had been carried out in this or that town, and then in another town, and that another ghetto had been eliminated. However, we were always telling ourselves and each other that perhaps we would be spared because we were working on this important road. You can talk yourself into all kinds of things when you are trying to hold on to the hope of survival.

Rumors spread that an aktion was scheduled in Ludvipol for anyone who ate more than was justified by their work output — infants, children, the elderly, and the sick. Then, Norgall told the Judenrat outright that these unproductive people would soon be killed in a mass slaughter. "Only their deaths can put an end to their miserable lives. No one has the right to prevent them from this death." He asked the Judenrat members to cooperate in order to finish up this business quickly and efficiently. Most people were still in denial about the Final Solution and believed that only the unproductive would be killed. All of the children who could do so then joined their parents at work.

On the twenty-fifth of August, I was awakened from my sleep by loud screaming and by police banging on doors and windows, forcing people out to the public square. The police were exceptionally rough, shouting and cursing. I heard children crying in distress and had a horrible feeling that this roundup was different from the others. I rushed to get dressed because in the past on such occasions, we quickly ducked into our hiding place to wait it out.

My father immediately ordered us to slide into the cellar. I ducked into the entrance with my mother and sisters, and my father assisted Manya Zuker and her baby; David Zuker had already been arrested and killed by then. Asreal's family of five — his wife, two older children, baby, and sister — appeared and slid into the shelter along with us. Thus, we were thirteen people in our small hiding space. There was barely room to stand, and breathing was difficult with so many people squeezed together. The shelter was not meant to accommodate us for more than a few hours at a time.

Then we heard people being driven out of their houses and pushed and beaten toward the square. We heard pounding on doors, screaming from every direction, and the sound of heavy boots running, then kicking and cries for mercy. It was terrible.

We waited an hour, two hours, three hours, four hours. Usually, the people had returned to their homes by then. It was hot and the air was fetid, but we did not dare to move and hardly breathed. We were afraid that someone would hear us. No one returned. This time it was different. Then we heard shrieking, smashing, and yelling again, and knew that this was the final hour. We could hear many, many people — over a thousand of our neighbors and friends — being forced out of the ghetto. If they fell behind or cried too much, they were beaten or shot. The sounds became fainter, receding in the direction of the kasharan, and then it was quiet. But not for long, because the silence was broken by the wailing of people being dragged from their houses and hiding places into the square.

We waited and waited, but there was only the eerie silence shattered by screams and the sounds of people being dragged and beaten.

In our cramped shelter, we had no food, no drinking water, and of course no sanitary facilities. It was pitch black and very hot. The smells of fear were nauseating. Some of us children slumped to the wet floor, where the air was slightly better, although it smelled of urine, and our eyes shut of their own accord for a few minutes at a time.

We had no way of knowing how much time had passed, but the next morning we heard some of our Christian "neighbors" break into our house and fight each other over our few possessions. It was terrifying when we heard them so close, tearing at our clothes. But it was more terrifying when it became quiet and we knew someone was in the house looking for us. There would be a faint whisper of movement in the house, and very quiet breathing, as some villager snuck around and strained for the slightest sound, hoping to flush out a family of Jews. We were paralyzed.

From time to time, we heard outbursts of shooting and screams. We knew that we were not the only ones with hiding places, and we could hear the Ukrainians and Germans searching every house, looking for fake ceilings and other hiding places like ours. Every time they discovered a group, they shouted in triumph. We could hear them kicking and shoving their prey into the street, where they were either shot, right in front of their homes, or beaten and driven into the street and then shot. We could hear all this, the gasping, the kicking, the sobbing, the shooting, and then the silence. We knew that this was really the Final Solution.

The police who were searching the houses for hidden Jews to kill were mostly Ukrainians, with Germans supervising and egging them on. That day, they came into our house and tapped all over the floors with the butts of their rifles to listen for the echo indicating a hollow space. We were desperate with fear, but our little basement was mostly under the yard of the house, and we were not discovered.

Amongst the thirteen of us in the basement, there were two small babies. The babies became hungry and uncomfortable. At the critical moment when the police had come to search the house again, the babies started to whimper. We did not know what to do. If the babies cried out, we were certain to be found and killed. The mothers tried fruitlessly to soothe the infants, and I thought it was the end of our lives. When the babies would not stop and there was no other choice, the men put pillows over the babies' faces to muffle the sounds of their crying. They had to press down hard so that no sounds would escape. Several agonized minutes passed while the Ukrainians searched for us. When they finally left, the pillows were removed from the babies' faces. Both had suffocated. One of the mothers became hysterical and started to moan and weep, and had to be subdued by the men. It was very painful to see both mothers howling silently, and tearing pieces of themselves. The men were in shock. It was a colossal tragedy. We did not talk about it.

No one talked to anyone. We remained hidden in this place for three days, shoulder to shoulder, head to head, with two dead babies, and the knowledge that our own lives, too, were worthless. At any moment, we thought we would be next.

Our condition was intolerable. After three nights, we figured we were going to die there anyway if we did not go out. So, during the night, we left the basement. I guess my father and the other adults decided that we had to go out because we were going to suffocate there. We opened the floor and went outside. It was dark and quiet, and we ran. We meant to run in the direction of the forest, but by mistake we ran away from the forest. The three families got separated and each one disappeared in the dark. But all five of us from my family ran together.

As we were running, we were intercepted by Ukrainians lying in ditches with rifles. We thought they were going to kill us, but apparently they did not want to make any noise that the Germans would hear, so they only robbed us of everything we wore, the few possessions we had on our bodies. They took our coats and shoes and stripped us practically naked. They confiscated everything they could, rings, clothes, whatever. Then they let us run away, almost naked. They left me my pants and shirt, but they took away my sweater, coat, hat, and shoes. They did the same to my mother, sisters, and father.

We were very, very nervous and very frightened, but we were delighted that they did not kill us. We continued running into the woods. My father remembered that one of our loyal workers, the Polish mechanic named Masik who used to run the factory and had collaborated with my father in happier times on ingenious solutions to factory problems, lived not too far away. We went in the direction of his home. It was still the middle of the night, and we knocked on his door. He received us fairly well. He put us in the barn, and he gave us some blankets and food. We had stayed for about two days in his barn when he came in, white and trembling. He said that there was serious danger to him, his family, and to us. He said that if one of his neighbors suspected that we were there and told the police, we would all be slaughtered. He suggested that we go into a secluded area of the forest that was two miles away.

We went. Masik's wife brought us food for about a week. The peasants in that area used to pick berries in the woods at that time of the year, early September. They collected berries in pails and when the pails were full, they would cover them with a white cloth to take home. Masik's wife would put the food into a pail and make it look as if she was going to collect berries.

Then Masik came and said that it was too dangerous to stay where we were. The forest there was small, relative to all the other forests in the area. He said he had heard that in another forest, quite a distance from where we were, there were other Jews hiding and perhaps if we went into that area, we would feel safer because we would be with other people. We understood that he wanted us to go because he could no longer risk his wife bringing us food, and he was afraid for their lives.

We thanked him for his help, and we walked, mostly during the night, to find the gathering place. Jews who had run away from

Koretz, a group of about forty people, were hiding there, and we settled next to them. What else could we do? The High Holidays had just passed and the nights were getting chilly. My father had a little knife, so he cut twigs and we had a fire burning all the time. We sat next to the fire most of the day and night. We built a little shelter from branches, just big enough to protect us from the dew in the morning.

Mostly Ukrainians lived in that area, and we used to go around begging the farmers for food. We could tell which farmers were Ukrainian and which were Polish by the language they spoke. There were also some visual clues. The Polish horses were generally in better shape; they were better groomed and better fed than the Ukrainian horses. The Polish farmers were dressed a little better, too. They were more affluent because the Polish government had given them the best land and had encouraged and subsidized them.

In terms of their physical appearance, the Polish and Ukrainian women and some of the men were blond and nice looking. You could not tell whether they were Polish or Ukrainian just by looking at them. We also knew which village we were in, and from its name we knew whether it was Polish or Ukrainian.

The Ukrainian villages could not be avoided, because the Ukrainians were the majority, but the Polish people were more sympathetic. This was not because they loved the Jews, but because they were a minority themselves and were constantly feuding with the Ukrainians for political reasons going back hundreds of years, so they had similar problems. The Ukrainians had been trying throughout history to gain independence from the Poles, and Jews were always victimized in the process.

Many times, the farmers sent their dogs to chase us off their property. Occasionally, people were nice and would give us some potatoes and bread. We were able to bake the potatoes in the coals of our fire to stay alive. We had no warm clothes. We were all very dirty and covered with lice. There was nowhere to wash, let alone bathe. There were no sanitary facilities of any kind. Drinking water was not the problem — there were streams, although it was too cold to wash in them. We lived from day to day and did not know what to do with ourselves.

At first we had matches that Masik had given us, but when they were gone, we started fires by placing some dry grass on the ground and focusing the sun's rays onto it with a piece of broken glass. In no time, the straw would start to smoke and then ignite. Lighting a fire was dangerous because we might be seen but we had no choice because we had to keep warm and roast our potatoes. The lice plagued us, so when a fire was already burning, we would put our clothes over the smoke, and the smoke would cause the lice to loosen their grip and fall off. You could hear the crackling of the lice as they fell into the fire.

The smoke from our fires put us at risk. The area was reasonably flat, with some small hills, so if someone looked at the forest from a distance, they would probably have seen the smoke on the horizon. Maybe that is how the Ukrainians later discovered where we were.

We were there for about a month until, suddenly, we were attacked by a group of Ukrainian police. They had hunted us down and came in shooting their machine guns from every side. We all ran in different directions and did not know what happened to the others. I hid in a bush.

When everything was over and things were quiet, I thought I was the only remaining survivor of the group. Then I heard a woman calling, "Children, where are you? Where are you?" Her voice did not sound familiar. Then she started to call names, my father's name, my sisters' names, and my name. I realized that it was my mother calling out, and I ran to find her. I saw she had been shot in the arm and the bullet had shattered the bone. She had been lying for hours and had lost, God knows, most of her blood. She was in terrible condition. I dragged her under the bush where I had been hiding, and after bandaging her wound, I made my mother a sling out of her underwear.

I remembered that we had left some potatoes lying on the ground near the fire, which had been burning for many days and was still hot. I ran and threw a few potatoes onto the coals, then ran back to our hiding place because I was afraid that the Ukrainian police might come back. A while later, when I estimated that the potatoes were baked, I made a dash to the campfire and pulled the potatoes out, and took them back to feed my mother. She was very weak and kept fainting. Somehow we slept through the night in the forest, just the two of us.

We heard no other human voices. It was frightening to be there in the woods, alone with my badly injured mother. I tried to reassure myself, but did not have much time to think because I was busy trying to take care of her.

We decided the next day to return to the forest where Masik lived because we did not know what else to do. It was a long way to walk. My mother leaned on me, and it took us a whole day because she kept fainting. On the way, I got some milk for her from some farmers. Some other farmers on the way told us that two little girls had passed through there the day before, and that one of them had said her name was Golub. The Ukrainians cannot pronounce the "G," so they say "Holub." I remember exactly how he said, "One of the little girls said she was Holub's daughter."

So I knew my little sister Esther was alive. To my surprise, we found her when we arrived. God knows how a little girl ever managed to find her way from such a distance. She had escaped the attack. She was practically naked when I found her. Apparently, Esther had taken her shirt off and put it over the smoke of the fire to de-louse it just before the attack and had run away without her clothes, just a little underwear. Some decent farmers along the way had given her an old dress.

When we arrived at the place near Masik's house, I found a woman who had been hiding there with her two daughters and a son. They had stayed there when we left. There was also a single woman named Leah, so we were a little group and it felt better not to be alone anymore.

My father had always kept a pocketknife with him, and it had been in his pocket when we made our escape from the ghetto. That three-inch pocketknife was our only weapon and our only tool. On the day my mother was shot and my father and sister Chava were killed, about half an hour before we were attacked, I had asked my father for the knife to cut some wood. By chance, I had escaped with that little knife.

I used it to make a small hut, about the size of a kitchen table, for my mother. I cut four or six V-shaped branches and stuck them in the ground, with the forked end pointing up. Then, I connected them with sticks of wood and overlaid the structure with lightweight leafy branches, leaving one side open for access. There were a lot of pine trees nearby, but I looked for trees with leaves and laid them on the floor for her to sleep on. By the time I finished cutting branches, I was exhausted. The structure protected us from the dew, which was very heavy, and provided a little shelter. In the morning, I felt lucky that no animals had attacked us.

I did not know what else I could do for my mother. She was so weak that she just lay there all day. I went back to Masik and told him what had happened to her, and he gave me some alcohol, perhaps vodka, and cotton. He told me to use it to put compresses on her wound. Believe it or not, the wound started to heal. The bone was shattered, but the wound itself started to look pinker and a little bit better. I changed her bandage with the alcohol every day. She cried so much because of the pain — it burned her terribly — but she knew that we had to do it.

The woman who had been there the whole time was well-to-do. She had owned the large dry goods store in Ludvipol. She was a very capable businesswoman who had been widowed for a long time. She had managed to salvage some gold that was sewn into her son's quilted vest and said that she was negotiating with some local farmers for a hiding place where we could all stay.

So again, we had some hope of surviving. Leah, the single woman from our group, had gone off to gather firewood when, suddenly, Ukrainians attacked us. Out of nowhere, they appeared with semiautomatic machine guns, firing from every side, taking us by surprise. I saw a policeman standing with his rifle aimed right at me, and I thought that was it, I was a goner. My mother, who was lying in the little hut I had built, heard the commotion and crawled out. When she saw that he was about to shoot me, she screamed, startling the man with the gun. He whirled around to see what was going on, and he shot her to death instead of me.

Somehow, I was able to run away in that split second. In a situation like that, you become like an animal. You just run and you hope everyone else is running too. I ran like a gazelle. They shot after me continuously, but they missed me.

I did not see what happened to my little sister Esther. But she was not around after that, and neither was the woman, nor the three children who were with her. I had to assume that they were all killed.

As I was running deeper into the woods, I stumbled upon Leah. She was hysterical. Apparently, one of the bullets fired after me had hit her in the thigh and she was bleeding profusely. She was lucky that the bullet had entered and exited her leg without damaging the bone, so I grabbed her hand and dragged her and she was able to limp along beside me until we finally felt we were a safe distance away. Since I already had the experience of handling my mother's wound, I tied up her leg with cloth torn from her undergarment to stop the bleeding. We walked together during the daylight and in the evening, we saw light from a farmer's house in the distance.

We knocked on the door of the farmhouse and asked for food. He gave us some food and told us about a place in the woods where Jewish people from Koretz were hiding. The farmers knew everything that was going on in their area — you could not hide anything from them. If they wanted to tell a Ukrainian or German policeman where there were Jews, they could give explicit directions and the Germans would not even need to look for smoke from our little fires. The farmer gave us perfect directions, in an area of forest that was about twenty square miles. It was quite a long walk but we made it.

There were about forty people there. Some of them had dug holes in the ground and constructed bunkers and huts. One group had built a large cabin. The cabin was dug down about three or four feet below ground level, with an entryway and steps leading down. The wood above was arranged like a gable. They had obtained a potbelly wood stove and a chimney, and their place was fairly warm.

Among them was a family I knew from Ludvipol. The father's name was Joseph Grosspich but his nickname was Diodia. My father had hired him from time to time to work with horses. That was how he made his living. In addition to his wife and two children, they had with them a younger boy I knew, Moshe Furshpan. The remaining people were from Koretz. But the cabin was crowded and the people were mean; they would not let me in.

Another group included five of the people who had been in the hiding place with us in the ghetto — the photographer Asreal and his wife, whose baby had been suffocated, their two surviving children, and his sister. They were dressed well; they had not been intercepted when they ran out of the hiding place and still had their clothes. That family had dug a bunker, about ten feet by ten feet, and all five of them slept in it. They slept huddled together, with their clothing and blankets. There was no heat in their bunker — a fire would have been too smoky — but their body heat kept them reasonably warm. They did not let me sleep with them. They left me in a corner by myself, without a blanket, just some rags wrapped around my feet. I do not know what subsequently happened to them, or to most of the people along the way.

The weather had become very cold. I did not have any shoes or clothing except some rags I had gotten along the way from some farmers. The rags around my feet got wet during the day and froze at night. No one in this hiding place gave me anything to keep me warm. My hands did not freeze because I always held them in my armpits. My nose and ears did not get frostbitten either.

The winter was especially severe and we went around begging for food from farmers, who would throw us a few potatoes. We could have survived if we had been left alone and not been attacked all the time. My feet were beginning to hurt me badly — I guess they were beginning to get frostbitten, but there was nothing I could do because the people who had the heated hut would not let me stay with them. Gradually, my condition became worse and worse, to the point where I was in such pain that I was no longer able to walk.

I have thought about this over the years. The feet are often the first part of the body to get frostbitten. I imagine that in prehistoric times human beings walked on all four limbs and the heart was in a more central position in the body. But when we started to walk upright, perhaps our legs grew bigger and longer, and the heart remained where it was, so the legs are now farther from the heart and have less efficient circulation.

Another group of about thirty-five Jews was hiding on the other side of the road that cut through the forest. Suddenly, we got word that during the morning hours the Ukrainians had attacked their camp and slaughtered most of the people; one or two escaped. One of the men knew we were hiding deep in the woods, and he came to warn us and to seek shelter. Our group was very concerned that we would be next.

Most of the villages on our side of the river were Ukrainian, but across the river, there were some Polish settlements, so people thought the other side of the river would be safer. They had heard rumors that the Jews were better off there and that some of them were armed with rifles. Our group decided to abandon the camp and go to the other side of the river. But because I could not walk anymore, they decided to leave me behind.

However, their attitude toward me seemed to improve and

they started to treat me better. They picked me up and put me into the hut with the stove. They left me some wood and a little food. Maybe they felt bad leaving me behind, saying, "We're sorry — we have to run because the people next to us just got killed the other day, and we might be next. But we can't drag you, we can't take you with us. We promise that when we get to the other side, we'll do whatever we can for you."

Although they did not say so, I think the leaders of the group realized that the people with rifles on the other side of the river were my relatives — Uncle Usher, Aunt Chava, and their sons Boris and Alex (Shalom). My uncle, who had always been respected — farmers used to tip their hats to him instead of setting their dogs to chase and bite him — was said to be "ruling" that area. Diodia knew my family and uncle well, and, if I am correct, the moment he heard the name "Usher Edelman," he became fearful; he knew that if my uncle held him responsible for what had happened to me, his life would not be worth much. He had not allowed me into his hut, not even in the most bitter cold, not even to just warm up a bit. He was a simpleton and very cruel.

Perhaps he thought he would have to answer for my life if the truth was revealed. Later, my suspicions were partially confirmed by his behavior. Although many people in the group came to my uncle for food or favors, he and his family never did, perhaps because they were afraid.

When the group left me behind, they said they would see what could be done. One of the men said, "Maybe someone will come back and get you." I think he meant my uncle.

They left me there, all alone in the woods. Fortunately, the hut was very strong. Wolves and coyotes came and scratched on the door all night. They became brazen because there was no one to frighten them off. I guess they knew there was a living person inside. I was very frightened. But eventually I realized they were not able to break through the door and got used to the fact that they would come every night. Anyway, there was nothing I could do since I could not walk.

I just waited there to die. God knows what I was thinking at that time. I was alone there for at least ten days.

Then one day, a farmer looking for wood in the forest saw the four or five log cabins, and must have thought they were abandoned. Dismantling the cabins would be simpler than chopping down trees. I could hear chopping noises from a distance. He must have noticed that smoke was coming out from my cabin, through a little metal chimney, so he came over. There was a small window in the roof for light, and he looked in and saw me lying there. I could see that he was hiding his face so that I would not be able to see him. I suppose he was afraid that if I were to be caught and interrogated, I would identify him. People were afraid for their lives — the Germans did terrible things to those who helped Jews stay alive. But he came back the next morning, opened the window and lowered down a bottle of milk for me on a string. Every day he came and brought me food.

Meanwhile, the people who left me behind had managed to cross the river and were looking for a place to stay. At this time, no Jews lived in houses; they had to live like animals in the woods. My uncle Usher, however, was a very unusual person, strong and tough. He somehow managed to get weapons and to live in a house in a secluded area, close to the edge of the woods near a swamp. God knows who owned the forest, but the owner had employed a Polish watchman, and this was the watchman's house. The watchman was in the army, but his young wife and her daughter lived there. My uncle, my aunt, and my cousin Boris were living with this woman.

To say that my uncle, a Jew, lived in a house was like saying a person had gone to the moon because for a Jew to live in a house at that time was incomprehensible. In this house, they baked bread and had food. Other people used to beg for food and would come to my uncle's house because he was, by those standards, a well-to-do person. My Aunt Chava was a very kind woman, and shared whatever she had with everybody. My uncle's older son, Alex, joined the Russian partisans and fought with them until the liberation.

Rescued

Apparently, a woman from the group who left my side of the river went to my aunt and asked for some food. My aunt put hot soup and bread on the table. A conversation developed, and my aunt asked, "Where are you coming from?" Little by little, the woman told her that she had come from the other side of the river. As an aside, she said, "Oy vey, we left a little boy there." After my aunt questioned her for a while, she realized that I was the little boy left behind. She practically fainted when she figured this out, and as soon as my uncle came back, she said she was going to commit suicide if he did not go and find me immediately.

The Germans closely guarded the only bridge across the river and checked everyone who crossed it. I do not know what he threatened or how he persuaded him to do it, but my uncle forced a farmer he knew to cross the river to look for me. My uncle had also heard about a little girl, Faygele Welman, whose parents he knew, who was being raised in another farmer's house as a Christian child, and he told the farmer to stop by that house and pick up the girl, too. Whatever the means of persuasion, they worked.

The farmer retrieved the girl first. Then, suddenly, as I lay in my cabin, I heard somebody calling my name. I got so excited that even though I could not walk, I managed to run out of the cabin before I fell in the snow. The farmer picked me up and put me in his wagon. During the night we traveled to the River Slusch.

There was only one route for him to take back over the river and that was by way of the bridge. The farmer was very scared, but my uncle must have really frightened him, and he decided to risk it. It was freezing cold, and the Germans were inside a tiny booth at the guard post by the bridge. A German came out and asked the farmer, "What's going on?" The farmer said that he was transporting a wagonload of hay to feed his cows. We were lying hidden on the bottom of the wagon, covered by a six-foot-deep layer of hay. Normally, the Germans would have stabbed their bayonets into the hay to search it thoroughly, but because it was so cold, the guard just waved us through.

The farmer brought Faygele and me to the house where my aunt and uncle were living. We had a joyous reunion. They immediately stripped me of my filthy clothes and burned them. They bathed me and dressed me in clean clothes. I got so excited that I asked them to turn on the electricity — I forgot that there was none, of course. People were lucky to have a little kerosene lamp or wood saturated with sap to burn for light.

Faygele Welman's brother Mordechai came to my uncle's house to pick her up the next day. She survived the war and settled in Israel.

I slept through the night, and when I woke up in the morning, the foul smell of my feet permeated the house. My feet had been frozen for a long time, but now that I was in the nice warm house, they thawed out. They were in terrible condition. Again, my uncle, because he had weapons and was a fighter, went out and pressured a Christian doctor from a nearby village to advise him on medical treatment. The doctor suggested that we should coat my legs with lard and wrap them in bandages. That was the only thing he could suggest under the circumstances.

My aunt and uncle tried this for a day or two, but my toes were just hanging off the end of my feet by the skin. My aunt took a pair of scissors and cut off all my toes. I watched her do this, but I did not feel it because everything was dead down there. After she cut off my toes, she put on bandages improvised from cotton cloth that they washed and reused. My aunt washed the wounds every day with warm water and she kept my feet very clean. I never got an infection and, gradually, my feet began to heal.

After a while, I began to feel as if I were living like a normal human being. I stayed in the house for a few weeks, perhaps a month. One day, a farmer came running in and informed us that the Germans were in the village. Since this house was about a half mile from the village, we only had a few minutes left in which to escape. In desperation, my uncle grabbed my aunt and the weapons, and ran into the woods.

I was left in the house with the Polish watchman's wife. Before I knew what was happening, I heard a German officer in the kitchen talking to her. She was a very attractive young woman. When the German officer walked into the house and saw her, he suddenly had things on his mind other than what he had come for. He befriended her, so to speak.

German policy at the time was that if they went into a house and found someone who was sick, they killed the sick person and burned the house down, because they were always afraid of typhus and other contagious diseases. The officer came in and looked me over. He asked her, "Who is this?" She told him that I was her sick little brother. Then he spoke to her in German and a little Polish. I heard a commotion in the kitchen when he did as he wished with her. Later, I heard him inviting her to come visit him where he was stationed nearby in a small town on the Russian border. He left in good spirits, on good terms with her, and he neither killed me nor burned down the house.

A few hours later the Germans left the village. The woman was hysterical, crying and screaming for hours, when my aunt and uncle returned. She said she would commit suicide if they did not remove me from the house. My uncle did not know what to do with me at this point. He knew, however, that they had to take me out of the house.

There was a bunker in the woods nearby where Jewish people had hidden several months before. The Germans had already raided the bunker and shot it full of bullet holes — the people had either escaped or been killed — but it was relatively safe now. The likelihood that the Germans would come back that night was very low. The bunker was dug into the ground, with logs stacked up against each other, and it had a very low roof.

My cousin Boris carried me there on his back because I could not walk. This was the first of many times that my cousin Boris carried me to safety. Every time we needed to change location to evade the Germans, Boris picked me up and carried me on his back. He was very devoted and saved my life more than once. Much later, on her deathbed, my aunt Chava told him to take care of me.

Out of sheer desperation, my uncle and aunt put me into this bunker for the night while they pondered what to do next. I remember them explaining to me that the woman was completely hysterical and would not let me stay in her house any longer. They said they could not force her to be quiet and let me stay in her house. There was a bench in the bunker, and my aunt and uncle made me as comfortable as possible on the bench, then secured the door and left. I am sure they felt terrible leaving me there, but they thought I would be safe for the one night.

The bunker was not as safe as they thought. During the night, again, animals came and scratched at the door, trying to break in. Coyotes howled all night long. It was the beginning of April and the snow was melting. I heard water seeping into the structure all night, flowing in under me. I could hear it coming and coming and coming. I put my hand down and touched the water as the level rose. I was frightened that the water would rise until I drowned. But the bench was at just about ground level, and when the water reached ground level it stopped coming in.

The next morning, my aunt opened the door, stepped down into the bunker, and fell into the water. When she had left me the night before, the bunker had been dry, but now it was half filled with water. She was horrified. She and Usher were always concerned for my safety.

After that, my uncle made a decision to move to another location altogether, because he thought that this one was too well known to the Germans as a hiding place where Jews might be found. Again, my cousin Boris carried me on his back, perhaps ten miles, maybe longer, and we went to Levaches, where my uncle managed to secure a room for us in a house at the edge of the village. The owner of the house was both a farmer and the tailor for the village and surrounding area. He had been crippled many years before and limped severely when he walked. We stayed there for a short time, while my uncle and Boris built a temporary hut for us in the forest nearby. I was unable to walk at that point, so they kept me in bed, and the tailor was very nervous about this. Every day, he asked my uncle, "When will you remove the one who is lying there?"

We relocated to the hut when it was completed and stayed there for the entire summer, perhaps six months or longer. Little by little, my feet improved slightly. They fashioned crutches for me from branches, and stuffed wads of cloth into big shoes to cushion my feet and hold them in place. I was finally able to get up off my bed and hobble around a bit.

Lots of Jews wanted to be near my uncle. They felt safe with him because he and my cousin Boris had rifles. The farmers in the area had great respect for him, too, although some were also afraid of him. My aunt was a very good-natured person. Word of her kindness spread like wildfire. If anybody had a wound or other problem, they came to Chava for help. We were surrounded with eighteen to twenty-five people. For safety reasons, the huts were spread over several locations. People used to come, even during daylight hours, to find food or help. My uncle always had enough food at that location.

This was the summer of 1943. The war was not going well for the Germans. I suppose they no longer had as much time to run around the woods hunting for the few individual Jews who had taken refuge there.

The Russian underground, the partisans, were establishing a stronger presence in our area and I would see them from time to time. We hid our weapons whenever they came so they wouldn't take them away; they were a military group and needed weapons themselves. They were fighting against the Germans, our enemies, but as much as we welcomed them, we were also afraid of them because they might confiscate our weapons and leave us with no means of self-defense.

The relationship between the Russian partisans, the Ukrainian nationalists, the local Poles and the Germans was complex and our fate was entwined with its outcome. After World War I, the Ukraine had been divided between Russia and Poland. The area we lived in, Ludvipol, belonged to Poland. The Ukrainians, who had for years been struggling for independence, were frustrated when their land was divided between the two countries. To secure their assistance, the Germans promised them an independent Ukrainian state in exchange for cooperation against Russia. Entire military divisions of Ukrainians went over to the German side, weapons and all. Civilian Ukrainians volunteered for militias that worked on behalf of Germany.

Eventually, however, they realized that the Germans were not going to give them an independent Ukraine. In fact, the Germans were also murdering them. The Ukrainians formed their own militia, called the Bandera, after their leader, Stepan Bandera. They were particularly desperate and cruel. They fought against both the Germans and the Russians, but most of their hatred was aimed at the Poles. They perpetrated horrendous atrocities, like raping women and then cutting off their breasts, or occupying Polish villages and killing all the inhabitants. They also were very happy to kill every Jew they came across.

Nevertheless, the woods gradually became safer. We had not heard of any searches or attacks by the Germans for a long time. My uncle decided it was safe enough to build a permanent log house for the winter. He and a Jewish carpenter built a log cabin together, which was partially dug into a mountain. It was almost a real house in the woods.

My uncle, by then, already owned a horse and a cow that we were able to milk for ourselves. My uncle was able to obtain enough food through his contacts and we no longer had to go begging for food. In comparison to what I had lived through previously, living in this house was like living in paradise. There was food and a big oven where we could bake our own bread, we had meat, and we ate reasonably well. We had enough wood from the surrounding forest, so the house was warm.

Because my aunt had mercy on anyone who asked for help, the new cabin quickly filled with people. Within a short time, we were fourteen people living in the house. We were crowded, but felt safe because we had weapons and were fairly secluded in an area away from major pathways.

We heard news from time to time that the Germans were retreating and the Russians were coming. The Russian partisans were becoming more active and raising their profile. Our hopes that perhaps, somehow, we were going to make it through the war were lifted once again.

I remember that one day during this period when we felt slightly safer I was walking outside. On the other side of the hill where our log cabin stood, I found the corpses of two Ukrainians lying frozen in a ditch. They were civilians, not soldiers. Boris and I were fascinated by the corpses, and every couple of days, we went back to look at them and check whether they were still there.

Earlier, Boris had been in a Polish village called Kozarnik, quite a distance away. He had seen the whole village chasing two guys who had run towards him shouting in Ukrainian, but the villagers caught them and locked them up. Then the Poles celebrated and drank vodka far into the night. Boris drank with them, but did not find out what the two Ukrainians had done wrong. He thought these were the two prisoners. We always wondered about what they had done, and why their corpses were in a ditch so far away from Kozarnik.

My life and that of my cousin, Boris Edelman, became closely linked, as I have described. To provide some additional perspective on what was going on at that time, Boris graciously agreed to share his story about what happened after the Germans came to Bistricht.

Boris Edelman's Story

"A few days after the Germans took over Bistricht, they came to our house and asked my mother to go and clean a barracks nearby that had been used in the past for Polish army cavalry shows. I went instead of my mother. As I started to walk up the steps, I saw a German coming down them. It was the first time I'd seen a German. The German saluted me without realizing that I was wearing the arm band with the Magen David (Star of David) on the wrong arm. Later that day, I had to go back to the barracks, and the same officer was there but this time he saw the Magen David on the wrong arm. He pushed me against the wall and said to another German, 'Shoot him. How can a Jew live that long?' The other man took a shot, but the bullet went into the wall near my head. He must have decided to let me go. The grit from the wall had flown into my eyes, so I couldn't see anything, but I could hear the noise from my father's flour mill, which was not too far away — the gas generator could be heard from as far as a kilometer away and these barracks were at most half of a kilometer away — and I walked toward the sound. When I got to our house, my mother rinsed my eyes with water.

"For the next couple of days, similar things happened. I was getting in trouble. The police came for my older brother, Alex, because a German needed someone to do something, and I went instead of him. The German had been watching the forest for Russian soldiers on the other side of the river, the Slusch, and wanted me to take a burnt cooking pot, dishes, and some other things to the river to wash. The pot was covered with soot from being used on a fire. I took the things and was starting to walk down the stairs when he said, 'No, you must crawl down the stairs,' so I crawled. He didn't give me anything to clean the pot and dishes with, but I did the best I could and then brought them back to him. He was sitting there, picking his teeth. He grabbed the pot and pushed it into my face, showing me some burnt part that was still there. Then he beat me in the face with the pot and said, 'Go back and make it clean.' I went back to the river and tried to get it cleaner, then came back, and he beat me some more. Finally I went home, my face all swollen.

"My father was not a poor man, and when the Germans put all the Jewish people into the ghetto in Ludvipol, some of the local farmers said, 'This is the best Jew. Don't put him in the ghetto. We want him here because he knows how to run the mill and we have no one else to do it.' So the Germans left us alone for a while. But one night, the Ukrainian police, who knew us, knocked on the door and then broke it and came in. They laid my brother, father, and me down in one of the bedrooms and said, 'Put your hands over your eyes. We're going to shoot you.' My mother started to beg them not to. 'Come,' she said, 'I'm going to give you gold!' She went to a shack where the valuables had been hidden underneath some firewood, and gave them the box of gold, jewelry, and who knows what. They grabbed it and took everything out of our house, and loaded up an entire wagon with our belongings, even our clothes. The only thing they left was a little jacket of my sister's that they dropped by mistake.

"At some point, we moved into the ghetto [in Ludvipol], but our house faced out. Later, we were permitted to move out of the ghetto, across the street. I suppose it was because my father was friends with some of the people on the Judenrat.

"Early one morning, a friend of our family came to our window and told my mother, 'They are assembling us and we are going to get killed.' He used a Jewish expression for going to die, going to go 'lulu.' Immediately, we got very panicky. My sister Riva started to put on one dress on top of another; I suppose we had gotten some clothes by then. I walked out to the door and saw Germans running to the houses and assembling the people, and there were people already standing on the main street in the square, ready to march to their graves. When I saw that, I told my older brother, 'Alex, let's run!' He said, 'I'm sick and cannot run.' I ran outside and saw a neighbor, Lazar Raber, get down on his knees and crawl between the weeds near a little creek, and I followed him. He was older than me and jumped over the water. I jumped, too, but fell. I grabbed hold of a fence, but it was rotten and collapsed on me. A German standing on a nearby bridge heard the noise and started to shoot. At that moment, my sister Riva came out of the house and when she saw the German aiming his rifle at me, she ran back into the house and shouted, 'Mommy, they have shot Boris!' My mother said, 'Don't worry. Boris has long legs. He's going to run away.'

"Riva ran out of the house in the same direction as me, and was shot and wounded. She was suffering. I learned later, from a woman who was watching from a hiding place in a double wall, that the German commissar, who knew her — she was pretty — went and shot her, and told the soldiers to bury her immediately, right there.

"Lazar and I, and a girl who was with us, wandered for a couple of days. Lazar went to a place in the woods where a few farmers lived and found his family there. But there were too many of us for the farmers, and Lazar's family said I had to leave. I went back towards Bistricht.

"As I went alone through the thick woods, I met up with five wolves, standing and looking at me, not fifty feet away. I understood that wolves are afraid of fire, and went down on my knees, grabbed some leaves — it was autumn — and made a small fire. The wolves were just standing there and staring at me. I was scared. Then they walked away. They did not run. Today, the thought occurs to me sometimes that we have to be afraid of two-legged animals, not four-legged.

"I crossed the river and went to a village where a good friend of my father, a farmer, lived. It was in the middle of the night when I knocked on his window to ask if he'd seen anyone from my family. He said he had not seen them, but that the mayor was going to the city, Ludvipol, the next day and maybe there would be some news soon. He let me stay overnight. The next night, he told me that there was a rumor that my father and two sisters had been killed. He also told me that I had to leave, because he did not trust the mayor or something like that. I stayed in his barn overnight and left the next night.

"I went back towards Bistricht and the house of another farmer, Schmidt, whose family was good friends with our family. On the way, a Ukrainian gave me food. I got to Schmidt's house and knocked. They were all having dinner and I asked Schmidt if he'd seen my father and my family. 'Where do you think your father is?' he quizzed me. 'I don't know,' I responded. And then he said to his daughter, Nadia, 'Take him to his father!' Nadia took me by the hand to the barn and showed me a ladder, and at the top of the ladder, in the hay, were my father, mother, brother, and two younger sisters, all having a meal.

"When the Germans had been rounding people up to kill, my mother had put up a ladder, and she, my father, my two sisters, and a cousin had climbed behind the chimney and hidden under the roof. My father's mother had stayed in the house because she had a cough and was afraid she would cough and give away the hiding place. The Germans had come into the house and said, 'Are you Jewish?' 'Yes,' she said, and they picked her up and put her in front of everyone, a few thousand people, in the square. And they had her walk with everyone else, marching behind town to the soldiers' barracks, where they made them dig their own graves, and killed them the next day.

"In the barn, my family asked me, 'Do you know where Riva is?' but I did not know. We did not stay there for long because the farmer's son was a policeman working for the Germans, and the police ate dinner there occasionally. The farmer's wife was very worried that they would come and find out about us, so we left one evening and crossed the river into the woods.

"For several days, we sat in the woods near Levaches with nothing over our heads. Then a farmer came. I remember that he took my brother's boots to be repaired, but never brought them back. He kept saying he would bring them but he never did. Then one time, he brought the Germans.

"By now our group consisted of my father, my mother, my two little sisters Chaya and Rosa, who were about six and seven or eight years old, my brother Alex, Judah and Devorah Raber, another girl, two sisters, Rachel and Cipa, and me. Some of us — I think it was my father, Judah Raber, Alex, and I — went to find a place that would be a little safer than where we were, and to start making a little camp. My sisters wanted to come, too. They begged to come with us. 'Please, take us. We can help,' they said. But my father said, 'No, you can't come. Mother will cook you some breakfast soup on the fire.' As soon as we started digging out the new camp, we heard shooting very close. We ran in different directions. For several hours, we hid and walked around. When we came back to the others, we found that they had chopped off my little sister Chaya's head. One of the sisters was lying there, beaten up, dead. Devorah Raber was dead. My mother and sister Rosa were missing.

"I somehow got lost after that. I remember that they were shooting at us. Eventually, I learned that my mother had been taken in by a local farmer, and I went there and asked, 'Maybe you've seen my mother? Everyone's dead, but she's missing.' The farmer said she had been there and he had sent her to another farmer, half a mile away.

"My mother was there, by the fire in the farmer's kitchen, warming up her bare feet. I said, 'Let's get out of here. It's dangerous.' We went to a barn and I found a big raincoat and took it. We went into the woods, and I made a fire and warmed her up and covered her with the coat. I told her what had happened, but she already knew about it. The next night, we went back to the place where we had been, and we found only a leg with one little boot. Haya is Hebrew for animal. Chaya was my sister's name. A haya ate up Chaya.

"Then we were just wandering around until we found my father and brother. Rosa was still missing. We were asking if anyone had seen her. And someone said, 'Yes, she is lying in the field about twenty feet from the creek.' It was the little creek where we used to get water. She had been running towards it and was shot. She apparently fainted and died. We found her dead, lying there with her eyes open, and her hair around her...and her beautiful dress. She was seven or eight years old. My father said, 'We have to bury her here,' and we dug a grave, and put her in it, and covered it with brush. Then my father lay down in it and said, 'I want to be buried here, with her.' He would not get out. We had to pull him out of it, finally.

"Often, we lost each other. One night, my father, brother, and I crossed the river to Bistricht. Ukrainian Banderas were there, preparing to attack the German police in the village, but when they saw us, they started to shoot at us. We ran in different directions. Apparently, my father fell and one of them said, 'Kill him!' but when they picked him up to kill him, my father recognized a neighbor, Alexander, and started to hug and kiss him, and said, 'Oh Alexander!' Alexander said, 'You can't kill him. He was my neighbor, and he owned the flour mill.' That night, we heard my father clearing his throat and recognized the sound. We were so happy. In the dark, we called out, 'Papa!' Really, we were all walking around those woods like lunatics.

"Somehow, the three of us got together with my mother and went into the woods again and built a camp next to where a Polish man, a Mazurian, lived. The Polish people of this area were Mazurians, who are a little different from the other Poles. The man was a forester for the government, a *gayurve*, so he had a little house there in the forest, although he was away, fighting somewhere, I think. We were there for several months. My mother was not well, however, so she stayed in the house with the man's wife and two small children; perhaps there was one child, not two. After a while, we started to stay in the house, too.

"While we were there, my father found out that Aharon was alive and lying somewhere across the river, maybe eight or ten miles away, and he persuaded a farmer to go across the river and bring him back. The farmer found Aharon and hid him on a wagon full of straw, and brought him to the house where my mother was hiding.

"Aharon was just bones, like a skeleton. He couldn't walk because his legs were frozen. My mother washed his legs and cleaned him — he was filthy, full of lice — and she gave him clothes. I remember how excited he was because my mother was cooking some peeled potatoes. 'Oh, you have peeled potatoes!' he said. Then his legs started to smell terribly. My mother and I were cleaning them as well as we could. And then his toes started to fall off. We put a knife in the fire to disinfect it, and cut them off, because they were already falling off.

"My mother was trying to keep his legs and feet clean with hot water, and maybe she had alcohol, but they were infected. Then one day we learned that there was a German doctor not too far away, about eight miles. This was one of the old-time Germans, people who had lived in the area for a long time. So I carried Aharon on my back — I always carried him on my back — and went through the woods to find the doctor. We knocked on the door, and when he opened it, we pushed ourselves in. We showed him Aharon's legs, and he gave us some bandages, medication, and liquid disinfectant, and told us that we needed a lot of melted fat because there was no ointment. After that, I went around begging for fat, and my mother melted it and applied it to Aharon's wounds. She would wash the wounds, put the disinfectant on, and bandage them. We needed a lot of bandages because they got smelly, and we went back to the doctor several times. I remember how my mother was hugging him all the time. It was going on and

131

on and on. Aharon was lying on the floor because there was no other place to put him. I went into the villages every night and got food, whatever I could find, for him. But we had to abandon the house because the Germans became aware that Jews were hiding nearby. At that time, Alex joined the partisans.

"My mother always told us, Aharon is not well and if something happens to him, we should take care of him. We were healthy and strong, and always tried to help him. I carried him, brought him food, and cleaned him when he couldn't move. I used to take him outside and hold him like a baby when he had to move his bowels. Until his wounds healed, which took a long time, and he got crutches, he was very helpless.

"By then, we were eleven people, and the farmers in the area knew we were there. It seemed dangerous, so we went somewhere else. At one point, we were staying in the house of a crippled farmer or tailor, and it was snowing and very cold. Then we heard from him that the Germans had come into the village nearby. 'Run!' he said. And we started to run, but nobody could carry Aharon. The tailor said, in Ukrainian, 'Take what's lying down there!' and I turned back and picked Aharon up. I put him on my back and ran into the woods. Some farmers had given us two rifles, one of which was very nice. Maybe they had sold them to us. Somehow my father had gotten them. When I couldn't carry Aharon anymore, I set him down in a tree, covered him with a blanket, and loaded the rifle and hid it under his blanket, and said, 'Stay quiet, and if they come into the woods and you see them, don't shoot unless you see that they're going to shoot you.' We survived.

"I remember when Aharon stood up for the first time. It was like the first time a child stands up. He was very excited. 'Look! Meme (auntie), look! Look! I'm standing on my feet!' he said. He was holding on to the roof, not really standing by himself, but we realized he would be able to walk a little bit. So my father got him crutches, and right away, he started to walk by himself and even jump.

"After the tailor's house, we crossed a swamp and got to a mountain. We started to dig into the mountain and made a log house. We got bricks from four or five miles away and made an oven, with a chimney, and were able to warm it up inside. We got a door and a window, and established ourselves. My mother's aunt was there. She had lost her son, and I remember that she was upset and kept saying that I should shoot her. We stayed in the log house over the winter. There was a lot of snow that winter. Sometimes, we were snowed in and couldn't open the door, although we made a way to climb out. We had a bucket, and for water, we went to the swamp, which wasn't too far, and made a hole in the ice. I was tall, strong, and healthy, and used to go out at night and bring back bread, maybe butter and potatoes. I always carried a rifle. I remember how Aharon used to sit and clean the rifle over and over again. There was nothing else for him to do, so he would clean the rifle. In the spring, it was easier because we could pick mushrooms on the mountainside and eat them, and we had some potatoes because my father knew farmers in the area. Salt was a big problem, but he was able to get a little bit of it.

"Spring and summer passed. Then Rosh Ha'Shana approached. In our house in Bistricht, my father had had a small synagogue with a Sefer Torah. We lived about eight to ten kilometers from town [Ludvipol], and my father used to invite all the people in the surrounding countryside to pray at our house. Now, my father said, 'Rosh Ha'Shana is coming. We should go and get the Torah and bring it here.' So my father and I went to get the Torah. We crossed the [Slusch] river, went to Bistricht, and got it from the Ukrainian farmer who was hiding it for my father. I was carrying the Torah, and my father was carrying a sack with potatoes and food on his back, and we had to cross the river again. My father said, 'Don't get the Torah wet. Hold it up high.' The water was so high it was almost in my mouth, and then it was in my ears, even though I was on my tiptoes, and I was stretching my arms up as high as I could. And finally, we were across the river. I had not let it get wet.

133

"We brought the Torah into the woods, and before Rosh Ha'Shana, my father got hold of a big, tall bull or ox, almost as tall as I was. Someone there was a kosher butcher, and he made the *brucha* (blessing) to make it kosher and slaughtered it. It made a lot of meat. My father invited anyone who had survived to come. The room was only big enough for eight or ten people, and there were maybe fifty there, peeling potatoes, making soup, and so on. We had some *siddurim* (prayer books), too, which my father had managed to get. My father, who was a very religious man, was praying loudly, begging that we be spared, and crying, bending and praying and crying. That was the autumn of 1943. We stayed there for another winter."

AHARON GOLUB'S JOURNEY

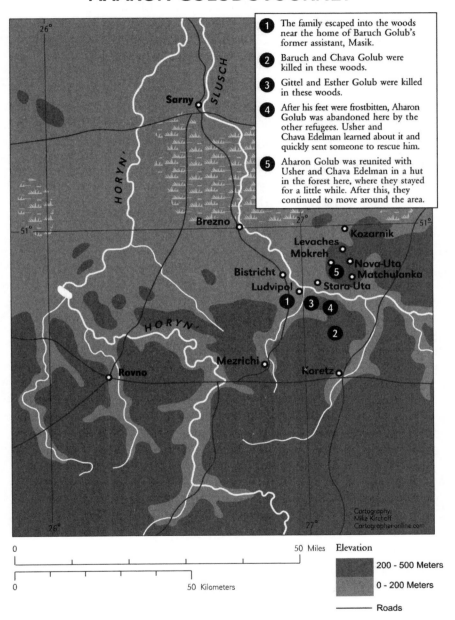

1 The family escaped into the woods near the home of Baruch Golub's former assistant, Masik.

2 Baruch and Chava Golub were killed in these woods.

3 Gittel and Esther Golub were killed in these woods.

4 After his feet were frostbitten, Aharon Golub was abandoned by the other refugees. Usher and Chava Edelman learned about it and quickly sent someone to rescue him.

5 Aharon Golub was reunited with Usher and Chava Edelman in a hut in the forest here, where they stayed for a little while. After this, they continued to move around the area.

Cartography:
Mike Kirchoff
Cartographer-online.com

| 0 | | | | | | 50 Miles |
| 0 | | | | | 50 Kilometers | |

Elevation

200 - 500 Meters

0 - 200 Meters

———— Roads

For Us, the War Ends

We knew the war was going badly for the Germans. There were fewer and fewer attacks or searches for Jews in the woods. My uncle had contacts with people in the villages. One day he brought us the news, "The Russians just occupied Ludvipol and they are on the way to Rovno. They've already passed us."

How was it that I survived? I think it was just luck. Or maybe, if there is a God, it was meant to be. I was not smarter than the others. It just happened this way. Every human being's instinct is to want to live and to do everything possible to stay alive. I did whatever I could. I had help from my cousins, uncle, and aunt; they played a great part in my survival. Without them, I would never have made it through that period when I was left behind in the forest.

After liberation by the Russian army on January 10, 1944, we moved out of the woods into a village called Matchulanka, about twelve kilometers from Ludvipol. Prior to the war, Ludvipol was the county seat, where the government administered the villages in the area. Before the Germans retreated, they burned Ludvipol to the ground, so the Russian government had to find another place for the county seat. They established a provisional township in Matchulanka, not far from where we had been hiding, while they continued to fight to the west, and my uncle went there after a few weeks to find us a place to live. Many other survivors from Ludvipol also settled in Matchulanka.

My uncle rented part of a house from a farmer's wife in Matchulanka. We used the living room, and the woman lived in the kitchen with her two children and slept on top of the big brick oven. Although security continued to be a major problem, we began to feel like normal human beings again, living in a village and surrounded by neighbors.

My cousin Alex, who had been fighting the Germans with the Russian partisans, returned and got a job with the Russian government fighting the remaining bands of Ukrainian nationalist terrorists (the Banderas), whom the Russians were trying to eradicate.

Meanwhile, my cousin Boris did some business distilling vodka with a man and his son in the village of Kozarnik and selling it to Russian soldiers coming into the village. The soldiers paid with food, which was in short supply, such as canned foods from the United States, received through the Lend-Lease Agreement. The cans had Russian labels printed over the English.

While we were waiting to see what was going to happen in this area, Jewish survivors started to emerge from the woods. Matchulanka almost doubled in population, and housing became a real problem. Jews started renting rooms in adjacent villages. After a few months, my uncle decided that we should move into a larger city, closer to civilization, to see what the future would bring.

The Russians announced that any former citizen of Poland could either remain in what was now Russia, or they could move west over the new border into what was now Poland proper. In keeping with the Jewish tradition of always moving west, farther away from the "czar," we decided to repatriate to Poland.

We had to wait for papers. We got a horse and wagon and, with our meager possessions, went to Koretz for a couple of days to stay with friends. From Koretz, there was a paved road to Rovno, and we were able to get into Rovno by truck. My uncle secured an apartment in Rovno at 22 Szkolna (School) Street in a Jewish area not far from the big synagogue. We lived there from February to August 1944, during which time we were notified that we would soon be repatriated to Poland.

Rovno was a big city with about twenty-six thousand Jews prior to the war. After the war, very few were left, but survivors came

from the surrounding areas, and there were two functioning synagogues. Little by little, people found friends and relatives. Life was
not too bad. My uncle got a government job with a Russian insurance company, and we all did everything possible to earn money.
I sold cigarettes on the street. Every Monday, there was a farmer's
market, and all the farmers came into the big city to sell their produce. Aunt Chava used to cook her wonderful Jewish soups and
sell them from a pail, with rolls, to the farmers. I brought food by
bicycle to the market and helped out in whatever way I could. The
Russians did not approve of private enterprise, but small-scale ini-
tiatives, such as selling soup, were not challenged. There were no
schools at that time for me to attend. We waited while my uncle
was making arrangements for us to go farther west.

When we were in Rovno, my uncle and aunt purchased a used
bed frame, made out of metal tubes, which could be dismantled.
Whatever valuables we had, such as jewelry and American dollars, were put into cylindrical cloth bags, like links of frankfurters,
and slipped into the pipes. This bed stayed with us for a long time.
When we arrived somewhere, we would take the bed apart, turn
the metal tubes upside down, and the bags would slide out. No one
ever suspected what was hidden in the bed, and we used to joke
about the bed being a border crosser. After I left my uncle and his
family much later on, they were still able to cross borders, even
when they were carefully searched, without their valuables in the
bed being discovered and confiscated. Even the heels of their shoes
might be removed during a search, but no one ever checked the
bed frame.

Near our apartment in Rovno, there was a passageway to the
Russian soldiers' barracks. One day, I saw some soldiers walking
with a boy about my age who was dressed in a Russian uniform. I
was curious so I spoke to him and he turned out to be Jewish. His
name was Leon, or Eliezer, Rubinstein, and he was from Koretz.
We had a short conversation, and I invited him to my aunt's house.
She was a very kind woman. Every time someone came who had

no place to stay, we made room for them; we only had two rooms, so we used to take a door off its hinges and put it between two chairs to make an extra bed. My aunt served Leon some of her famous soup and other homemade foods that he had not tasted for a long time. Leon and I became very good friends, and we have been close friends ever since.

We left Rovno at the beginning of 1945. One day in March, we were told that a special transport train would take us to our destination in Poland. All the people who were registered were supposed to be there at a specific time and were assigned room on the train based on the size of their family.

My cousin Alex had returned from his assignment with the Russian security forces and was ready to repatriate with us. He had met a beautiful young widow named Sally, whose husband had been killed not long before by the Banderas, and we decided to take her and her baby, Lila, with us. My uncle had also arranged to take a man who was otherwise alone. Thus, we were a large enough "family" to qualify for our own car on the train.

When we were allowed to leave Rovno, we were going to go to the new borders of Poland on the transport train with thousands of other people leaving the Ukraine. The journey was long. Every so often, when the tracks were needed for important trains to pass, we were put on the siding to wait for clearance. Sometimes, we waited two or three days. My uncle was imaginative and very capable, and we had enough food; maybe it was provided for us. We were as comfortable as we could be in transit. Eventually, we wound up in Bitom, a mining city in southern Poland that was full of Jewish refugees from all over.

I recall that my cousin Boris always carried a pistol, during and after the war, and everyone begged him not to take the pistol on the train because the Russians might discover it and throw us off the train. I remember walking with him and another man, and noticing the grease boxes between the wheels of the train. We wrapped the pistol in plastic and rags, and threw it into one of the grease boxes. The pistol survived the trip. When we arrived at our destination, I stood watch while Boris retrieved the pistol.[1]

My uncle managed to get us a nice furnished apartment in Bitom. It had once been a German home and its previous occupants were Jewish refugees who were ready to head farther west. We settled there for a while.

At that time, the German people were quite devastated and in great need of food. Many people used to buy food in Poland and take it by train to Germany, where they would exchange it for anything of value, like watches, suits, and coats. Boris and Alex tried their luck at this business and earned some money. My uncle also did some buying and selling of other items. There was a market where people exchanged money, too. My uncle was always able to provide sustenance for us; we never received any help from any organizations.

One day, we were sitting and talking on the couch in the living room. I was a restless teenager and was sliding my hands between the cushions. I felt some little packages in the seam between the back and the seat. I pointed them out to my uncle and he removed the cushions and found bundles of money neatly laid in there. It was American occupation money, the official currency used in Germany. We were excited about this bonanza, but my uncle said, "The money must belong to the people who lived in the apartment before, and they will come to retrieve it at some point." A month or so later, someone knocked on the door and explained that he had left something behind by mistake. He went to the couch, put his hand in the seam, and there was nothing there. My uncle said, "Don't worry, we found the money, and here it is." The man was very grateful. He gave me a reward, thanked us for being honest, wished us good luck, and left.

Alex married Sally at a wedding in the apartment and things began to seem almost normal again. We felt reasonably safe in the streets, and life returned to some semblance of normalcy. Although the war continued, farther west, deep into Germany, it was over where we were.

We were busy trying to reestablish our lives and survive. There was a mixture of Poles and Germans in Bitom, but millions of Germans from that area had left for what later became East Germany.[2]

In Bitom, I heard that Jewish organizations from Eretz Yisrael were offering shelter to Jewish orphans and would eventually bring them to a permanent home in Israel. One day, when I was out in the market, I came across someone who told me about such a group. I went to visit them and made up my mind that I was going to join this organization and go to Israel. I had already decided that I did not want to live in the Diaspora any longer, and that I wanted to go to Israel, to a Jewish state where I could defend myself and no longer be easy prey for others. I had always been brought up as a Zionist, so the idea of going to Israel was not foreign to me.

My entire family, — my uncle, my aunt, and my cousins, — made up their minds to go to the United States, and I realized that this meant that we would have to part.

I am sometimes surprised that I had the courage to make such a bold and independent decision, considering that my feet were in poor shape and I was giving up the umbrella of protection I enjoyed while living with my uncle, who was such a capable and able man; my aunt, who was such a nice woman; and their sons. But my desire to go to Israel was so strong that I decided that no matter what else happened, even if they did not want to, I had to go to Israel.

Apparently, some of the Edelmans also considered going to Israel. Boris has said that when the war finally ended, he, too, wanted to go to Israel but the people gathering refugees for Palestine were only taking orphans at that time.

My aunt and uncle were very sad about my decision, but they did not stand in my way. They said that if I felt so strongly about not living in the Diaspora anymore, they would not object. They loved me as if I were their own child. Many years later, when my uncle died, he said in his will that whatever he had must be "equally divided between my nephew and my two sons." I was like a son to them, and they were like parents to me.

After living in Prague, Czechoslovakia for several years, Usher, Chava, and Boris immigrated to Canada, arriving on August 15, 1949 on the *Samaria*. Alex (Shalom), Sally, Lila, whom Shalom had adopted, and their infant, Bobby, were already in Brooklyn. Shalom immigrated with papers saying he was going to be a yeshiva student. Later, they moved to Canada to join the rest of their family. Usher worked as a builder in Canada and also served as a chazzan. Coming from Europe, he already knew everything necessary to be a chazzan and, since he was a *macher* (Yiddish for a person who gets things done), it was not difficult for him. He was a fine gentleman, a modern religious man who prayed every day, even when we were in the woods.

Chava Edelman

Usher Edelman

1. Boris has a different memory of this; he recalls being too cautious to risk bringing a pistol.
2. Subsequently, Germans who relocated to East Germany after the war established a strong political organization to regain the land from Poland. After the unification of East and West Germany, an irrevocable agreement saying that the land had been given up to Poland for good was signed.

Aharon Golub in Bitom
(about 1945)

Left to right, Shalom
(Alex) Edelman, Boris
Edelman, Sally Edelman,
Usher Edelman, Chava
Edelman, and Aharon
Golub (Bitom 1945)

Lila Edelman (Feinstein),
Usher Edelman, Sally
Edelman, Chava
Edelman, holding Bobby
(Sally and Shalom's
infant) Edelman in a
Displaced Persons' camp
(Prague, about 1947)

Legal Papers for Palestine

I gathered my possessions and joined the children's organization, one of many Jewish organizations trying to sort things out. I moved into a nice home run by survivors of the Warsaw ghetto uprising who were connected with Israeli organizations. Many Jewish refugees were still coming to Bitom. Suddenly, we felt safety in numbers. Since I was one of the older boys in the group, almost eighteen, and spoke Hebrew fluently, I became a Hebrew teacher and a leader. I felt good about becoming a useful person again.

I was very fortunate to have already lived with my uncle and aunt for quite a while, so I did not show signs of distress from my wartime experiences. Most of the other kids appeared to be normal, but were still suffering from traumas. They had lived in the group's home for a while and were well fed, clean, and dressed in decent clothing, but they had nightmares and often cried. Some of them remained withdrawn and were unable to communicate or express themselves. Part of my job was to help them. We started to teach them Hebrew with singing lessons, dancing, and games, so it became a happy place for them.

After staying with the group for some time, we were notified that we were ready to set out for Israel. Meanwhile, the war had ended. The British controlled Palestine, and because of oil interests and political interests, they went along with the Arabs to limit the immigration of Jews into Palestine. The British White Paper allowed only 1,500 legal certificates per month for immigration to Israel. Because most of the thirty-two children in our group were under eighteen years old, we were told that we would be able to legally go to Palestine. That made life easier because we did not have to sail on one of the illegal ships, which were often caught, and their passengers taken to detention camps in Cyprus or sent back to Europe.

One day, we were picked up by trucks and taken to Poland's border with Czechoslovakia, but we could not cross this border legally. The organization had arranged fake documents identifying us as the children of Greek refugees who were returning to Greece. We were told not to speak Polish or any other Slavic language. We could, however, speak Hebrew, which would sound like Greek to the Poles. The leaders also taught us a few Greek words, which I still remember. The Polish guards took their time looking over our papers, but let us pass through the border. I remember their crude sexual remarks about the girls in our group. We understood what they were saying and had to force ourselves not to react, not to smile and not to laugh. We passed the border and, on the other side, boarded a train to Prague.

Our appearance was relatively normal and our past experiences did not overtly affect how we looked or acted. We really did look like we could be the children of Greek refugees returning home. On the train, we overheard some of the passengers speaking Czech, a language similar enough to Polish for us to understand. They felt sorry for us and kept on making remarks like, "Oh, look at those poor children without parents." Some of the other passengers gave us little gifts. I remember that one salesman, who apparently sold spools of thread, opened his little attaché case and gave almost each and every one of us a spool of thread. God knows what he thought we were going to do with them, but we accepted them because it was much easier to smile than to say, "We don't need it" in a language that would expose our identity. So we accepted the gifts, shook their hands, and said in Hebrew, "Todah," which means "thank you." They did not realize it was Hebrew.

In Prague, some buildings were occupied by Jewish and Israeli organizations, such as the Joint Distribution Committee. We got identity cards from the Joint Distribution Committee and we no longer had to pretend we were Greek refugee children. We were taken to a place where there were clean rooms, beds, food, and everything else we needed, and we stayed there about a week. I believe it was an unused military base. Prague's streetcars were running, and we rode them into the city. Once we got to Czechoslovakia, we were free to speak any language we chose and so could explore the city without fear of giving ourselves away.

After about a week, we were told to get ready to go to Germany. We would be crossing the border illegally, on foot. I was concerned because I could not walk any significant distance. The young man in charge of taking us, an Israeli from the *Haganah* (the underground military arm of the *Yishuv,* the organized Jewish leadership in Palestine), told me not to worry. Because it was winter, they would have sleds to carry what little we were taking along. If I had trouble walking, they would pull me on a sled. I was able to speak to this young man in Hebrew, and we developed a friendship.

I asked him what would happen if we were stopped at the border. We were going to cross the border in a secluded area, he said, and hopefully it was prearranged with the guards that they would look the other way. He then lifted up his jacket, showed me a pistol, and said, "We're crossing the border one way or the other — if we're stopped, the people who stop us will not live. We are going to cross." I had a wonderful feeling of true liberation because someone was carrying a weapon to protect us, rather than to kill us.

As it happened, no one was guarding the border when we got there. There was always the danger that Russian officers might appear at the station unexpectedly — although Czechoslovakia was independent, Russia was beginning to assert itself there — and that the Czech border guards, wanting to show how efficient they were, would intercept us. But we crossed to the other side without incident.

Trucks from the American armed forces took us to the Leipheim Displaced Persons (DP) camp, a former SS officers' camp in the American-occupied zone near Munich that then housed about three thousand refugees. It had opened in December 1945. Before we could settle in, we had to go through an American health inspection to make sure we did not have lice and were not carriers of typhus or other contagious diseases. They lined us up in a room with a huge gasoline-powdered DDT duster. Today, we know that DDT is extremely dangerous, but in those days nobody knew. They put the nozzle of the compressor into the neckline of our clothes, pressed the button, and so much powder shot out that it came out from our sleeves and pant legs. When we walked away, there was powder all over the ground except for a clear spot where our feet had been. Whatever we had or did not have definitely got killed.

The boys and girls were split up so we could strip naked and dress in the new clothing that was waiting for us. All they had were military uniforms, and the smallest shirts and pants I could find were still too long. We were each given brand new clothes and assigned rooms in the former SS barracks, two to a room. The barracks were charming little houses with nice clean beds and carpets.

The new place was so beautiful, and our rooms were so clean and well furnished, that we could not help but feel that we were finally liberated and living in a new world. At four o'clock, we went to the main dining room. There were many young Jewish men and women there, all waiting to go to Palestine. We were treated with special care because we were children. They gave us tables that were charmingly set, with plentiful food. They gave us chocolate, and the American soldiers gave us other goodies. We could not believe our good fortune! When we finished eating, everybody took a pile of food back to his room.

We felt very comfortable in Leipheim because there were Jewish activities, including a newspaper committee and classes. We got along well, too. We were kids, so of course there was a certain amount of mischief. I already had a few friends from the group. Leon Rubinstein was there, having arrived about a month earlier. Another young fellow who became a lifelong friend, Ezra Sherman, was there with his brother and sister-in-law. Since he was a young boy, they brought him in to stay with us.

We managed to find a little electric waffle maker and a lot of wonderful bread and margarine, so we decided to make toast in our room. The aroma was so delicious that all the other kids came knocking on our door to see what was going on. Since we did not have a lock on our door, Ezra hooked up an electrical wire to the handle of the door, so that anyone who touched it got an electric shock. This kept all the unwanted kids out of the room while we were making our toast and other goodies. Finally, we had gotten some spunk back in us! Even though we were a little old for it, some of us started to "relive" the childhood days that we had never had.

After a couple of weeks in Leipheim, the camp organizers decided that we should not stay there any longer. Maybe they felt that it was not healthy for a small group of children to stay among so many grown-ups who were struggling with their own traumas. We were moved to Landsberg, which was also in the American zone of occupation. We found a large number of people there from our organization, Dror. Not only were we all going to Palestine, but we were all in the same political movement. Things were good for us there.

Since our schooling had been interrupted, the leaders thought it was time for us to be educated and arranged with the American administration for the use of an empty German school. The building had a number of classrooms and a kitchen, so folding beds were brought in and we lived in the school where we attended our lessons. A German woman cooked for us. While we were staying there, we visited a nearby prison, located very close to the school, where Hitler had written his book, *Mein Kampf.*

There was a big celebration when we were notified that the papers had come through allowing us to enter Palestine legally. My papers stated my age as sixteen so that I could stay with the group, though I was really eighteen. The British did not permit eighteen-year-old Jewish males to enter Palestine. Their concern was that young men might fight with the Jewish underground against the Mandate or help illegal refugees get into Palestine.

Somehow, the Jewish organization worked with the American army to move us; it is my understanding that Jewish American soldiers had a lot to do with helping organize our transportation. We were allowed to use American trucks. In addition, the Joint Distribution Committee and other organizations provided us with food, clothing, and other necessities. The trucks delivered us to the railway station, where we boarded a special transport train to Marseilles; there were approximately fifteen hundred passengers, mostly children. I would imagine that we represented almost all of the Jews allowed to enter Palestine that month. Getting to Marseilles took over a week because this train, too, had to wait on sidings now and again. But there was plenty of food. The train had benches that were long enough to sleep on. We also climbed up and slept on the luggage shelves. We were young and excited.

We arrived in Marseilles, and were amazed to see how well organized everything was. They drove us in trucks to a provisional camp, told us exactly which buildings we should go to, and gave us cots and food. We stayed there for about ten days for medical exams. We were not permitted to leave the camp, but since there were so many youngsters there, we had a good time.

Subsequently, we were picked up by U.S. Army trucks and brought to the *Champollion*, where we were assigned to quarters according to the group and political organization with which we were traveling. The ship itself was too crowded to be comfortable. Most of us slept in hammocks. My feet were not in very good condition. I did not have special shoes, only regular shoes lined with cotton, and they caused me constant pain. It was an ongoing struggle, but I was young and felt as if I was coming to life again, like a flower in April starting to bloom after a hard winter, so my pain did not matter that much to me.

We met another group, fifty youngsters from Hungary, and we passed the time very pleasantly. I got to know one of the girls well enough to keep in touch with her for a while in Israel. The ship was also transporting four or five hundred French soldiers. We left Marseilles and went to Morocco; Algeria; Bizerte, Tunisia; and Alexandria, Egypt. At some point, perhaps in Algeria or Bizerte, the soldiers got off the boat, but we were not allowed to disembark. In Alexandria, we exchanged chocolate for oranges with the Egyptian stevedores. Growing up in Poland, we had rarely had oranges, which were an expensive commodity in Europe at that time. From the ship, we threw chocolate, which had been given to us by the American soldiers, down to the Egyptians on the pier, while they threw oranges up to us. Some of the oranges fell in the water, which to them was no big deal since they had cases of oranges. But when we saw oranges fall into the sea, we felt like jumping into the water to retrieve them because they were so precious to us.

From this juncture forward, no one ever talked about what had happened during the war. I could never speak about it myself until recently. For many years afterward, talking about my painful past, even to my wife and children, was impossible.

The *Champollion*, the boat that carried the Dror children to Palestine

Back, left to right, Miriam Peltz, Aharon Golub, Behira Zakay, Shimshon Klakstein. *Middle,* Hannah Haklay, and Shmuel Peleg. *Front,* two of the younger children (Landsberg, Germany 1946)

Aharon Golub (*back left*) and some of the Dror youths (Landsberg, Germany 1946)

Aharon Golub (*back right*) and some of the Dror youths, including the mothers of several of the children and the leader, Natka (*center*). The younger children did not go to Yagur. (Landsberg, Germany 1946)

Aharon Golub's immigration document (1946)

III

A New
Beginning

New Life in Our Ancient Land

We arrived in Haifa on April 27, 1946 when I was almost eighteen years old. We were legal immigrants and were treated well at every turn. Israeli buses with Israeli drivers, displaying big smiles on their faces, were waiting to take us to a nearby absorption camp called Atlit, where immigrants and refugees were processed.

We were assigned a tent and again underwent medical examinations. Our paperwork was filled out, and our pictures were taken. During the week or so we were there, we were treated well, fed wonderfully and eventually given our identification cards. The various groups from the boat were assigned to different destinations, with the Jewish Agency or Va'ad Leumi making the arrangements. When it was time to leave, the Hungarian group of forty or fifty children was sent to a kibbutz called Naan. Our group of about forty, the original thirty-two plus eight who joined us in transit, was sent to Yagur, a prominent kibbutz near Haifa with about 1,200 members.

From that point on, our lives changed completely. Just knowing that we were in Israel and riding a bus through Haifa was one of the peak experiences of my life. The weather was perfect — the sun shone brighter, the sky was bluer — and the atmosphere was festive. We were finally home.

When we arrived at Kibbutz Yagur, at the foot of Mount Carmel, everyone stopped work and came out to welcome us. I cried — I feel like crying now, just thinking about it. There was great excitement. People lined up on both sides of the long driveway, and cheered as we drove by. The dining room was decorated with flags and filled with wonderful food. We were treated like celebrities, with dancing, singing, and baskets of gifts at a wonderful reception. This was one of the finest days of my life, like a fairy tale come true.

The kibbutz was proud to have us and treated us very well. For us, it was like one big family, even though they allowed us some autonomy as a group. At first, they tried to assign us to families, but we were already older, and we did not have a great deal of time to spend with the families. Nor did the families have time to devote to us. They had their own children and, in the evenings, they would take their children back to the children's houses at about nine, tuck them into bed, and kiss them goodnight. We worked and studied all day and had many activities in the evening as well, after which we went straight to sleep because we woke up early in the morning.

A number of the senior kibbutz members made a great sacrifice on our behalf, they gave up their quarters for us, despite having waited ten or fifteen years to get them. Most of the members lived in wooden houses; cement homes were being built as fast as finances allowed and were typically given to the oldest and most senior members. Thus, we were quartered in the best housing in the kibbutz.

Our building was two stories high, with outside stairs to the second-floor rooms. We occupied about twelve rooms, with each room large enough for up to four people. I was given a small ground-floor room so that I would not have to climb steps. The room had a private entryway and two windows, and I shared it with my friend Shimshon. It was convenient and comfortable.

There was not yet indoor plumbing at the kibbutz. Every house had a faucet out front for washing up, and there were several bath houses within walking distance. Everyone ate in the communal dining room. Today, kibbutz members have an apartment of two or three rooms, a private bath, and their own kitchen, although they can choose to eat in the communal dining room when they want to.

For the "older" people — age forty or fifty — who had arthritis and other ailments, a woman maintained special tubs of mud from the Dead Sea. Because of my condition, I was given a key to access them and could go there whenever I wanted to take a shower or bath. I felt comfortable taking off my shoes there because it was private.

Within a few days, I went to have my feet examined. The kibbutz doctors sent me to specialists in Haifa, including a plastic surgeon who decided to remove the metatarsal bones and much of the scar tissue. The surgery was performed at Carmel Hospital. After two weeks of excellent treatment, I was fitted with orthopedic shoes and released. Back at Yagur, I stayed in bed for a while, and my friends visited me every day. Gradually, my condition improved and life became much easier. I had much less pain when I walked. I became a normal guy, almost like everyone else.

At the kibbutz, we were tested and grouped by level of education — some of the Dror children had never gone to school. Two *madrichim* (counselors), Shoshana and Shlomo, were assigned to be our teachers and leaders, and they stayed with us from morning until late in the evening. We went to them with our problems. Shoshana was a *sabra* (a native-born Israeli) and not yet married. She taught the more advanced group, of which I was a part. Shlomo taught the other class. I am not sure whether he was born in Israel. He was married with three children. Being back in school was exciting, and we all worked very hard to advance our studies.

There were problems to overcome, such as sickness and the emotional scars from the war, but we received unbelievably sensitive care. For instance, if the housemother found lice on one of the girls, she waited until the middle of the night to wash her hair, to spare her embarrassment, although her wet hair still gave her away in the morning. Kerosene was used for treating lice. If a child had a habit of bed-wetting, the night patrol would wake him up and take him to the bathroom. If someone needed medication in the middle of the night, they always got it. About five of the children in our group were sent to convalescent homes in the mountains or near the sea, because of their extremely poor health, such as anemia, late development, depression, or severe problems of the throat and eyes.

Soon after our arrival, the complicated political situation in Palestine caused a major event in the history of Kibbutz Yagur. By 1946, when we arrived, there were three distinct military groups in Israel. Some of the freedom fighters — the British called them terrorists — did not see eye to eye with the Haganah, which was the "official" underground army. Neither the Haganah nor the Palmach, which was like the Green Berets of the Haganah, carried out independent actions. They took the long-term perspective of shaping a moderate national policy. The other two groups, the larger being the Irgun (Etzel), headed by Menachem Begin, who later became Israel's prime minister, and the smaller being Lechi, acted independently and were considered breakaway groups. At Yagur, we worked only with the "official" Jewish leadership and the Haganah.

My feelings about the breakaway groups, the Irgun and Lechi, were mixed. The three groups did not always coordinate their actions, to say the least. The Irgun and Lechi made a number of daring moves on their own; they worked on their own and made their own decisions. Often, this caused problems because suddenly, while certain accommodations were being negotiated between the Haganah and the British, they would do something, such as kill British policemen, and the good will that the Haganah was trying to create would go down the drain. There were times when the Haganah was planning a major national action and a day before it was to take place, the breakaway underground would do something rash that alerted the British and brought out the patrols and policemen, so the national action could not be carried out.

But many of us now feel that the Irgun and Lechi caused Great Britain so much misery that, in their own way, they probably expedited its departure from Palestine. Great Britain had as many as

100,000 soldiers in Israel, due in large part to the activities of these groups. The Irgun and Lechi routinely killed people and blew up bridges.

In 1946, Etzel carried out a major attack, blowing up a wing of the King David Hotel that housed the British government offices and the headquarters of its Criminal Investigation Division and killing many British officers and civilians. To do this, they managed to hijack the milk delivery truck, emptied out a few canisters of milk, load them up with dynamite, and deliver them to the lower level of the hotel. After the canisters were unloaded, the blast was set off, either by remote control or a timer, and an entire wing of the hotel was demolished. One hour before the explosion, they warned the British to evacuate the King David Hotel, but the British ignored the warning.

I lived in the kibbutz at that time, and we knew what was going on. Of course, the British reacted decisively, with curfews and all kinds of restrictions. They kept bringing more policemen and reinforcing their bases. The whole country was put on a war footing, and they decided to crack down on the Jewish establishment. They started to search for weapons, not only those of Etzel and Lechi, but everywhere. That led to the events of Black Sabbath.

On Black Sabbath, June 29, 1946, the British stormed Yagur and arrested all the men, hauling them off for questioning. They left the old people, the women, and the children, but confined us to our living area with a barbed wire fence. Even the bathrooms were off limits, and we could only use them if we were escorted there and back by a British soldier. All we could do to harass them was to go to the bathroom constantly. A few times, the women started walking toward them as if they were going to try to break through their cordon. Although the soldiers stood with their bayonets ready, they backed off, rather than using them. As individuals, the British soldiers acted with a great deal of restraint while they were at Yagur.

Unfortunately, however, they succeeded in finding our caches of illegal weapons, which had been smuggled in and were extremely important to our cause. Only a select group of members knew about the existence of the secret weapons (I was not one of them). The weapons had been covered with paper and wax for protection. Using huge magnets, the British found a large number of rifles, ammunition, mines, and machine guns. They emptied us out. We mourned the loss.

It was a very difficult time in Israel and Yagur, but we did not give up. We were intent on working and training, learning discipline, judo, the firing of weapons, and other combat skills.

Kibbutz Yagur's economy combined manufacturing, agricultural products, and income from outside work. We produced tin cans that were used for soda, fruits, vegetables, fish, and other goods. At the time, we were actually the largest can factory in the Middle East. We bought fully automated machinery that was considered obsolete in the United States. We fed the metal in at one end and a complete can emerged at the other, properly rolled and soldered. Older members, for whom work in the fields was too physically strenuous, could sit and work in the factory. We also had a large agricultural training school on our grounds, with its own facilities and dormitories. The school belonged to the Jewish Agency and students came from all over the country to study.

Agricultural products were very lucrative for the kibbutz. We sold chickens, eggs, milk from our hundreds of cows, sheep, wool, flowers, especially roses, and fruit, such as apples, pears, and grapes. Dairy products were distributed from the kibbutz, using at least ten of our own trucks, via a dairy cooperative called Tnuva. Some of our members taught at colleges and six of the kibbutz members were bus drivers — bus drivers and college professors had equal status, though driving a bus might have been slightly more prestigious. All outside salaries went into the kibbutz treasury.

There were a small number of permanent, full-time jobs within the kibbutz, such as the secretary and some of the senior people in the bookkeeping department, but everyone else worked wherever they were needed most. Each person checked in when he went to work, and every division submitted a roster of who had worked and who had not at the end of the week. The management handled the finances and reported the results, so all members were aware of our financial condition.

One of the key principles of the kibbutz charter was to be self-sufficient and to live by our own sweat — not to exploit others. We were a communal system and believed that we should not enrich ourselves through other people's labor. Thus, when we hired workers, who were usually from the refugee camp, they not only received their wages, but also a bonus, proportionate to the kibbutz's profit, at the end of the year. These new immigrants were often shocked when they received this extra payment.

On May 1, 1947, exactly one year after their arrival, the Dror group created a pamphlet with written contributions from each member, including memories from the war, the journey, and their new lives as part of the kibbutz. The children described their work, the hikes in surrounding areas, and their thoughts. The pamphlet was written in a literary, almost academic Hebrew, probably with help from older kibbutz members. I wrote the following introduction to it:

"When I realized it's been a year of my life in Eretz Yisrael, many thoughts crossed my mind. I remembered all the difficult past; I remembered myself standing in front of a cruel death without knowing why and what for. I've heard in stories and legends about heroes who died while protecting their people and honor, and others who died for their crimes and sins, but us...us!!! I did not protect and I did not sin, and with no trial or justice, I was about to die. I did not understand much but I was accepting my destiny.

"The days have passed, an entire year is over. I have felt I am free. Yes, I am free of the Germans, but am left without parents. I had to make up my own mind, what to do and where to turn. When I came from Poland, I joined the *Hevrat HaNoar* (youth community) of Dror. Together we lived, together we were happy, and together we suffered. At difficult moments, everyone was willing to sacrifice everything, sacrifice the present, in order to reach the future, to reach a point that seemed sacred to us.

"There is no way to describe the instant when we boarded the train to go to Germany. We were beginning the journey to the Holy Land! We were so excited that we could hardly speak. But this moment was forgotten soon. More important moments on our way to our destination arrived. Such was the time when we boarded the ship, the ship that steamed bravely to the shore of our homeland. The days felt like years, especially the last day on board. We descended in Atlit, and the bus came to take us to our new, permanent home. In this home, people work their land, and with hard work they provide for themselves — these people standing near the gate and waiting with open arms for us to arrive.

"On that day, we crossed through Haifa. We saw workers and youngsters demonstrate with red flags and, with these flags, express the freedom they achieved in their land. And here, we were accepted in Yagur. We felt the people wanted the best for us, with all their hearts. And now a year has passed. We are now an organized *chevra* (community). Now, we are not just people brought together around one table by conditions or a situation. Each member of the group knows that he is building a home for the future, that he is building a strong foundation for generations. We feel our own progress. We have achieved great things in our chevra. We have a common treasury, which is the base for collective and social life, and we strive with all our hearts for progress, and to fulfill our goals.

"When I recall the first days of our arrival, I do not recognize myself. Getting used to normal life was difficult for us. For several years, we had gotten used to arriving in a place and waiting for the day we would leave it, and getting closer to our destination.

And now we have arrived. Believing that we are actually supposed to stay here and build our lives was hard. In my vision, it was a holy thing. In reality, it is not perfect. When you return to a normal life, you start to notice details that you did not notice before. Everything that was wrong in exile, we hoped would change here in this country. In the first days in Yagur, we noticed small details that went against what we had hoped for in Israel. They were small things, but important, and it was puzzling. We hoped that social conditions would be better, and here and there we realize different things, such as that among the kibbutz children, one has a watch and the other does not, one has a bicycle and the other one does not. How it influences them, I do not know, but it had a bad effect on us. Our ideals were hurt....

"Now we are working youth, youths of the Land of Israel. All of our energies are directed toward work and study, for the future, and for the concerns of the children — those who suffered with us and those who still suffer there now, far away from the homeland."

Getting caught up in the world of the kibbutz was easy. We did not think about the past. Life was totally different now. The place hummed with activities and training, and we were always busy. Work started at 6:00 AM, and we had our main meal at about noon in the dining room, where we ate all of our meals. Mealtimes and seating were flexible. After lunch we showered and rested, and then we went to school from about two in the afternoon until five or six o'clock. Dinner was from about six to eight, and then we went to lectures, concerts, performances, movies, or discussions. We could visit the well-stocked library, or attend classes in such subjects as photography, dance, and music. I took a photography course. Many of the activities were conducted by intellectuals and artists who had come to the kibbutz from Germany in 1937 or 1938.

One man in particular, Mr. Glass, was a skilled musician. In the evenings, we used to gather on the Mediterranean-style roof of the dining room — flat and quite large, almost the size of a football field — to listen to Mr. Glass play recordings of classical music and operas. He would play excerpts from an opera, such as *Aïda*, and explain the music and the libretto as he went on, so that we could understand what the opera was all about.

I had a good singing voice and joined the choir. Yagur was well known nationally, and even internationally, for its choir, which had made some popular recordings. (When I met my future wife in the United States years later, she had recordings from Kibbutz Yagur.) The conductor of the choir was the brother of Moshe Shertok (Sharett, in Hebrew), the future foreign minister and second prime minister of Israel.

As I was already fluent in Hebrew, I had a very easy time in school. Most of the other kids picked up the language quickly because they were bright and had an intense interest in learning. People at the kibbutz were quite intellectual and we read constantly; our library had over thirty thousand books, all in Hebrew. We read classics like Tolstoy, Sienkiewicz, and the French writer Romain Rolland. I loved to read, and I got a good education. Our teachers were skilled and well-qualified.

The kibbutz accepted tuition-paying outside students, some of whom boarded at the kibbutz. Under British rule, there was free education at the elementary school level, but not for the upper grades; I helped arrange for a sixteen-year-old girl, Rivka, who was from the city and could not afford high school, to live on the kibbutz and get her diploma. Usually, however, we did not interact with the paying students or the other kibbutz children. For one thing, we attended classes at different times. Also, we had different backgrounds and interests. Our relationship with the sabras was good but not close.

People at the kibbutz generally got along with each other. Interpersonal disputes were rare. In the eight years I lived at Yagur, I was never aware of any quarrel that had to be settled by the au-

165

thorities, nor any situation where someone physically attacked someone else on the kibbutz. The only problem I recall was when a man refused to go to his assigned job and was punished by not being assigned work for a week. He was so embarrassed that he did not show up at the dining room that entire period of time; his wife brought him food back to their room.

The kibbutz commissary was run on an honor system; everything was free for the asking. If you said you needed seven packs of cigarettes for the week, you were given seven packs of cigarettes for the week. If you said you needed toothbrushes, toothpaste, soap, or anything else, you got it. You were never questioned. And to the best of my knowledge, no one deliberately took advantage of the system.

Laundry was identified by its owner's number, sewn in red thread inside each garment. My number was 476. We left our dirty clothes at a central place and then on Fridays, we picked them up at the laundry, where every member of the kibbutz had a shelf labeled with his or her number. Waiting at your spot would be your clean, ironed, and folded laundry.

Because the kibbutz did not want to create a hierarchy or ruling class, the constitution of the kibbutz decreed that no one could serve as head of the kibbutz for more than two terms, or two years. At the weekly membership meeting, we debated the kibbutz's internal problems, such as whether to buy a new truck, install air conditioning in a particular room, enlarge the library, put up another building, or accelerate some programs.

Everyone in the Dror group was treated fairly and with respect, and we had a good life. We were an independent unit within the kibbutz, but we were friendly with all the kibbutz members and had a good relationship with them. The Germans had robbed us of four years of our lives, but at Yagur we regained our youth and started to behave like normal teenagers again.

Although the kibbutz had no hierarchy, a number of national leaders were members or were associated with Yagur, including

Eliyahu Golomb, the father of the Haganah, and Yitzchak Tabenkin, a labor movement leader, whose wife lived in Yagur. Tabenkin's son, Josef, became the head of the Palmach. Israel Bar Yehuda, who later became Israel's minister of the interior, and Moshe Carmel, who was commander of the Northern Front and later became the minister of transportation, were members of Yagur.

Uzi Gal, who invented Israel's famous Uzi submachine gun, was also a member of the kibbutz. He was one of about eight people working in the tool shop when I worked there and was about three years my senior. During this period, he and I worked side by side in the tool shop and ate lunch and dinner together. He was secretly developing the Uzi. I never knew about this project, but he was later jailed by the British on suspicion of making weapons. He was the son of Mr. Glass, the music lover from Germany.

I had a good social life during those years. Sometimes when I went to Haifa for driving lessons, I would see a movie or do something with a friend. Occasionally one of the girls would come along. Our group was very close, like brothers and sisters; not a single marriage took place within the group. This is the usual pattern for children that grow up together on a kibbutz. That did not stop us from carrying out mischief and pranks, like drilling a peephole into the shower so that we could spy on the girls, or climbing a tree and looking in through a window. I suppose the girls played tricks on us, too.

We used to go on hikes in the country, often to caves or mountains. Since I had difficulty walking, the kibbutz allowed me to buy a bicycle with money that my grandfather sent me from the United States. It helped immensely. While others were walking, I rode my bicycle. Even on rocky paths, I could go faster and served as a scout, and became somewhat of a celebrity. I was even more in demand because I gave rides to the girls. Life was good.

The kibbutz was very liberal in general. Sex, for instance, was not a secret, and unmarried people occasionally lived together. Some couples separated or divorced. Nevertheless, the children felt secure. They lived separately from their parents and received wonderful care from women whose full-time job was to take care of them. The children used to bathe together, which helps explain why sex was not a big mystery to them. The body was accepted as natural and normal. For instance, seeing a woman nurse a baby was not a big deal.

Yagur was completely secular, to the best of my knowledge, and there were no religious observances or services run by the kibbutz itself. Shabbat was a special day, but no kibbutz members went to shul, nor did we celebrate with ritual observance beyond a modest party, though some elderly parents of members had a small synagogue and observed the Sabbath. The Bible was studied as history, but no one was bar mitzvahed and no rabbi lived at the kibbutz. Traditional Jewish holidays, even the high holidays Rosh Ha'Shana and Yom Kippur, were celebrated symbolically, without a rabbi and without praying or fasting. When a rabbi was needed for an occasional marriage ceremony or for a funeral, an older man who had been a rabbi in Poland would come from a nearby kibbutz and perform the ceremony. The fact that everyone knew that they were Jewish, Zionist, and in Israel gave sufficient Jewish content to our lives without our calling it "religion."

Hope for a Jewish state was increasing, and we could almost taste the possibility of having our own country. We dreamed of gaining world respect as we took a normal place among the nations. Appeals were being made to the United States and, at one point, during Truman's administration, a United States commission suggested that 100,000 Jews be permitted to enter Israel. Politics was discussed constantly. This was an exciting time.

A strong labor union, the Histadrut, practically ran the country. Most of the kibbutzim (except for the minority of Orthodox kibbutzim) belonged to the labor movement and it bred most of the country's future leaders, including David Ben-Gurion. Within the Histadrut, there were several groups of kibbutzim, as well as individual members who lived in cities. Yagur belonged to *HaKibbutz HaMeuchad* (United Kibbutzim), an association of about forty-eight kibbutzim. Another association of kibbutzim was HaShomer HaTzair, which was politically to the left of us. But despite their other differences, all the kibbutzim that were associated with the Labor Party belonged to the Histadrut.

We passionately debated about how the government should be organized and how it should accomplish its goals; the security and future of Israel, its form of government, worker benefits, health insurance, and similar matters were among our leading concerns. In our kibbutz movement, called Meuchad for short, two political parties were prominent: Achdut HaAvodah, to which about 80 percent of Yagur belonged, and Mapai, Ben-Gurion's party. In the Histadrut in general, Mapai held the majority, Achdut HaAvodah was second largest, and HaShomer HaTzair came third.

We had come from a place where our lives had seemed worthless, and now, suddenly, we felt equal to other people and even dared to have hope for the future. New settlements were being established almost daily in strategic areas. Our entire Dror group was working towards the establishment of our own settlement, and we wondered where we would be sent. Along with Hebrew, we studied the skills we would need to run our own settlement, including self-defense. Eventually it was decided that our group would start a new settlement called Kibbutz Mash'abei Sadeh in the Negev, south of Beer Sheva.

Everyone had a role to fulfill. Some learned how to work the fields, plowing, seeding, and harvesting crops, some to tend flowers and fruit trees. Some learned to work with the cows, sheep, and chickens, others to repair tools and tractors.

Because it was difficult for me to be on my feet for any length of time, I worked in the metal shop where Uzi Gal also worked. The shop was very modern. I was taught how to handle metal, and soon could solder and weld. We made and repaired everything the kibbutz needed. I made pails and fixed children's potties, which were always being damaged by the constant scraping along the cement floors. Little by little, I learned how to do the more sophisticated, creative work. I used electric welders, soldering irons, shears, brakes to bend metal, drills, and more. I enjoyed the work and was good at it.

Then another challenge arose. A self-sustaining settlement would need managers. I was given an IQ test, which I apparently passed with flying colors, and was assigned to work in the bookkeeping office of the kibbutz management. The kibbutz also got approval from the Children and Youth Migration Bureau to enroll me in a two-year accounting management program at the BaMa'aleh Institute for Business Training in Haifa, with the Bureau and Yagur sharing the cost of tuition. For the next two years, 1948 to 1950, I studied bookkeeping, finance, money management, and other business courses in Haifa in parallel with my work in the bookkeeping office. Once again, I liked the work and was good at it.

I wanted very much, though, to do farm work, and when I saw all of my friends returning dirty, tanned, and muscular from the fields, I was jealous. Some of them drove tractors and would come in wearing dirt-covered goggles. I felt envy when I sat next to them in my clean white shirt. Our ideology was that a kibbutznik's most important job was to till the land.

I told some of my friends how I felt and they agreed to secretly teach me, after work, to drive the tractors and other farm vehicles. In particular, Ezra Sherman, who worked in the garage repairing combines, tractors, and other agricultural equipment, taught me how to drive and handle a tractor.

Normally, we shared all of our money, even gifts from relatives, but when I next received some money from my grandfather in the United States and relatives in Argentina, I enrolled in a Haifa driving school to qualify for a truck driver's license. I used my vacation time and sick leave and took the bus to the school; the bus only cost about twenty cents each way. Getting away was not hard. I did not have to ask anyone's permission; I said something like, "I'm going to be away for half a day."

I finally got the license, which was not easy — one of the tests, for instance, involved starting up a truck that was parked facing uphill on a steep slope without damaging a small matchbox that had been tucked behind the rear wheels of the truck.

I went to Yagur's manager of agriculture, which was the biggest department, and said, "Listen, I have a truck driver's license. I can drive a truck. I can do any work. I want to work in agriculture." I was so determined to be assigned to farm work that I considered threatening to leave if he did not agree. Fortunately, we struck a compromise. I would work fulltime at agriculture for the two or three busy months of harvest season and then go back to the office. From then on, I had two jobs, doing agricultural work during the harvest season and office work the rest of the year.

During the harvest, the fields were worked twenty-four hours a day in three eight-hour shifts, with a snack break halfway through each shift. The people from the agriculture department sat in the dining room every night after dinner to work out the next day's schedule and assign people to fields. One of the old-timers took me out for my first shift, and when he saw how well I handled the equipment, he made himself comfortable under a tree and took a nap. I was very happy to have won his approval. I worked the entire three months of the season doing various tasks.

I never simply accepted the way things were done, but always tried to innovate better ideas. For instance, when wheat is harvested, a combine separates the grain from the straw, which is then baled and dropped along the field every twenty feet or so. The bales are then loaded onto a platform pulled by a tractor. When I saw that the bales were often precariously balanced and fell off the platform as they were hauled away, I figured out a way to stack and interlock them so that the pile would be stable. Then, after they were loaded and hauled away, we used the time to collect new bales in one place, ready to be loaded at once.

I also told the workers from the *ma'abara* (temporary refugee

171

camp) who worked for the kibbutz, "If we collect a certain number of bales, we can go home early." Everyone worked hard and benefited from it.

My system allowed us to bring in twice as many bales a day while reducing the time to six hours rather than eight. I received recognition for this and was proud of having improved the system.

Working in the fields at night was a little scary. Some of our fields were far from the kibbutz and, although I carried a rifle, I felt like a sitting duck riding on top of a big tractor with front and rear lights shining brightly in the dark. One night, I was plowing with an eight-disk International Harvester tractor when some hungry-looking coyotes appeared and began to follow me. They followed the tractor as I went up and down each row. They followed me as I went back and forth. They then began gaining confidence and drew closer to the tractor. At some point, I climbed down from the tractor and removed the pin that connected the tractor to the disks; then I chased them with the tractor, but they were persistent.

Finally it dawned on me that they were picking up the scent of the meatloaf sandwiches I was carrying for a midnight snack. I threw the sandwiches down to them. They gobbled them up and disappeared. I wish every problem could be solved so easily.

After about a year, we considered ourselves established at Yagur. New people were constantly arriving and our group decided that the time had come for us to return the rooms we were occupying to the senior members of the kibbutz. We moved into tents in a wooded area of the kibbutz. We decided to house two boys and two girls in each tent. We respected each other's privacy completely. If one of the girls wanted to get undressed, she would say the word and we looked away, and it was the same for the boys. Although we may have peeked elsewhere, this was our home and we lived by the honor system. For better or worse, it was part of our culture. We lived like that for almost a year. At that point, our group joined the Palmach, and I remained at Yagur.

I moved into a room in a wooden building next to the *wadi* (dry riverbed) that ran through the center of the kibbutz. Both sides of the wadi were lined with houses, and small bridges crossed from one side to the other. During the rainy season, the wadi would fill with water from Mount Carmel that ran off into the Kishon Creek.

In the autumn of 1948, heavy rains caught us by surprise. I was in my room, one of six in a wooden building with concrete floors, when we heard a loud noise at the back wall. An avalanche of water had hit the wadi, which overflowed with such force that in no time at all, half the floor of my room was torn away and part of the building collapsed; the rest was standing on just a third of the foundation. Along the way, the current dragged with it many small dwellings and some trees, as well as hundreds of boards, windows, beds, quilts, and other household items. Nothing like this had happened in Yagur for as far back as anyone could remember.

We stood on the part of the building that had not collapsed and planned our escape through the rushing water. I hesitated because I did not want to get my orthopedic shoes wet, but someone helped me get to higher ground. The water raged on for perhaps two hours. Then, suddenly, it stopped and everything gradually returned to normal. Deposits of rock and lime, yellow and red from the layers of the mountain, were everywhere and the bridges were destroyed. But by some minor miracle, although some of my furniture was lost, my bed with its custom-made mattress stood untouched.

We were always aware of the Arab presence nearby. A large contingent of the Arab Legion was located in Jelamy, a British military camp about three miles from us. The Legion had originally been set up to patrol the Hashemite Kingdom, or Transjordan, which the British created when the Palestinian Mandate was divided along the Jordan River. The Legion was led by a British general, John Bagot Glubb, who took the name Glubb Pasha and continued to lead the Arab Legion after Britain left. British officers taught the Jordanians the techniques of warfare that they still follow; they are the best-armed force of the Arab world, even today. During my earliest years in Yagur, we rarely had trouble with the Arab Legion.

However, we feared the Arab Legion's soldiers because they zealously took the Arabs' side against the Jews. One time, for instance, they suspected that we were holding training exercises behind Yagur's vineyards. The Arab Legion soldiers came in armored cars along the main road and fired cannons into the vineyards. No one was hit, fortunately, but from then on, we were very careful because we realized that they were constantly patrolling the area. This disturbed us because they were officially part of the British military. Later on, before the British departed, we had a lot more trouble with the Arab Legion. Fortunately, when the British left Israel, the Arab Legion was also evacuated to Jordan.

We had little contact with Arabs, even though the road to Haifa went right through a large Arab village about two miles from the kibbutz. Just beyond it was Nesher, a small Jewish settlement with a large cement factory and shops we liked to visit for soda and other things not available on the kibbutz. Occasionally, we would go to the other Jewish settlements in the vicinity. There was a Hasidic village, Kfar Hasidim, with many well-tended gardens and agricultural products for sale. But we never went to the Arab village, even though the people there were not hostile during those years. The residents of Nesher probably did business with them, and there were no problems.

The Arabs were much better off because of the Jewish immigration to Palestine. Jews developed the land and created many jobs for them, jobs that paid well and provided benefits, especially if workers joined the Labor Union, the Histadrut. But the benefits did not offset the terrible fear created by the Islamic clergy, in particular the Grand Mufti of Jerusalem, Haj Amin Muhammad al Husseini. The Mufti constantly agitated the villagers against the Jewish entity, saying, "The Jews are coming to take your land away!" He organized the massacre of Jews in Hebron in 1929, most of them ultra-Orthodox, non-Zionist and even anti-Zionist. He made a personal agreement with Franco, Mussolini, and Adolf Hitler to support the Nazis, in return for which he would be the official spokesman of the Arab world.

In contrast, we were always friendly with the Druze villages and had good relations with them. Every so often, a Druze leader would come to Yagur from one of their villages on Mount Carmel, and we would all talk politics. One of the villages, Usifia, is very large now, with about eleven thousand people. Today, when we go to Israel, we usually visit Usifia and another of the Druze towns, Daliyat el Karmel. The Druze were, and are, loyal and friendly, unlike the other Arabs. They are the only Arabs who routinely serve in the Israeli army today.

Sadly, before the War of Independence, the Arab villagers near Yagur started throwing rocks at our vehicles. Protective metal shields had to be installed on the windows of buses that passed through the area. Relations became strained. Then, during the War of Independence, the village was attacked by the Jewish underground, and the villagers abandoned it completely and never came back. Today, it is a heavily populated Jewish settlement and has grown all the way up the mountain.

The British were also our enemy, constantly placating the Arabs, whose oil they needed. They kept tight control over Jewish immigration to Israel and only allowed 1,500 refugees a month into Israel, while hundreds of thousands of Holocaust survivors were waiting in Displaced Persons camps for British permission to enter. The United States proposed that 100,000 Jews be immediately allowed into Israel, but the British were sitting on the Suez Canal, and not antagonizing the Arabs was very important for their empire. They continued to do what was politically expedient for them, regardless of the human consequences.

The British had two police forces: the British police, who wore round hats, and the *Notrim*, a secondary force that was half-Jewish and half-Arab and wore a different type of hat. The Jews patrolled Jewish areas and the Arabs patrolled the Arab areas.

In front of our kibbutz was a British police station manned by Jewish policemen, mostly from Yagur. The station had a machine gun in a glass case and a supply of rifles. The kibbutz would frequently take the weapons out and trained our underground with them. But one day, with half of the British weapons out for training, a high-ranking British officer arrived with a group of policemen to visit the station. We rounded up some of the best-looking girls in the kibbutz to welcome and chat with them and invited them to the dining room for a meal that was served with long pauses between courses. Meanwhile, messengers went out to the field and gathered up all the weapons. We cleaned the dirt off them with lightning speed and spirited them to their spots in the station. When the girls got the signal that all was back in place, the atmosphere in the dining room became more relaxed. The officer said, "I think it's time I go to make my inspection." Perhaps he suspected a deliberate delay, and saw a little dust when he finally inspected the weapons — we will never know.

The *Yishuv* (Jewish community of Palestine) sensed that the possibility of our own country was within reach. We were looking ahead and preparing for what was to come; we were anxious to establish the State of Israel. After all that had happened to the Jewish people, we thought the world might have a conscience. Somehow, we hoped, something might bend our way.

The British did not permit us to possess any kind of weapons to defend ourselves, so in anticipation of establishing the State, we were busy with attempts to smuggle them in. Illegal weapons from Czechoslovakia were being delivered at night by small planes. In prearranged locations, small fires were lit to show the planes where to land and the landing fields were protected by Palmach units. The weapons were then quickly unloaded and removed from the area. Many of them were brand new rifles, delivered with their wooden butts still unvarnished and unstained. These beautiful new guns were needed badly. The Haganah also received many machine guns. In April 1948, it smuggled two hundred rifles and four light machine guns into the country from Czechoslovakia flown on United States aircraft. However, the Haganah did not have many heavy weapons until after the establishment of the State, when Israel was able to buy airplanes and weapons from Czechoslovakia. Payment had to be in U.S. dollars, and the money was raised privately in the United States.

At the same time, a lot of paramilitary training was taking place. Training and hiding weapons was easier on a kibbutz than in a city. The kibbutzim formed the backbone of the Haganah and Palmach. They were fierce and well trained, and they always got the best weapons available. Everyone at Kibbutz Yagur belonged to the Haganah, and the best of the best belonged to the Palmach.

The kibbutz was large and profoundly dedicated to the security of the nation; the members were idealistic, devoted, and trained to defend our land. Our group of forty, including the girls, was accepted into the Palmach, which had a policy of accepting entire groups, and we secretly trained in the use of weapons, including Sten guns, as well as judo and other skills. Though there were some things I could not do, such as military-style running with a rifle, I could drive a jeep and do other tasks, and I trained with the rest of the group. We did this out in the open with someone always watching the gate so that the British would not surprise us.

After the UN vote on November 29, 1947 in favor of the partitioning of Palestine, the British began to plan their departure. They did not realize that they would leave us some presents. Some Israelis knew which British contingent would be the last to evacuate and prearranged that three large British-made Centurion tanks and their crews would "disappear" on their way to being evacuated and thus remain in Israel. One tank got stuck in a ditch, and the crew fled. The other two tanks were hidden under camouflage. The British were furious and searched like crazy for the tanks until two minutes before their scheduled time of departure. However, being punctilious, they kept to their schedule.

Those tanks eventually saved many lives. The Haganah did not have any cannons, and the weapons the British had taken on Black Sabbath were never restored to us. All the Haganah had were old rifles from the days of the Turks, rifles that fired one bullet at a time. Now, suddenly, they had these tanks, and the tanks had two cannons. During the War of Independence, every time there was a major catastrophe, or an area had to be occupied, or cement walls needed to be blown up, those tanks were used. They were constantly loaded onto a truck platform and moved to the spots that needed help, wherever these were.

Meanwhile, the Grand Mufti in Jerusalem was agitating against the Jews and trying to stir up trouble. After the UN vote on partition, he and his contingent preached to the Arabs, "Don't worry about the Jews! Go and hide, because four or five Arab armies are going to attack Israel, and Israel does not stand a chance! As soon as it is overrun, you will be able to go back to your homes — and you will be able to take the Jews' possessions. Pick any of their houses you want! They will all be yours!"

Of course, the Arabs now claim that the Israelis gave some of them a little push to encourage them to leave. We had never expected help from the local Arabs during the war and would not have trusted them anyway. In Haifa, the Arab majority fled when Egypt, Jordan, Syria, and Iraq attacked. It was frightening to see them abandoning the city and running to Lebanon. Israeli trucks with loudspeakers went around the streets of Haifa, urging the Arabs not to leave, saying, "Why are you leaving?" Some Arabs were persuaded to stay. Today a substantial Arab population still lives in Haifa, but nothing compared to the size it used to be. Most of Haifa is now settled by Jews, and it is a flourishing modern city.

Dror group in Yagur, creating a topographical map of Israel (1947)

Dror group in Yagur (1947)

Kalman Offir, Chaviva Uberman, Leon Rubinstein

Shimshon Klakstein and Aharon Golub

Mordecai Aviv, Cylla Stornberg, Eliezer Fox, Aharon Golub, Shlomo Goldin (1947)

Back left, Shmuel Peleg, Aharon Golub, Yasha Steinberg, and one of Shmuel's relatives, rowing on the Yarkon River, Tel Aviv (about 1947)

Aharon Golub (1948)

The War of Independence

David Ben-Gurion declared the State of Israel on May 14, 1948 in Tel Aviv and formed a government. The Haganah became the nation's army. At first, its elite fighting unit, the Palmach, remained in place because the Palmach officers were the best trained and most experienced.

When the War of Independence broke out, our group moved into military barracks and actively participated in battle. We were part of the Harel Brigade, one of the three brigades of the Palmach; the other two were *Iftach* and *Chativat HaNegev* (the Negev Brigade). I did not go with our group to their field assignments because of my physical problem. I had to accept this. I remained at the kibbutz and continued to study business management in Haifa. I felt I was making a contribution by helping prepare for the future. My apartment at Yagur became a gathering place for us and whenever a member of the group had a few days off, he stayed with me.

Our group was assigned to defend the corridor to Jerusalem, which the Arabs were blocking. The Arabs had laid siege to the city and conditions there were bad, with no food and not enough water. The Haganah sent convoys of armored trucks carrying food, water, and medical supplies and the Arabs attacked them when they went through the Castell area. The road there was very narrow and passed between two mountains. The Arabs would sit on the mountains and throw hand grenades down onto any passing trucks, buses, or cars and blow them up. This was true even before 1948, when the British were still there, so the Jews had to do everything clandestinely and could not show any force. Most actions were carried out at night and everything had to be dismantled by daybreak.

Israel built a bypass route called the Burma Road, a reference to a similar road built into China during World War II, and even erected bridges so that it would be passable. This was an unbelievably heroic achievement and was accomplished with limited provisions and supplies. Some members of our group were wounded in the process, but none were killed. However, a tragedy occurred in connection with this road. Colonel David (Mickey) Marcus, an American Jew who had volunteered to fight for Israel, was walking in a military zone when a refugee who had just been recruited stopped him and asked for the password. When he was unable to provide it for some reason, or he answered in English instead of Hebrew, the recruit shot him. A number of books were written about the incident and it became the subject of the movie *Cast a Giant Shadow*.

Next, our group was transferred to the Negev to join the battle against the Egyptians and assigned to guard a particular road. The avant-garde of the Egyptian forces had advanced very close to Tel Aviv and were confident that they would have an easy time getting through the rest of Israel. After all, the Israelis had very few weapons, just the two cannons from the English tanks, some homemade mines, and old weapons.

The Egyptian advance troops had reached an intersection of two roads at Abu Agheila near Tel Aviv. They never expected the Palmach to come through the forbidding desert. But the Palmach cleared an abandoned ancient Roman road, improvised as needed, and moved in from behind them, cutting the Egyptians off from their base, and lay there silently in wait. Suspecting nothing, assuming that they were in Egyptian-held territory and that no Jews were there, the Egyptians kept coming, including a cousin of the country's King Farouk himself. My friends who where there described how he was all decked out in a fancy uniform with tassels and epaulets.

The Palmach ambushed them. The King's cousin got out of his car and signaled for them to stop — he thought the attackers were Egyptians — and was shot. When the Palmach realized he was an important dignitary, they rushed him to a field hospital, but I do not think he survived. One of my friends kept his little silver pistol and later turned it over to the Palmach commander.

After the establishment of the State of Israel in 1948, U.S. President Harry Truman gave Chaim Weizmann, the first president of Israel, an American Constellation airplane for his official use. This gift was greatly appreciated by the people of Israel. However, one of the Centurion tanks that had been stolen from the British and was desperately needed for its cannon developed engine trouble. It was rumored that an engine was taken off this plane and installed in the tank. This demonstrates how desperate the Israeli defense forces were for heavy weapons.

A tragic incident took place in Israel's early days of nationhood. When the State of Israel was first established, it had very few weapons and could not quickly import any. At the same time, efforts were being made to unify the Haganah, Lechi, and Etzel. Etzel independently arranged for a ship called the Altalena to bring weapons and ammunition to Israel in June. When the ship approached Tel Aviv, it became clear that Etzel was not going to share the weapons and ammunition with the Haganah, which was now the nation's official army. Etzel was planning to keep the weapons for its own fighters, who were defending Jerusalem.

Rightly or wrongly, Ben-Gurion took a stand, saying that weapons coming into the country had to be turned over to the central military command for distribution. When Etzel refused to surrender the weapons and ammunition, they were told, "If the weapons are not surrendered to the State, we will fire on the boat." Eventually, the government attacked the ship while it was anchored outside Tel Aviv at Kfar Vitkin. Several people were killed and most of the cargo of weapons, desperately needed by Israel, was destroyed. This was a shameful chapter in our history, in part because Israel needed the weapons so badly, and in part because the government acted in such a manner. This episode almost sparked a civil war and remains a heavy black cloud in our history.

After the War of Independence, the Palmach disbanded and most of our group returned to the kibbutz, although those who had become specialists in certain military areas remained in the newly unified army. Many high-ranking Palmach officers were appointed to the general staff of the army or remained until replacements were found.

The Beginnings of a Normal Life

With the war over and my schooling completed, I had a debt to repay to the kibbutz. The kibbutz had supported me through my studies and now I owed it about six months of work. In early 1949, our group was ready to move to the Negev to found Kibbutz Mash'abei Sadeh. Two other groups joined the approximately 40 from Yagur, so there would be the 120 needed for a settlement. I intended to stay on at Yagur for only a short while, then join the group.

But physical conditions were very difficult at the new kibbutz. People lived in wooden huts and had to walk through sand to get to the dining room, as sidewalks had not yet been built. Sanitation was poor, and the bathroom was a long way from the living quarters. There were no bathtubs, only showers. I could not stand on a cement floor without my special shoes, which made it impossible for me to shower at the new kibbutz.

I concluded, for this and other reasons, that I could not join the rest of the group at that time, and I decided to remain in Yagur for the present. Ultimately, due to my physical problems, I never did join the group at Mash'abei Sadeh. If I had gone to the Negev with the group then, I would still be living there today. I am realizing for the first time why I made the decision to stay in Yagur. Until now, I have never shared these thoughts with anyone.

I was able to assist my group, however, from Yagur. Surplus vehicles from the United States were made available to the kibbutzim and other groups by the Israeli government. I helped procure one of the trucks for the group. When it arrived, the truck needed new tires. I went to the head of Yagur and pleaded their case, and eventually they got a loan from Yagur to buy the tires. Even before the settlement was established, the truck was earning money for the new kibbutz.

At about this time, I faced a tragic personal loss. When our group was discharged from the Palmach, they returned to Yagur and lived in tents on the kibbutz. In November 1949, the group left for Mash'abei Sadeh. However, a smaller group, including Shimshon, my roommate for all those early years in Israel, went first to a place in Herzliya that functioned as a transfer location for provisions to be shipped to the Negev. Shimshon contracted a case of meningitis that was not diagnosed in time, and it proved to be fatal. He was only twenty years old. His death was a great loss to me. When Mash'abei Sadeh was established, his was the first grave in its cemetery. Even today, I am still very much saddened by Shimshon's death.

Life at Yagur evolved after independence. Despite the terrible recession, known as the *Tzena*, when we survived on dried milk, dried potatoes, dried eggs, and frozen fish filets — I will never eat them again — we were building the new State of Israel. Each person was doing his part and we were very dedicated. I was no longer considered a child, and developed friendships with kibbutzniks outside of the Dror group.

Immigrants were arriving from all over the world, including Algeria, Tunisia, and especially Morocco. There was no housing or jobs, and they had to live in tin boxes and tiny bungalows in *ma'abarot* (transfer camps).

Earlier on, Yemeni immigrants had come to Israel on planes, which many of them had never seen or been on before. They were wonderful people and very industrious, but they came from a very primitive country. A popular story was told that after the plane landed in Lod Airport and they were put into buses to go to the transfer camp, the Yemeni immigrants started to scream because the bus did not lift off into the air.

Next came the Moroccans. In order to help smooth the transition to a new life in Israel, the government sent the young Moroccans to camps in France first, where they could learn Hebrew and how to use knives, forks, toilets, and so on. They were to pass on this knowledge to their parents when they were reunited in Israel. One of these groups from France was assigned to Yagur and, in the process of welcoming them to Yagur, I met a beautiful young woman from Marrakesh. She had gone to an Alliance School supported by Women's American ORT (Jewish Trade Schools) and spoke French well. She learned Hebrew quickly and worked on the kibbutz. She became my girlfriend, and we lived together quite pleasantly for about a year before parting ways. Afterwards, she went to Mash'abei Sadeh for a while and then to Haifa, where we lost contact. I understand she married and had children.

At about the same time that I finished repaying my obligation to the kibbutz, an interesting opportunity arose to work as a driver for the Kibbutz Administration in Tel Aviv. This organization served as a resource center for about forty-five kibbutzim in the movement, including Yagur, and was headquartered in Tel Aviv. It was a good offer, one I thought I should not pass up. I signed on.

If any of the kibbutzim had a problem, such as disease striking their livestock or produce, they would call the Kibbutz Administration. If the Arabs were attacking and a kibbutz needed help with security problems (this was especially frequent for kibbutzim on the Lebanese and Syrian borders, and in the Negev), they would call the Kibbutz Administration for help. Its specialists in many fields, including medical personnel, would be dispatched to help out at a kibbutz that requested assistance. They needed transportation, so the Kibbutz Administration had many cars. I worked as a driver for a while, which gave me exposure to many different people and places and was also good for my social life. After all, I was a single guy. Driving a private car in Israel was a big deal in those days, and it contributed greatly to my status.

When the supervisor of the drivers took sick, I was offered

the position of running the department. The position was a paid one, and the salary was sent directly to the kibbutz, although I was given a food allowance. Whenever something happened and people were dispatched to a kibbutz or needed transportation from a kibbutz to another destination, they would inform the Kibbutz Administration that "So-and-so has to go to the Galilee for two days." I had to figure out how to provide a car and driver.

I used my imagination to accomplish this economically. Sometimes, I would combine several trips to the same area. Often, the driver would deliver someone to one place, and then go to another place that needed help, and on the way back, pick up the first guy.

I tried to get our drivers to keep their expenditures to a reasonable level. To do this, I established an acceptable average monthly figure. If a driver went over this budget, I would politely ask, "Have you had unusual troubles this month?" The next month, the bill usually returned to its normal level. Kibbutzim ran on the honor system, and you could not chastise or talk down to anyone. There was very little friction, and it was very satisfying to work with people who were all considered equals doing equally important jobs.

There were other logistical problems to solve. The seemingly simple task of filling the cars' gasoline tanks was in itself quite a challenge. We had coupons for gas and an account at a station south of Tel Aviv, but we did not always go south. To improve efficiency, I established a relationship with a station to the north.

Our cars were not new and they needed constant repairs. I improved that process, too. The garage we used was in a former military barracks and the repairs were done in pits, which was not an efficient solution. I arranged for funding from the central kibbutz office so the garage could put in lifts. In return, the garage owner gave our cars first priority for repairs, and as a result, our entire fleet was usually fully available for use. A side benefit for me was that, because all our cars were now in commission, one was usually available for my use.

Fridays were a constant scheduling challenge. We had many kibbutzniks who worked in Tel Aviv, and they usually signed up to go home to Yagur or other kibbutzim for Shabbat. I would design a plan every weekend to work them all in, and try to avoid making anyone take a bus. Our drivers went home on Fridays and came back on Sundays. They would drop people off along the way home and pick them up on the way back. There was always a car going to Yagur — I was in charge, after all. More importantly, well-known dignitaries and prominent leaders in the labor movement lived at Yagur, including Yitzchak Tabenkin and Israel Bar Yehuda.

This was a good period in my life. I was an eligible young bachelor of twenty-five with a private room in a private house and access to a car, which was quite unusual in Israel during those days. The organization rented rooms for us in Tel Aviv, and since we came from kibbutzim, we were in demand as tenants: honest and straightforward, unlikely to cause problems, and certain to pay the rent on time. Moreover, since most of us went home every weekend, the owners saved on precious hot water and other expenses. Our rooms were in the nicest neighborhood, near the Yarkon River. We ate breakfast and dinner together in a communal kitchen and received an allowance for lunch.

I enjoyed the job very much, in part because the car made me equal to other people, despite my handicap. There was another benefit: I was exposed to new people and places, which broadened my horizons.

I also stayed in close touch with survivors from Ludvipol, my landtzmen. Even before I began working in Tel Aviv, I went there on vacations and stayed with my old friend from Ludvipol, Eliahu Kleinman, whose large family had practically grown up next door to me. When I moved to Tel Aviv, I felt very happy to renew our warm relationship and reawaken some happy childhood memories.[1]

Romance came my way again. While I was working for the Kibbutz Administration in Tel Aviv, I met a young woman, a Holocaust survivor, who lived in the Tel Aviv area and was very

Aharon Golub driving a tractor in Yagur (1950)

Aharon Golub working for the Kibbutz Administration in Tel Aviv (1954)

Wedding of Dror group member in Ramat Gan. *Back, left to right*, Miriam Chayon, Aharon Golub, Shoshana Bronstein Dannenberg, Shmuel Peleg, Sarah Guss, Moshe Trosman, leader Yasha Steinberg. *Middle, left to right*, Regina, Bluma Musman Levy. *Front*, Bella Kalmanowitch Kopatch and her husband, Michael Kopatch

191

bright and well educated. She had spent a few years living and going to school at a kibbutz until she left to live in the city with her parents. We had much in common, including our political views. We both belonged to the Labor movement, the Histadrut, and were very committed to social justice. We learned a lot from each other during the year I was in Tel Aviv. She later married and had children, and still lives in Israel.

I had a good life in Israel — the kibbutz years were the best years of my life.

---

1. Eliahu Kleinman died in 2002. His cousin Pesach lives in Ramat Gan.

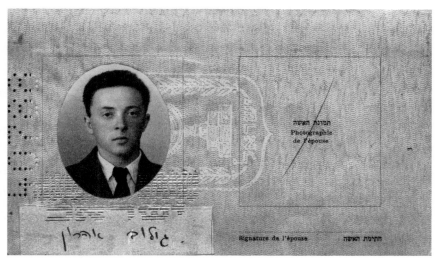

Aharon Golub's Israeli passport, No. 40788. Aharon's passport erroneously lists 1930 as his year of birth.

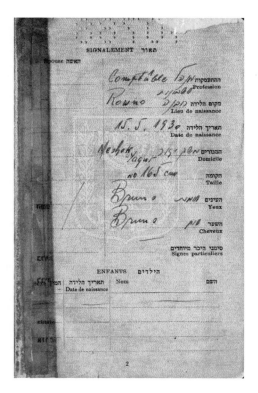

IV

Starting Again

Another Country, a New Family

All during my years on Yagur, I was in touch with my uncle Usher in Montreal, and my relatives in the United States were constantly urging me in their letters to come visit them and resettle in the U.S. I always refused. I definitely did not want to move to the U.S. and I was reluctant even to visit because I did not have money for the fare. I was proud of the way everyone in the kibbutz shared everything, and I felt it would be unfair to take such a trip, even if my relatives paid for it.

I had not seen my Uncle Usher and Aunt Chava for eight years. They had settled in Canada because they had not been allowed into the United States. My cousin Shalom (Alex) and his wife Sally, who had obtained a visa to the United States and now lived in Brooklyn, urged me to come to visit. My father's brothers, Alex and Jack, who had been in the United States since 1925, were also urging me to come.

When my grandfather Shlomo Golub died in 1954, he left a small apartment house in Brooklyn to his five children and my father's share reverted to me. The value of each share was between $1,000 and $1,200, which was a lot of money in 1954. Upon inheriting this sum, I finally felt that I could let my relatives buy me a ticket because I would be able to repay them when the estate was settled. On that condition, I accepted a ticket from them.

During the six months it took to get a visa, I saved money by skipping lunch. With the money I saved, I bought gifts for my relatives from the Bezalel Art Gallery, books about the War of Independence, and other souvenirs. I wanted to be able to give everyone at least a

En route to the U.S., Aharon Golub, *(left)*, with fellow travelers at the Acropolis, Athens (1954)

small gift. I boarded an Israeli ship named the *Jerusalem* on October 24, 1954 for a visit to the United States. When I went aboard I had no intention of remaining permanently in the United States.

The *Jerusalem* was a slow old ship and it took a long time to sail from Haifa to New York. But I had a good time during the voyage. Israelis were only allowed to take ten dollars in foreign currency out of the country because Israel was in a tight financial crunch and dollars were very scarce, but we were given some special boat currency that could be used only aboard the ship.

The ship stopped in Athens for a day. Even though I only had ten dollars, I debated with myself the whole night before we docked whether or not to splurge two of my precious dollars on a tour of Athens.

"I'm going to America," I thought. "I don't know what's going to be there, and I need at least a stamp to write a letter to my girlfriend. What should I do? On the other hand, who knows when I'll be back in Greece? I'm here," and I decided to take advantage of the opportunity. It was a wonderful tour and well worth the money and, as things turned out, I never have gotten back to Greece. I went to the Acropolis, which was not fenced in at that time, and was able to go all over the place. A nice lunch was provided in the package deal, for good measure.

Next, the ship stopped in Spanish Morocco. By then, I had become acquainted with a sailor who said, "You spent two dollars for a sightseeing trip? You're out of your mind! Come with us. If six of us share a cab and expenses it will only cost us seventy-five cents apiece." Another benefit of going with the sailors was the sense of safety it gave me to know that the ship would not sail without them. If I ventured forth on my own, I might be held up by a flat tire, a traffic jam, or other mishap, and not be back in time. So I went with the six sailors and, for seventy-five cents, toured Spanish Morocco.

The ship then crossed the Atlantic and docked in Halifax for a day, but the Canadian government only allowed holders of British and French passports to disembark. Israelis were not allowed ashore, so my remaining funds remained intact.

On November 10, 1954, I arrived in New York. My devoted cousins Shalom and Sally closed their fruit store so that they could greet me at the ship. I stayed with them in the house my grandfather left to us, 555 Hopkinson Avenue between Sutter and Pitkin Avenues in Brooklyn, which was a thriving Jewish neighborhood.

Pitkin Avenue was a major commercial street with many fine stores and the Loew's Pitkin Theater, a large, glamorous movie house. On Friday nights, thousands of people strolled in the neighborhood, and it was delightful.

My U.S. relatives, who had lived in Brooklyn for over twenty years, received me warmly though we had never met before they left Europe, and they made me feel at home. Shalom and Sally's four-room apartment was small and quite crowded with their four children and me. But my Uncle Jack, a widower who lived with his daughter in a three-bedroom apartment on the first floor of the same building, came to like me so much that, after a couple of weeks, he said, "Come, move down to my house. I have much more room." He had a big bedroom with two single beds, so I moved in with him. This arrangement was much more comfortable.

Uncle Jack's butcher shop was on Mermaid Avenue in Coney Island, near the rides and games. I used to help him every day in his store. As a visitor to the country, I did not have a work permit, but I wanted to be productive and pay for my keep. We were taught in Israel to pay our own way.

I also adjusted my religious practices out of respect for my uncle. He was not extremely religious, but he was traditional and followed Jewish customs. While I stayed with him, I adapted to his way of life. I felt, "When in Rome, do as the Romans do." I was Jewish, after all, and had come from a traditional home, so it was not too difficult. On the holidays, especially the High Holidays, I went with Uncle Jack to shul, and for the first time in many years, I fasted on Yom Kippur. I knew Hebrew of course, and was quite familiar with the traditional melodies because I had attended shul with my father.

My relatives wanted me to stay to manage the building we had jointly inherited. Uncle Jack was too busy and the other three heirs lived far away — one uncle and aunt lived in Canada, one uncle in California, and one in Argentina. Still, I planned to return to Israel after six months.

Then I met my future wife, Ruthie.

I had been invited to an Israeli dance, and Ruthie was there. She and her whole family were Zionists and very involved with Israel and organizations that raised money to support Israel. Ruthie and I started going out and, over the months, we became very serious about each other. We had many values and interests in common. As our relationship developed, I got to know her family as well.

Ruthie's parents, Phillip and Gertrude Silverstein, were deeply devoted to Israel. Their home felt like an Israeli home and this made me feel very comfortable there. Israeli records were playing all the time, and it was full of pictures and mementoes with Jewish themes.

Her sister, Helen, was very active in Beitar. In fact, some of the crew of the Altalena stayed at Helen's house while the ship was loaded with weapons in the United States. This had to be done clandestinely because the United States did not permit weapons to be exported to Israel.

Ruthie's parents embraced me. They had never had a son, and once Ruthie and I were seriously involved, her father said to me, "I finally have a son in the family." I was very moved. Belonging to that household gave me a warm feeling.

Ruth and Aharon Golub, happily married. (1958)

We married about six months after we met. I had asked Ruthie to move back to Israel with me, but she did not want to leave her family. I had good friends in Israel but no relatives, whereas Ruthie had a large extended family, with many uncles and aunts, in the United States. I felt that it would be unfair to pressure her to leave them. Her family members were loyal Americans and felt strongly that the U.S. was their home. So when Ruthie and I decided to get married, I knew I would remain in the United States.

During our courtship, Kibbutz Yagur sent a representative to try to convince me to return to the kibbutz. We entertained him well (I remember taking him to see *Damn Yankees* on Broadway), but I did not go back.

This decision saddened me. I remember calling my friends at the kibbutz and telling them that they could have my things, including my treasured books and my excellent mattress. The Kibbutz Administration had given me gifts every so often in appreciation for the work I had done in Tel Aviv. My most precious possession was a famous book they had given me called *The Book of the Palmach*. I gave all of these possessions to my friends.

But I felt very comfortable with Ruthie's family. Her parents lived in a two-story, one-family house with stained-glass windows in the living and dining rooms, on Shepherd Avenue in East New York, Brooklyn. They grew grapes in their large garden, which they pressed to make wine, a process they learned from their Italian neighbors. They grew raspberries and other fruits in their garden. They even had a permanent sukkah with a movable roof, which made it kosher. I was giving up my kibbutz home and family, but I was joining a new family and home.

In his own way, Ruthie's father Phillip was a warrior, a unique person who was deeply concerned about the welfare of the Jewish people. He was a major contributor to the United Jewish Appeal, giving thousands of dollars to the organization. He and his family genuinely lived more modestly than they had to so that they could support the UJA. Prior to the war, Phillip had had the good sense to get his entire family, and Ruthie's mother's family from the Pultusk area, out of Poland. When he came to the U.S. he worked hard and sent money to Europe to bring over additional relatives. Phillip was able to get about fifteen people out of Europe. Thank God for his foresight.

Many people were barely making ends meet at the time, and my father-in-law's business was to enable people to buy items on credit. He worked hard, going from customer to customer and arranging for the sale of general merchandise. He had connections with several appliance, furniture, and clothing stores, and would go to a customer, agree on a price for an item, such as a new refrigerator, and then give him a letter of credit to take to the store in exchange for the merchandise.

Phillip received a dealer discount from the stores. The customer would pay my father-in-law in weekly installments, perhaps five dollars a week for a big item, or three dollars a week for a small item. Once a week, he would drive around and collect the payments. He never charged interest. His profit came from the dealer discount he received from the stores; he took on himself the risk of extending credit to the customers. He worked with quality stores; I used to patronize the stores to which he sent his customers. I also remember that he had a big box of dress samples in various sizes, but I do not recall the details of those transactions.

I know a lot about Phillip's business because I used to fill in for him occasionally after work when he was sick. By the time I met him, he had been in business for about thirty-five years, and his customers were the grandchildren of his original customers. He loved his customers and had genuinely warm relationships with them. They talked about him with great respect and invited him to their children's weddings and so forth. But some of the neighborhoods he worked in were rough and he was beaten up by several times by local hoodlums who thought Jews had horns.

Ruthie's father was also a big supporter of the Orthodox synagogue to which he belonged, a *shtibel*, a traditional, Eastern European style synagogue where the women and men sat separately. Once a year, the United Jewish Appeal made an appeal for Israel there. I happened to see one of the lists of UJA contributors from the shtibel: the total contribution that year was $4,136, with some members giving $18, some $5, some $3, and Phillip Silverstein giving $4,000. Money was very dear at that time; people did not earn much. In those days, you could buy a fully equipped new car for about $2,000, meaning that my father-in-law's contribution for one year was the equivalent of two cars. He was not a rich man, but he put his money where his mouth was.

For his seventy-fifth birthday, three years before he died, Phillip donated the bulk of his estate to build a new retirement home in Israel. Ruthie says, "He took everything he owned, whatever money he saved up over his lifetime, and he gave it away to Israel." A plaque at the retirement home reads, "Donated by Gertrude and Phillip Silverstein." Although we did not profit financially from this decision, we were extremely proud that he had left his life savings to a noble cause. I can attest that everyone in the family survived financially and none of us are starving. Phillip lived up to his ideals, and I hope we all follow in his footsteps.

My mother-in-law was a busy woman. She helped with her husband's business; packages were always arriving from suppliers, and there were lots of things to do. They always invited people to their home for dinner on Friday nights and the Jewish holidays, especially Passover. Sometimes they would have as many as thirty-five guests. These dinners were major undertakings, and my mother-in-law never had help. She was from the old school, and she believed in doing things herself. She prepared all the food and handled everything personally.

With my marriage to Ruthie, my immigration status changed to permanent resident. I received a Green Card, which allowed me to be legally employed. From then on, I was always gainfully employed and was never unemployed for even a single day. Ruthie also worked outside of the house until we had children; she returned to work when our daughter was twelve years old.

At first I worked for Ruthie's father, driving and helping to expand the business. But after a few months, I realized I would not have a great future in his business. I was not eager to run around collecting money, a type of work that was difficult for me because of my disability. Also, Phillip was fairly set in his ways and strenuously resisted my suggestions for improving the business. He would say, "Look, I was successful with the way I did things until now. Why should I start doing things differently?"

To her credit, my wife was against my working with her father from the start, and she was right. Telling my wife that she was right was difficult. We tried not to hurt Phillip's feelings; I ascribed my leaving to the fact that all the walking around required to do the job was problematic for me. We parted ways with no hard feelings and I looked for another job.

We lived with Ruthie's parents for a few months until we got our own apartment. When you live in someone else's home, you have to conform to their way of life, but we were young and had our own ideas about how we wanted to do things. So we decided to move into our own apartment, not too far away from their home.

Our son, Bennett William, was born about ten months after we were married. We named him after my father, Baruch, and Ruthie's grandfather William. We chose the name Bennett because it means "blessed" in Latin, which is the meaning of Baruch in Hebrew. Ben was born on Ruthie's birthday, April 9.

We took to parenthood naturally and did what we had to do. We tried to give our children, first Bennett and later Elizabeth, a proper education. Bennett attended the Pride of Judea Nursery School, and then kindergarten and first grade at a yeshiva located in a trailer on Linden Boulevard in Brooklyn. We liked the rabbi there. I worked not too far away from home, and every time Ben was in a school performance, I went to see it. Usually, I was the only father amongst many mothers. I enjoyed being able to attend.

I started my independent career in the United States working for a real estate broker in Borough Park. I got my sales license, but the job was far from ideal. The broker turned out to be dishonest, and, since most real estate business is conducted in the afternoons, evenings, and on weekends, it interfered with my family life. I started thinking about making a change.

I saw a help-wanted ad in a Jewish newspaper for a part-time bookkeeper. They hired me on the spot. The job was at a catering hall, Chateau Gardens, on East Houston Street in Manhattan, close to Little Italy. I worked there in the mornings and at the real estate office in the afternoons and on weekends. Now I hardly saw my wife at all.

Chateau Gardens was a large hall with five ballrooms, located in a converted stone church. Some weekends, there were as many as thirteen affairs. Most of the customers were of Italian descent, but some were Orthodox Jews, especially for events in the ballroom that seated nine hundred. A kitchen in the former rectory accommodated kosher catering.

They liked me very much, and gradually, they asked me to stay an extra hour, then another. Little by little, they persuaded me to work full time. Finally, I gave up the real estate job and began working full-time for Chateau Gardens. I was treated very well, earned a nice salary, and enjoyed good benefits. Many times I earned overtime for working weekends. We did well.

I especially enjoyed one rather unique benefit. Chateau Gardens bought forty-pound turkeys for the Italian buffets, but used only the breasts. I was free to take home the legs, necks, and livers. The liver sometimes weighed close to a pound. Sometimes, I would bring home 200 chicken livers at a time. I even distributed them to the neighbors for a while, but at some point, I got fed up dragging the bloody packages home.

After I had been working there for two and a half years, New York City decided to build a subway station, connecting two existing lines, directly under our building. The planners were concerned that the church might collapse during the excavation process. The building was condemned, and my boss was paid a lump sum in compensation. This left me without a job.

We had just bought a house in Brooklyn on Atkins Avenue, near

Ruthie's family, and were planning a major renovation. I decided to handle my own contract work, expecting to be unemployed for a while. But after I had been home for only a day or so, the accountant who handled the books for the catering hall called and said he had a job for me at Sacher's, a large restaurant on Madison Avenue between Forty-first and Forty-second streets in Manhattan.

I always considered myself a working man, and I felt I had no right to reject a job. I went there for an interview, and they too hired me immediately. I became the business manager, doing the buying, controlling the provisions, processing the payroll, and so forth.

I did some innovative work for them. For instance, I established a credit card system for their clientele. Many of the customers were mining engineers who worked for two weeks, then came back to New York and hung around for two weeks, not doing much except eating and drinking in our restaurant. They were big customers, but they sometimes got so drunk that their signatures were illegible. I came up with the idea of creating an identification card for each of them, with their name and a number on it. They were always able to remember their number when the waitress asked for it, no matter how drunk they were, so we always knew whom to charge.

I also invested in a few small houses in Brooklyn. The attorney who handled the closings had a sister who owned an employment agency; she sent me to interview for a job as a purchasing agent at Templet Industries, a large metal stamping company on Atkins Avenue in Brooklyn, practically walking distance from my house. They offered me a better salary and I took the job.

Elizabeth Gabrielle, our daughter, was born at about this time, on October 19, 1961. She was named after my younger sister, Esther. Her Hebrew middle name is Chava, after my older sister. Gabrielle was after Ruthie's uncle, Gabriel (Gabby), who died not long before her birth.

I was working at Templet and owned or co-owned five buildings: two four-family houses, one six-family house, an eleven-family house in partnership with my brother-in-law, Jack Daniels, and an eight-family house in partnership with my uncle, Jack Golub. After work, I drove to the buildings and personally managed their maintenance. I handled the paperwork, collected the rents, and hired repairmen. I was fastidious about my properties and constantly improved and upgraded them. I made sure that the buildings were properly painted and that the heating always worked. I installed and maintained locks on all the doors, curtains in the hallways, padded carpeting on the steps, and trees in front of the buildings. The tenants were grateful for the improvements, and I had the satisfaction of knowing that my properties were well maintained.

In 1964, Templet Industries relocated to Plainview, Long Island. They received a government subsidy to construct a new building, which I helped plan. They gave me a nice private office. For three or four months, I traveled from Brooklyn to Plainview, but it was a long commute.

At about that time, our old neighborhood began to deteriorate. People became afraid, almost panicky, about the changes, and started selling their properties. We held out for quite a while, as did a lot of our immediate neighbors, but eventually we decided to sell the house and move closer to my job. We sold it to nice people because this was important to our remaining neighbors.

We bought a house in Old Bethpage, New York, where we have lived ever since. Later, I sold all of my investment properties because I felt that I would not be able to manage them well from Long Island. Since they were small properties, they could not support a superintendent.

Old Bethpage was a distance from Ruthie's mother, Gertrude, who still lived in East New York, in the same house in which Ruth grew up. She used to visit us for holidays and other occasions. Ruthie's sister, Helen, lived in West Hempstead and both families looked out for Gertrude. When her neighborhood became dangerous — vandals used to break windows with bricks — she moved in with a widowed brother who lived in Bensonhurst. Her house sold for next to nothing.

Helen moved to Florida and Gertrude followed her after her brother died. A few years later, Helen's leg started feeling numb when she climbed stairs. At Mount Sinai Hospital in New York, they discovered a long, thin cyst on her spine. They tried to drain it, but this damaged her spinal cord. She went into the hospital numb but walking. She came out confined to a wheelchair and paralyzed. She never walked again.

Toward the end of her life, we brought Ruthie's mother, Gertrude, to an excellent UJA/Federation facility on Long Island, the Gurwin Geriatric Center. She lived there for eighteen months until she died at the age of ninety-two. After about ten years, Helen moved to Long Island to be near her children, where she lived in the Franklin Hospital Nursing Home until she died.

The management at Templet changed after I had been working there for almost twenty years. The new management decided to relocate the company to New Jersey. I opposed the move for business reasons and resigned; not only was the move a poor business decision, but I did not want to move my family. My wife was working, my children were in school, and we were established in our synagogue. I was not going to follow what I believed to be a failing venture. And that is exactly what happened. Templet moved to New Jersey and went bankrupt within two years.

Templet abandoned its metal stamping operation, as part of its move, in order to concentrate on electronics and solar water heaters. The stamping operations were sold to a Brooklyn company named Lomart Industries, which was a big outfit known for manufacturing stainless steel swimming pool filters. Lomart also had a stamping operation that they wanted to expand. They were eager for me to come work for them. I told them I would think about it and let them know.

I started a job with Grumman, a large aerospace firm on Long Island, but within a week realized that I could not adjust to the way they did business. I resigned and went to join Lomart in Brooklyn.

They were happy to have me. I worked there for a few years, and though the job was good, commuting to Brooklyn was difficult.

We had always been active with the United Jewish Appeal. One day, at the kickoff of the eastern Long Island annual campaign, I sat at a table with other dignitaries and businesspeople. One of them offered me a job at General Aerospace, a large metal distribution company that sold mostly to aircraft manufacturers all over the country, such as Grumman and Fairchild. By then, I had become an expert in buying steel and was familiar with every type of aluminum and alloy, so I was in demand; people with my skills always were. I had twenty years' experience in the field and was well networked. I went to work at General Aerospace in Plainview.

I worked there for two years, but found no opportunity for creativity. At my other jobs, I had always enjoyed being creative, and I missed it. All we did was buy and sell aluminum sheets or extrusions.

Over the years, I would often have lunch in the same coffee shop with Mel Greenberg and Frank Marchhart, the owners of a local lighting company, Aluminum Louver. One day during lunch, they sensed that I was unhappy with my current job and invited me to work for them. Their offer was attractive, and I agreed to join their company. Finally I had a job that was literally around the corner from my house.

I enjoyed working for Aluminum Louver because we created things. We manufactured tubular lighting, built fixtures, and made louvers (the slots that diffuse light in fixtures). We designed and produced custom made lighting for places like Trump Towers in New York, Atlantic City casinos, and the Fort Lauderdale airport. The Gap and Casual Corner had us reequip all of their stores. We had to find sources for new materials, unusual switches, custom-made items, and fulfill the specifications for each new design. The work was quite interesting, the products were of high quality, and I was involved in every phase of the design and creation of the new product.

I worked for Aluminum Louver for twelve years until I retired. Bob Marchhart, Frank's son, kindly let me retain an office there. I enjoy being in a business atmosphere. I do some work for my son, Ben, because after I had heart surgery, I was somewhat depressed. Ben felt that, after a lifetime of being productive, I was just not built to be idle. He had certain work he wanted me to handle for him; mostly, he wanted to encourage me and get me out of the house. Retirement can be too quiet. Going to work has always been good for me.

My feet remained a constant problem throughout my life. My left foot developed carcinoma and had to be amputated in 1973, in the days before micro-surgery became available, to save my life. I now wear a prosthetic below the knee, so I am able to bend my leg. Walking with a prosthetic is not easy, but my lifelong agility stands me in good stead.

My right foot was also in bad shape. Because my toes were amputated by my aunt in the forest and the metatarsals were removed in Israel, the foot is now very small. In the mid-1990s, my right heel developed an oozing ulcer and the tissues started to deteriorate. I had been living in fear of this happening. I went to every conceivable doctor and endured painful procedures, trying to find a solution to save my remaining foot. Finally, in 1999, we went to Columbia Presbyterian and consulted a plastic surgeon. We did not see eye to eye on my first visit, but Cindy, my daughter-in-law, came with us on the next visit and charmed him. The doctor and I became friendly. He insisted on doing a biopsy of my heel.

Reluctantly, I let him do the painful procedure. To my great sorrow, the results showed malignancy in the area, including the heel bone. The doctor recommended surgery to save the leg, though he was uncertain as to whether the foot could be saved. He explained in detail how he planned to proceed with the microsurgery to try to save my foot. He would remove the malignant tissue and shave off the infected part of the heel bone. He would then graft a muscle from the side of my chest, under my arm, to the heel. Then, he would graft a large piece of skin from my thigh onto the muscle graft, to protect it. In order for the graft to succeed, circulation would have to be established by connecting an artery and vein from the muscle to an artery and vein in the leg. The doctor emphasized that this procedure depended on his ability to locate a viable vein and artery in my leg.

Many tests were performed that were inconclusive, and no suitable vein could be located. The doctor was willing to perform the surgery, hoping to locate a vein during surgery. He told me that I had nothing to lose because if a vein was not found, my leg would have to be amputated. With a heavy heart, I agreed to have the surgery.

The surgery lasted 11½ hours because the doctor refused to give up. My poor wife, son and daughter just sat and waited for news. Eventually, the doctor found veins hidden deep inside the leg and connected them to the transplanted muscle.

I was intensely anxious, when I woke after the surgery, to find out whether the new connections would succeed. The leg was heavily bandaged, with a big hole in the middle of the bandage where the doctor inserted an instrument to amplify the sounds of the pulse. I heard *voosh, voosh, voosh!* The connection had been made! But the vein might still collapse, and we waited through the first six hours, then the next twelve, then the next twenty-four. Finally, after thirty-six hours, there was still a pulse, and the danger had passed. My leg was spared.

As happened long ago in Haifa, special orthopedic shoes were designed to compensate for the missing part of my foot. I walk well, although with difficulty, and only for brief stretches. But how can I complain, when I am still able to ride a bike and dance? In fact, I am a good dancer. Onlookers do not even realize that I have a problem.

The *Yizkor* Book

For many years, the survivors of Ludvipol tried not to think about Ludvipol, the Holocaust, and our loved ones who had been tortured and murdered. Even so, the first Ludvipol memorial service was held in Jaffa, Israel in 1950, as soon as the survivors were in a position to do so. An annual memorial service has been held there every year since.

But people wanted a written remembrance of Ludvipol, a *yizkor* book. Creating the book was a long and emotional process and required significant financial resources.

A Commemoration Committee was established in 1952 by Nahum Feldman, Abraham Stadlin, Judah Raber, Mordechai Ostrovsky, Zvi Tuchman, Abraham Shlifer, Nachum Ayalon, and Shmuel Shafir. Six years later, the committee sent a letter to all the surviving members of the town's Jewish community. It read, "People of Ludvipol, remember! The *Yizkor* book is your book. Contribute to it whatever you can afford, and do it today, because tomorrow will be too late!"

People contributed funds, photographs, information and recollections. Baruch Guttman, among others, wrote extensive testimony for the book and elsewhere. The book was published in 1965, twenty-three years after the liquidation of the community, on the Hebrew date Yud Gimmel Elul.

The *Ludvipol Yizkor Book* begins, "The decision to publish a yizkor book and to commemorate the terrible Holocaust that afflicted our community was conceived in the hearts of the few survivors left after the war. Those who survived, who saw with their

212

own eyes the atrocities of the terrible Holocaust, and succeeded in escaping the swords of the brutal killers, swore not to forget and not to erase from our memory what was done to us, our families, and our people by the bloodthirsty predators, the Nazis and their Ukrainian assistants — may their names and memory be erased. The blood of our dear ones and family members who were murdered, through no fault of their own, the women, the elderly, and the children who gave their lives…is crying to us and forcing us to write down their last chapters of life, so that their memory will remain forever, and the world will know what the murderers did to our holy ones."

The introduction also describes what it had been like for the survivors: "A mental oppressiveness took over our hearts after the liberation. Our dear ones' souls stood in front of our eyes, day and night. We asked ourselves, 'Who am I to be so fortunate as to survive the Nazi hell, while my pure and innocent parents did not?' This feeling pursues us even today."

It took even longer for me to begin talking about Ludvipol and the Holocaust. I did not want to dwell on the past. Only after a great deal of urging from my family did I finally agree, in 1995, to be interviewed on videotape by the Shoah Foundation. That interview was an important turning point for me. Since then, I have spoken about the Holocaust at synagogues and local elementary schools. But no matter how often I do it, I still find remembering and speaking about these events very, very difficult.

The Bones of Ludvipol

In 1988, my son Ben and his wife Cindy journeyed to Ludvipol to search for our family roots. The Ukrainian terrain is still rough and my feet were not up to the trip, so I did not accompany them. But I put Ben in touch with Samuel Tiktin, the son of Alter and Chava Tiktin (Chava, my great aunt, was my paternal grandmother's sister), who was still living in Rovno. Samuel was by then a prominent man, an English-speaking college professor.

By 1988, Rovno was part of the USSR and Mikhail Gorbachev was in power. Access was starting to open up and the tight control of the Communist era was beginning to loosen, although travel from town to town was still restricted. Samuel's connections enabled Ben and Cindy to make the necessary arrangements for their trip to the Ukraine.

As a wounded Soviet war veteran who lost his arm in fighting the Nazis, Samuel had a government-provided car. Samuel and one of his Ukrainian friends drove Ben and Cindy to the site of Ludvipol. Formerly lovely Ludvipol had been burned down and rebuilt into a rundown little town called Sosnovoye.

The group visited the forest near Ludvipol to see where our people had been killed. It was a frightening experience for Ben and Cindy, the first Westerners to visit the site of the mass grave. The road they were driving on into the woods ended, then they had to proceed on foot for about half a mile. Suddenly, out of nowhere, a man appeared, shouting and aiming his gun at them. Tiktin yelled in Ukrainian — "What are you doing? These people have come back to look for the grave of their relatives." The man lowered his gun.

It turned out that this man was a guard responsible for protecting the site of the former kasharan, the fenced-in Polish military barracks where the Jews of Ludvipol had been taken the day before their murder. The site was now used by the Russians for storing dynamite and other chemicals. The guard was not accustomed to seeing people wandering around, which is why he was so rattled and almost opened fire against the intruders.

Once the guard calmed down, Ben gave him some of the Marlboros he had brought along to encourage cooperation. I had warned Ben not to tip with American dollars, for which he could have been arrested, but to use American cigarettes instead. The guard was so excited to have the cigarettes that he became almost friendly. He knew where the mass grave was and guided them to the spot.

It had been many years since anyone had come to the grave, so the surrounding area was as overgrown as a jungle. It was difficult to get to the location of the grave, though it was only two hundred feet or so from where they first met the guard. Once they had battled their way through the undergrowth to reach the site, it struck Ben that not even a blade of grass grew in the place where the people were buried. It was barren. Nothing grew on this soil that was so saturated with blood.

Ben and Cindy found a small monument on the site. There was no mention of Jews on the monument, which noted that in the year 1942 victims of German fascism were killed on this spot. This monument had been erected by two brothers named Yasnobolka, Jewish survivors from Ludvipol who now lived in Kharkov. Due to their prominent positions in the Russian army, they had connections and influence. They persuaded the Russian government to order the local authorities to place a small monument on the site of the mass slaughter. No other survivors from Ludvipol had seen the monument until Ben and Cindy's arrival.

The guard helped Ben and Cindy to gather stones to place on the monument, in keeping with the Jewish custom of leaving stones when you visit a grave.

Ben and Cindy returned to the U.S. with photographs of Ludvipol. I mailed copies of the pictures to our landtzmen in the U.S. and Israel, which caused a great deal of excitement.[1] Ben's visit triggered a plan by the Ludvipol organization for the survivors to return to Ludvipol as a group and erect a proper memorial for those who had been slaughtered.

A committee, which included Arje Katz, himself an important supporter of the memorial project, raised funds, mostly in the United States and Canada, from Ludvipol survivors, myself included. Shmuel Shafir, president in Israel of the Jewish Organization of Ludvipol Survivors in Israel, who has dedicated his life to the project of remembering our martyrs and keeps the organization alive, made arrangements with Viktor Borisovitz Palchovsky and other local Ukrainian authorities for the preparation of the site and memorial stones. A Jewish contractor from Rovno was hired, and he enclosed a 180-meter by 90-meter memorial site with an iron fence.

In 1993, a delegation of twenty-three Ludvipol survivors from Israel and the United States returned to the town for the unveiling of the memorial stones. It was a long journey for them, literally and emotionally. Most of them flew to Kiev and then rode seven hours by bus to Rovno. Proudly walking through Ludvipol (now Sosnovoye) with flags, they showed the community that the remnants of the Jews are still very much alive and kicking.

A big ceremony was held to dedicate the new memorial. The survivors participated, as well as about a thousand local villagers and officials.

After the ceremony, Shafir approached the local officials and asked for their help in locating additional mass graves. One survivor, now in her nineties and living in Israel, had been hiding in nearby bushes and witnessed the killing of about sixty people, who had been shot in the street by the Germans after being dragged out of their hiding places during and after the liquidation. Their bodies had been dumped into two mass graves in the middle of town. Shafir and the others were insistent that these graves, too, be located, and the skeletons dug up and buried properly at the memorial site.

Three years later, in 1996, Shmuel Shafir and the committee made a second trip to Ludvipol, armed with details provided by the woman who had watched from the bushes. It was a team effort to accomplish the project. Viktor Borisovitz Palchovsky helped by convincing residents who knew the graves' location to reveal the secret. A young Ukrainian laborer from the Russian army found the unmarked mass graves in the yard of a local family. The effort was assisted by Michel Kostoztensky, a secret Jew whose real name was Meir Eisenstein. He had been living in Rovno as a Christian ever since the German occupation and had only disclosed his true identity when Jews started to visit the area in the 1990s. Contributions from the community, including my son Ben and myself, Arje Katz, Samuel Keck, and Moshe Furshpan, helped fund the project.

On July 18, 1997, survivors, their children, and their grandchildren went back to Ludvipol to rebury the skeletons from the mass graves in town at the memorial site. They opened the grave and worked all day to remove the bones and personally carry the skeletons to a decent burial. A memorial service was conducted.

During the ceremony, Shafir said, "I don't think there is one of us...who is not moved to the bottom of our hearts and souls in the face of the atrocity we witnessed. What we have heard today from the survivors, which is minor compared to the horrible things we have seen, will be marked deep in our hearts and consciousness. This thing will never be forgotten. It is extremely important to transfer it to the younger generation, the children and the grandchildren. We, the survivors, are obligated not to repress it anymore, but to talk, to tell, and, most important, to remember."

I could not go on that trip, either. Some others were not willing to visit Ludvipol. My friend Itzak Gurfinkel, for instance, said, "For me, there was no reason to go back there. It is only a place. And it has bad memories for me...it is where my family lived and died."[2]

In addition to the main monument in Ludvipol, there are two smaller monuments. One was erected at the main site in memory of my father, mother, and two sisters, whose remains could not be found. The other is in the woods at the approximate location where my father and sister Chava were shot. I am very grateful that the survivors of Ludvipol displayed the willingness and generosity to erect a special memorial for them. I am especially grateful to Shmuel Shafir and his brother Isser, who helped to make this happen.

Shmuel went back to Ludvipol in July 2002 with a group of survivors from Koretz, and he found that both the cemetery and monuments were being well maintained by the local authorities. Today, visitors can pay their respects at the memorial site without being harassed by guards.

In Holon, Israel, there is another memorial to the Jews of Ludvipol. I had the honor of placing a glass box of soil, gathered from the memorial site in Ludvipol, at the Holon memorial.

---

1. Rabbi Arje Katz writes, in his unpublished Memorial Book for the Men, Women and Children from Ludvipol and Volynia (p. 73):

"The Monument commemorating the mass killing of the Jews of Ludvipol was brought to our attention by the devoted son of Ruth and Aharon Golub, Bennett Golub. And this happened during a period of great danger ... God sent angels to watch over them on this trip. At that time it was still dangerous to travel in the Ukraine. They were accompanied by their cousin of Blessed Memory [Samuel Tiktin], who lived in Rovno after the war. While they were searching for the place of the "cemetery" or, to be more correct, the killing fields of all the dear ones from our town, an armed-guard from the military depot from previous times stopped them in a threatening manner. There used to be a Polish Military garrison that was guarding the border between Poland and Russia. The guard was convinced by Samuel Tiktin that they were here to look for the graves of their family that lived in the area for generations. The ones we are looking for are my family. 'As Joseph said, I am searching for my brothers.' ... The soldier left them alone after the explanation.

"Bennett, you lovely son, you were the first one to pass in front of the multitudes, like the children of Gad and Reuven, and they said to God, 'We will walk as front-runners for the people on the way to Canaan.' [Numbers 32]. You promised to go, and you did. God give you strength! To our great sorrow, your father was not able to be there because of his physical problems, but it is written that God blessed your father with an asset like you. Go and succeed in all your deeds, and the best wishes to your family."

"This blessing comes to you from Arje Leib Katz, Rabbi."

2. Itzak Gurfinkel immigrated to Israel illegally in 1948 with HaShomer HaTzair. He lived in Kibbutz Mishmar HaEmek, served in the Israeli Defense Force for twenty-seven years, and helped establish Kibbutz Megiddo. Today he lives in Ramat Gan.

"The path ended here" when Ben and Cindy Golub, and Samuel Tiktin attempted to drive to the nearly hidden memorial stone in honor of the murdered Jews of Ludvipol. (1988)

Ben Golub and Samuel Tiktin found the memorial stone in honor of the murdered Jews of Ludvipol. Nothing grew there, although the surrounding area was lush. (1988)

Left, the memorial stone erected in 1993 in honor of the murdered Jews of Ludvipol by the Jewish Organization of Ludvipol Survivors. *Right*, the stone for the Golub family (September 1993)

"A memorial for the Jewish community of Ludvipol and its surroundings, 1942"

The martyrs are listed by family, with the eighth line from the top reading, *Golub, Baruch, Gittel, Chava, and Esther*. (September 1993)

The Golub family's memorial stone in Ludvipol (September 1993)

The memorial stone erected in the forest where Baruch and Chava Golub were murdered, near Glubachoc (September 1993)

The delegation of Ludvipol survivors who came from Israel and the United States for the unveiling of the memorial stones in 1993, walking proudly through the streets of the town. *Left to right*, Shmuel Shafir, Yona Raber, Baruch Guttman, Arje Katz. (September 1993)

221

Aharon and Ruth Golub in Holon, Israel at the memorial to the Jews of Ludvipol. The stone says, "In memory of the holy community of Ludvipol (Selishtch) and the surrounding area, county of Volhyn." (May 1996)

Aharon was honored to represent the community in placing this box of soil in front of the Holon memorial to Ludvipol's Jews. The soil was gathered at the site of the mass grave in Ludvipol. Six yarhzeit candles were lit for the six million European Jews murdered during the Holocaust. (May 1996)

Reunions

I remain very close to my friends in Israel, and we speak often by phone. Most of their children are now married and have their own families. Little by little, we are all getting older.

Many of our Israeli friends have stayed with us when visiting the United States. We go to Israel often and get together with them. We are frequently invited to someone's place for a party or get-together with five or six other couples. Ruth even jokes that trips to Israel are bad for her figure because she gains weight whenever we go there.

I have two groups of friends in Israel. One is the "Dror children," from Kibbutz Yagur. All of them are established, married with families, and well-positioned in business or professions. Some have excelled in their work. Mordechai Aviv became one of the largest real estate developers in Jerusalem. Eleazer Fuchs earned a Ph.D. in Economics and was the head of Israel's national adult education program.

On my first trip back to Israel, Moshe Trosman heard I was arriving and came to welcome me at the airport. I was excited and surprised to see him and asked what he was doing there.

"I came to welcome a friend," he said.

"Who?" I asked.

"The man I'm talking to now!"

We have not forgotten Shimshon, my friend and roommate during my first years in Israel. Leon Rubinstein, his wife Estelle, and Kalman Offir once noticed when they visited Shimshon's grave that it had only a cement marker while the other graves had marble overlays. Leon paid for an engraved marble overlay so that Shimshon's grave looks like the other graves. At the Dror group's Fiftieth Reunion, we gathered to honor Shimshon at his grave.

My other group of friends is my landtzmen, with whom we are very close. Most of the surviving Jews from Ludvipol are in Israel, although there are several families in New York, a few in Detroit, a few in Canada (Winnipeg and Montreal), and one in Vienna.

We see many friends from Ludvipol and their families, such as Pesach Kleinman, whose grandfather was our next-door neighbor and Tibel Tuchman, who saved the pictures of my family. Several years ago, Eliahu Kleinman and his wife Ada hosted a party for us. Nearly all of the survivors from Ludvipol who lived in Israel participated. The party was at Eliahu and Ada's beautiful apartment in an exclusive area of Tel Aviv, with a breathtaking view of the whole city. Ada hired an accordion player, prepared wonderful food, and did everything possible to make the party one of the most memorable evenings we have had. After food and a few drinks, we sang the old Russian, Ukrainian, and Hebrew songs we had learned as children, accompanied by the accordionist, far into the night. We shall always treasure the memory of that evening.

Another time, my son Ben and Moshe Trosman organized a surprise party in Israel for my seventieth birthday. When I walked into the room and realized it was a surprise party for me, I almost collapsed. Over eighty people attended, including the children of Samuel Tiktin, the "Dror children," and my landtzmen. I was very happy.

Matty and Moshe Trosman at home in
Ramat Gan (November 1989)

Aharon Golub and Zipora Glick — Tsipi
(Faygele) Velman — the girl rescued by
Uncle Usher at the same time as Aharon
(November 1989)

Rivka and Shmuel Shafir in Israel
(November 1994)

Eli, *standing*, and Ada Kleinman, Pesach
Kleinman, Tibel and Zvi (Hershel)
Tuchman, and Ruth Golub, *standing*
(November 1989)

Inseparable friends Ezra Sherman, Leon Rubinstein, and
Aharon Golub at Ben Golub's bar mitzvah (April 1970)

225

The Fiftieth Reunion of the Dror group, at Yagur (May 4, 1996)

Chava's Rosh Ha'Shana Card

At the end of August 2001, on the last day of summer vacation before classes resumed at their Solomon Schechter School, I visited my son and daughter-in-law to celebrate my twin grandchildren Phillip and Alexandra's ninth birthday. In my role as host grandfather, I greeted guests and introduced myself. I struck up a conversation with a young couple from Riverdale, Israel and Manya Eiger, whose son was about to begin his first year at the school and whom Cindy had thoughtfully included.

I noticed that Israel spoke with an accent that sounded like a blend of Israeli and Polish, so I asked him, "Where are you originally from?"

"My family is from Ludvipol, in Poland," he told me.

I was amazed. I rarely run across someone from my hometown. I asked him his parents' names. Sure enough, his mother, Miriam Eiger, nee Eisenstein, was a dear friend from Ludvipol. I had known her well. During my period in Kibbutz Yagur, when I vacationed in Tel Aviv I would stay with Eliahu and Pesach Kleinman from Ludvipol. A group of us would go out together on Friday and Saturday nights, including Miriam and her sister.

I called Ben and Cindy over and told them, "You see, when you do good deeds, and you have kind intentions, something special comes of it!"

The next morning, Miriam called me from Israel. Israel had phoned and told her of our meeting, and she was excited to relocate an old friend. We chatted and promised to get together the next time Ruthie and I came to Israel.

Miriam has a friend named Chaia, with whom she had renewed her friendship when they both went on the expedition from Israel to Ludvipol to set up the new memorial. Chaia is none other than the girl who left Ludvipol in 1936 with her grandfather Mottel the shochet and her brother Shlomo to join her father, Joseph Schwartzman, in the Holy Land.

Miriam called Chaia to tell her the news. "Imagine what happened! My son met Aharon Golub."

Chaia exclaimed, "Oh, my God. I still have a picture of Arieh's sister, Chava, on a Rosh Ha'Shana card that she mailed to me from Ludvipol!"

For the 1936 Jewish New Year, being the daughter of a family who ran a photography studio, Chava had sent Chaia a Rosh Ha'Shana card personalized with her photograph. She had written her greeting on the back in her beautiful Hebrew handwriting.

Miriam convinced Chaia to give me the card. When Israel and Manya Eiger visited Miriam in Israel, they brought me back this precious memento of my sister.

Since then, we old Ludvipol friends maintain closer contact. Ruthie and I have seen Miriam and her sister several times in Israel when the old crowd gathers at parties. I remembered Miriam from 1950 as a young woman, and now we are both grandparents of children who study together in a Jewish school in America. Chava's New Year greeting to her girlhood friend traveled to Israel and then to me in the United States.

This is indeed a small world.

Chava Golub, pictured on a 1936 Rosh Ha'Shana greeting card she sent to Chaia
Schwartzman, the shochet's granddaughter, in Israel. The card was given to Aharon
in 2002.

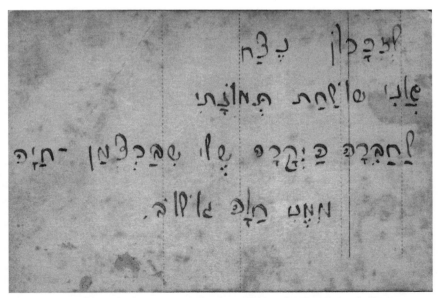

On the back of the card, Chava wrote in her beautiful handwriting, "For a lasting memory,
I send my photograph to you, my dearest friend, Chaia Schwartzman. From me, Chava
Golub."

V

Reflections
on My Life
and Times

M y family, my children, and my grandchildren have been the most wonderful and important part of my life.

The next two greatest events of my lifetime were witnessing the creation of the State of Israel and the liberation of the Jews of Russia. Being fortunate enough to see these events was worth all the suffering I have endured. A great injustice was done to us, but what can we do about it? God works in mysterious ways. Perhaps this was the price we had to pay for the Jewish state.

During the Holocaust, I learned the art of survival and experienced firsthand the vulnerability of the Jewish people. I believe that Jews are basically good, straightforward people who do not harm anyone, and I have always wondered why some people do not like us. I am a proud Jew. I am happy to be Jewish. From early in my life, I have believed that the Jewish people must make every effort to have an independent homeland of their own — and that it was my responsibility to help it become a reality.

I think we are a wonderful people. We work, we earn a living, we are charitable, and we help others. We do not bother other people. Perhaps others have been jealous of our accomplishments and resent that we believe in our God so deeply that we resist attempts to convert us to Christianity.

When I was approached, several years ago, to videotape an interview for the Shoah Foundation, I was just beginning to feel comfortable talking about my past. I hesitated to do the interview because I knew it would be very stressful. However, despite the pain of recalling details, I believed that I had an obligation to leave testimony for future generations. What happened to our people was unbelievable. I feel it is important that someone who actually experienced it should inform and educate future generations. By knowing what happened, future generations of Jews will be more vigilant and understand the necessity for strong support for Israel, so that we are never again as vulnerable as we were in Europe. I hope that this book will contribute to accomplishing this task.

At the time of Hitler's rise to power, the Jewish people were unprepared to fight or defend themselves against such an atrocity. I hope that the coming generations, knowing what happened, will be better prepared. Perhaps they will be able to prevent another disaster before it occurs. Perhaps they will be able to defuse it in its earliest stages, at the first signs of serious anti-Semitism. Jews must be strong, and we cannot permit anti-Semitism to flourish.

In this world, the weak do not get privileges. No one is generous enough to hand things over to weaker people for a prolonged period of time. Some may throw a bone or be "charitable," but the weak and the poor never have much say in this world. Thus, Israel must be a nation equal to other nations. Only by being strong and having our own state, one that is economically viable and militarily strong, will our people be respected. Only then will old prejudices, inborn hatred, and negative stereotypes vanish. Only by having our own proud and vibrant nation will this change. Only by having our own state will people stop blaming us for all of their troubles.

The Jewish people have had a miserable past. For hundreds of years, we were persecuted, held back, and pushed from one country to another. In many cases, we were used as scapegoats because we were a people without a land, with no one to stand up for us. When we were exiled from the Land of Israel by the Romans, we made a choice not to be warriors, not to be a military people. Instead, we chose to accept our fate and to focus on being scholars. Realizing that we would have to live within other nations, we left ourselves to the mercy of other rulers.

Of course, Jews have served in the militaries of their countries.

They did their duty and then went back into civilian life. Few developed military careers. As a result, we were ill prepared in Europe, and the Germans encountered little organized resistance.

The Germans also broke the morale of the people in the countries they occupied, gradually bringing them to a point of feeling that their lives were worthless and hardly worth fighting for. In Israel today, the situation is finally different — we now have several generations of military people, out of necessity. We have a country to protect. We do not depend on others to protect us.

The roots of anti-Semitism go back thousands of years and stem directly from the church, in particular the Catholic Church. Its leaders fanned the flames of hatred and kept them alive for centuries. They did not condemn the hatred they observed and kept generations of people in ignorance. People I knew in Poland and the Ukraine never even knew that Christ was born a Jew.

Perhaps it was in the church's interest to eradicate the Jewish faith. Our belief in the same values — the sanctity of life and one God — might have allowed us to get along well if this hatred had not been encouraged. Perhaps the early Christian leaders were ashamed that their religion originated from a small group of people called Jews and felt it would be best for them if we could all be converted or eliminated.

Only in recent times has there been meaningful dialogue between the religions, and only lately are efforts being made to explain these basic truths. Perhaps this is partly because so many people are better educated now and the truth can no longer be hidden. Hopefully, although it might take hundreds of years, these dialogues will make life better for all of humanity and not just the Jewish people.

The Jewish Chatauqua Society, for instance, arranges for Jewish scholars to speak at universities, especially Christian universities. Their courses were completely extracurricular at first and taught on a volunteer basis, but they became so popular that they are now accredited, remunerated, and oversubscribed. My wife and I are contributors to the Jewish Chatauqua Society because we believe that students should be getting proper information about our religion and our people. Perhaps in due time, some clarity can be achieved. At the beginning of World War II, many European intellectuals became anti-Semitic, perhaps out of fear, perhaps out of ignorance. Understanding or pinpointing exactly what happened is difficult, but clearly the intelligentsia of Europe did not do its job.

Moslems are a different story altogether. Jews did not experience extreme religious persecution from the Arabs in the Middle East until recent generations. However, as I understand it, Islam is not very charitable to other religions in general. It does not regard people from other religions as fully equal to Moslems. Islamic regimes have traditionally held Jews as second-class citizens, called *dhimmis*, but these regimes have not persecuted the Jews as happened in Europe, and they have not endorsed and encouraged pogroms as happened in Russia. Some of the most influential Jewish writers and sages emerged during the Moslem renaissance in Spain.

Perhaps Moslems cannot accept a Western-style state in lands they consider to be within the Moslem sphere. Perhaps their leaders see Israel as a foreign body in their region and are concerned that its democratic way of life will contaminate the region and draw power away from them. In my opinion, what we are experiencing is due largely to political, rather than religious, considerations.

As I write this, there are over five million Jews living in Israel. The country is economically viable, with a high standard of living that is, in some cases, over ten times higher than that in neighboring Arab countries. We have a democratic society, and the people and the press can speak freely. The Arabs in Israel are citizens who vote and have all the rights of citizens, except for service in the military and, in some cases, the right to hold certain positions of power. Nevertheless, Arabs are entitled to the same educational, medical, and other opportunities as other Israeli citizens, and they have the right to elect members to the Knesset. Nor are they shy to speak out against the State. Israel is a free country.

I would like to see a more peaceful world and the end of blood-shed in Israel. We have suffered enough. Perhaps we can find some accommodation with our Arab neighbors and try to live with them in peace. However, while we have the conflict with our neighbors, Israel has to be militarily strong. Unquestionably, our military might is superior to that of the Arabs, but we are about five million people surrounded by over a hundred million Arabs. Egypt alone has over seventy million people.

Perhaps, as the Bible says, we must be a "light unto the nations." The push for learning and creative use of knowledge is very important in Israel. Israel is advanced in science and medicine, pioneering in such fields as laser surgery, and second only to the United States in electronics, Internet, and communications. Numerous inventions come from Israel. Its immigrants from all over the world have contributed their trades and talents. What motivates the country is a combination of the drive for knowledge and education and the need to be accepted as an equal partner in the region.

I do not think we Jews are special people, or that we are exceptionally bright or smarter than others. We are equal to everyone else, but we have certain priorities, including the deeply held belief in the importance of education. This desire, this thirst for knowledge, is a major trait of the Jewish people. Parents may go without food, but they will still send their children to the best schools they can. In the long run, it adds up.

I do not know if other religions or cultures share this passion to the extent we do, or whether it is an obsession with them as much as it is with the Jewish people, who push their children to excel and learn at all costs.

Where does all this interest in education lead to? We are decent people who have brought a great deal of goodness into this world in varied areas, such as the arts, theater, music, medicine, and philosophy. I think that this obsession with knowledge and education has been a good thing for our people and for the world — witness the many scientific and technological advances that have come from Israel. If all the people in the world were well educated, it would be a better place to live.

I see the problems of other people, such as the recent problems of Cambodians, as being different from the problems of the Jews. The Cambodians were dominated by a cruel regime and were left devastated by the time Pol Pot was defeated. But Cambodia is a nation with no enemies at this point, so it will get back on its feet.

In comparison, I ponder the mind-boggling prospect of how Israel, its citizens, and the region would prosper if they were not constantly engaged in ongoing hostilities with their neighbors. Billions of dollars now spent on weaponry and defense could be used for education and the advancement of our people and people all over the world. We are proud of our military accomplishments, with one of the finest air forces in the world and tanks that are second to none, but I wish that we did not need all those weapons. Israel is a poor country constantly at war. If peace or settlement could be achieved with the Arabs, we could use that money for other things.

Jews need to look out for each other, no matter where in the world we are. Currently, the Argentinean Jews are in a difficult situation. Argentina is economically desperate, and many Jews, especially in Buenos Aires, said to have the third largest Jewish community in the world, are feeling the pinch. Their lives have been devastated. Many, including my first cousin, have lost their businesses and jobs, and have needed financial assistance from the world Jewish community. The United Jewish Appeal is setting up soup kitchens in Buenos Aires to feed the hungry, not only among the Jews, but whomever needs help. Many Holocaust survivors who have lived in Argentina for the past fifty years are even now immigrating to Israel, despite their fears of the security situation, suicide bombers and other acts of violence. For those people, being in a country where you can earn a living is better than starving in Argentina.

I believe that, eventually, the internal problems in Israel between secular and Orthodox Jews will be resolved because we have a common goal: to live in peace in a prosperous country. Extremism is, in my view, unacceptable, including the Jewish extreme. In the long run, the Orthodox, Conservative, and Reform Jews will manage to find a way to live together. At present, the Orthodox faction dominates the Israeli religious establishment, but Conservative, Reform, and secular Judaism should also have a place, including the right to help determine the country's direction. All segments of a society should be recognized as legitimate and viable.

It is my hope that the Jews spread across the world in the Diaspora will gradually make their homes in Israel. If my grandchildren were to decide to move to Israel, Ruth and I would probably move with them. I still think about returning to Israel, but my children and grandchildren live in the United States and my wife's extended family is here. Living near family is important and precious to me.

I am concerned about Israel's safety and contribute beyond my means to the United Jewish Appeal and other Jewish organizations. My hand shakes if I have to throw out a request for a contribution from a good cause. I have been a UJA volunteer, soliciting contributions from larger donors for the past twenty years. I do this because I feel it is my obligation.

The UJA was instrumental in helping Jews get out of the Soviet Union. I participated in rallies and wrote letters to legislators urging the United States to put pressure on Russia to free the Jews. It took many years, but eventually the Soviets relented and released people. Ben and Cindy were also active in campaigns on behalf of Soviet Jewry. Ben raised enough money among his professional colleagues to pay for the complete flight of a 747 jet from Moscow to Israel; it carried more than four hundred people. That flight alone cost hundreds of thousands of dollars. And this occurred during the time that Iraq was attacking Israel with Scud missiles.

I believe that we learn from the personal example set by those within our families. The person who had the greatest influence on me was my father. He was my idol, a courteous, charitable man with a deep respect for others. He was a wonderful father and a wonderful human being, deeply involved in education. I also had great respect for my mother, who was a good mother and enormously devoted to her family. I remember how she was always concerned for our well-being and intent on keeping us well-fed. I would like to think that my mother and father have been looking down on my life, though I don't really believe in life after death.

My family observes Jewish traditions. We celebrate the Jewish holidays and are proud of our Jewish identity and our heritage. We belong to and are active in various Jewish organizations, including our temple, where we have been members for almost forty years.

My two children, Ben and Elizabeth, are wonderful human beings. I am glad to see that they follow our tradition in many respects, are good people, active in Jewish organizations, and generous to charitable causes. Ruth and I have tried to instill in them the importance of giving to others, of being involved in Jewish affairs, of supporting Jewish organizations, and of helping the needy of all nations.

My son, Ben, a graduate of MIT with a Ph.D. in Applied Economics and Finance, is a successful young man. His wife Cindy is a wonderfully decent woman, also well educated and active in Jewish affairs. She retired from a successful professional career to be a full-time mother. I have three lovely grandchildren, Jill, Phillip, and Alexandra Golub, at the time of this writing. My daughter Elizabeth is a graduate of Oswego College, and now she works as a senior paralegal in an excellent professional position. Elizabeth recently married Kenneth Martin, a fine young man. I am very proud of both of my children and very proud of our family's accomplishments.

Family heritage expresses itself through both genes and values. Some say that my son looks like my side of the family, others that he resembles my wife's father. Perhaps he inherited a little from both sides. Physically, my daughter resembles my mother and often reminds me of her. Most of all, I am proud that our children inherited our family's compassion for others. I would like to believe they learned from us how to respect other people, to be honest, and to be law abiding. I do not think either of them has ever deliberately deceived anyone.

I wish for my children and grandchildren, first of all, good health. I want them to be good, fair, and honest people. I want them to be well educated. I am pleased that my grandchildren's school, the Solomon Schechter School in White Plains, is giving them a good education and an intimate knowledge of Judaism and Jewish values.

True success in life is to be a *mentsch*, a decent person, who tries to do the right thing and does not confine oneself to one's own little world. Not everyone can climb to great heights. Some do. Some are great writers, some are great musicians, some achieve great things in other ways, but every individual has to do something for the world as a whole. I believe this and try to follow that path, and this is what I want for my children and grandchildren — to use their lives to contribute to the betterment of the world.

Aharon Golub, United Jewish Appeal
Federation Inaugural Dinner (October
1993)

Aharon and Ruth Golub at the UJA Federation
Inaugural Dinner (North Shore Synagogue, Syosset,
New York, November 19, 1994)

241

Left to right, Cindy, Alex, Jill, Phillip, and Ben Golub in Venice (June 2002)

Jill, Phillip, and Alexandra Golub, Ben and
Cindy's children, Haifa (April 2000)

Elizabeth (Golub) Martin and Aharon
Golub (October 7, 2001)

242

Historical Background and Interviews

I. Ludvipol: A Modern Shtetl

A Brief History of the Region

Today the map shows a town called Sosnovoye, but for hundreds of years it was called Ludvipol. Now it is in the Ukraine, but for the first three centuries of its recorded existence, it was in eastern Poland. It is a small but resilient village, home to hundreds of Jewish families.

The region around Ludvipol, known as Volhynia (Volyn in Yiddish), is a flat, fertile country drained by the Bug and Prypet rivers and the Prypet's tributaries, among them the Slusch River. Many of its towns made their first appearance on the historic record as properties of Polish and Kievan nobles, as did Ludvipol and Kostopol, the administrative center, rather like a county seat, of the district that included Ludvipol.

From ancient times Volhynia had a rich rural landscape. Wild horses, deer, and bison roamed its forests before Tatar invaders burned away large tracts; extensive woodlands, still remaining, yielded timber, skins, wild berries, and mushrooms. On its large farming estates, orchards of pear, apple, and cherry blossomed white in springtime and fields of grain ripened in summer, while both small farmers and large landowners raised potatoes, sugar beets, cattle, chickens, hogs, and geese.

The large estates were owned by Polish gentry, who often employed Jews as estate managers and rent collectors. As the centuries went by, that economic symbiosis caused the larger but less wealthy Ukrainian population of Volhynia to identify Jews with the Poles, from whom the Ukrainians were often — but unsuccessfully

— trying to gain their independence.

The roots of Jewish culture in eastern Poland and the Ukraine were very old and very deep, and Jews are believed to have lived in the area as early as the tenth century. It was not until late in that century that the *Polacy* (people of the fields) became Christianized and their country, Poland, became a nation in the eyes of the Pope and other European powers.

As early as the eleventh century, Jews in Lutsk (Luck, in Polish; Lodz, in Yiddish), the ancient provincial capital of Volhynia — located about seventy miles west of the site that later became Ludvipol — formed craft guilds and participated in city council decisions about the levying of taxes. Lutsk eventually became a famous center for Torah study, with many yeshivas.

Many of the earliest Jews to arrive in Poland were Yiddish-speaking Ashkenazim migrating from France and Germany. In their new home, "they seem to have been welcomed. In 1264, the Statute of Kalisz, signed by Prince Boleslaw the Pious, gave Jews a wide range of rights, including equal treatment in Polish courts.... In the mid-fourteenth century, Kazimierz the Great, known to Jews as 'the king who was good to the Jews,' provided a haven for refugees fleeing the Hundred Years' War, the Black Death, widespread famine, and anti-Jewish atrocities [and] confirmed the rights given to them in the Statute of Kalisz."[1] King Kazimierz also gave the Jews a prime tract of land near the Vistula River in the royal city of Krakow. That neighborhood, where Jewish institutions destroyed during the Holocaust are now being rebuilt with help from Jewish communities in America and elsewhere, is still known as Kazimierz in his honor. In addition, Jews clustered in *shtetlach* (small towns and villages) where they were a majority or near-majority of the population. By the seventeenth century, Jewish merchants, so wealthy that they rode in coaches-and-six and had pages to attend them, were a common sight in Lvov, a large, cosmopolitan city about 140 miles southwest of Ludvipol.[2]

Jews formed a vital part of the connective tissue of the economy in this region and all of Poland. They worked as doctors, lawyers, moneylenders, accountants, commodity brokers, manufacturers, brewers, and craftspeople, and held leases and mortgages on mills, inns, and other properties. All this brought occasional rumbles of anti-Semitism from non-Jewish businesspeople who were their competitors. A fourteenth-century middle-class Pole complained: "In our country, the leaseholder is a Jew, the doctor is a Jew, the merchant is Jewish, and so is the miller, the secretary and the most faithful servant, since they've gained the upper hand in everything."[3]

Farther down the social scale, anti-Semitism took on the darker coloring of superstitious fear: "In peasant lore, Jews were believed to have supernatural powers and dark, peculiar customs. According to one folk belief, all Jews were born blind and needed blood to become sighted."[4] There was less anti-Semitism in Poland than elsewhere in Europe, however, and Poland's liberal religious toleration laws continued to make it a place of refuge for Protestants and Jews fleeing religious persecution in nations to the west.

Jews seem to have lived in the village of Hovkov, near the Slusch River and, later, Ludvipol, until it was overrun by Genghis Khan's Tatars in 1241.[5] The Tatars struck again in the 1640s and carried many residents of Volhynia into slavery before they were finally defeated. The complicated series of battles sparked by the Tatar invasion culminated in a bloody showdown between the Poles and the Ukrainians, who were irritated by Poland's hegemony over Volhynia but were no match for the Polish hetmani (regional military commanders). Some Tatars settled permanently and peacefully in Poland; from the fifteenth century there were dozens of mosques in the vicinity of Lutsk.

Records at the Beth Hatefutsoth Museum of the Jewish Diaspora in Tel Aviv mention a seventeenth-century Jewish cemetery near a fortress in Hovkov, about three and a half miles from Ludvipol; the fortress was destroyed during a war in the eighteenth century. After the war, the Jews of Hovkov may have resettled on the other side of the Slusch in the large village of Wielkie Siedliszcze (large settlement, in Polish) — some families, such as Mordechai Velman's, traced their roots in Ludvipol to 1780 or earlier — but their graveyard remained in Hovkov. There are rumors of an older graveyard in the Hovkov area, as well.

Wielkie Siedliszcze became known as Ludvipol when a Polish nobleman named Siemaszek began to develop the area. A romantic explanation for the name change is that a *poritz* (Polish landlord, in Yiddish) named Ludwik lived in a palace on a hill there and changed the name to Ludwipol when he married a woman named Paula. The Jews of Ludvipol usually called the town by a Yiddish name, Selishtch Gadol (Big Selishtch), distinguishing it from the small Ukrainian village at its edge, Selishtch. Still, it consisted of only two main streets, two alleys, and a marketplace.

Globally speaking, it was no accident that there is definite evidence of activity at this time in Jewish settlements like Ludvipol. By the early 1770s, according to historian Adam Zamoyski, four-fifths of all Jews lived in the Polish Commonwealth.[6]

Exhilarated by the revolutions in America and France, Poland's parliament, the Sejm, produced the first written constitution in Europe in 1791. This progressive action angered Poland's powerful neighbors and the nation soon found itself partitioned and occupied by Russia, Prussia, and Austria.

Jews and Poles fought together against the partition in a 1794 uprising led by Tadeusz Kosciusko, a Polish nobleman famous for his participation in the American Revolution. But this effort was unsuccessful, as were other uprisings in the nineteenth century in which Poles — and Jews — attempted to free their country. Punishment by the occupying powers was extremely harsh; after a failed uprising in the 1830s, the Russians sent thousands of Polish noble families from Volhynia into exile in Siberia and executed thousands more Poles at home. The partition lasted for 125 years, until the agreements that ended World War I restored Poland's independence in 1918. There were periodic surges of Jewish emigration from the region, especially during the early part of the twentieth century. One factor was the danger of conscription into the Czar's army.

A writer in the Ludvipol Yizkor book, a collection of remembrance essays published in 1965 by the Jewish organization of survivors from Ludvipol, recalled the time when a messenger arrived in town and put up notices ordering all men between sixteen and sixty to register for the czar's army and fight the Bolshevik revolutionaries. Boys conscripted into the army served for as many as twenty-five years, losing touch with their families and Jewish traditions. Those who did not die were exposed to vicious anti-Semitic attacks. Because single sons were not required to join, some families gave each of their sons a different last name. Occasionally, a release was obtained by the boy sustaining injuries and paying a fee. A third way to avoid conscription was to leave everything behind and move to distant lands.

For many middle- and lower-class people, the partition made little difference in daily life, but it fanned a smoldering Polish nationalism, one component of which was deep rancor against both czarist Russia and, later, Russian socialism. Though both Jews and Poles suffered under the Russian occupation, "common victimization does not necessarily make good bedfellows."[7] Poles distrusted Jews, fearing that they might side with the Russian oppressors. On the other hand, Jews in Poland, caught in waves of anti-Semitism for over a hundred years there, had little reason to risk everything for the Polish national cause. The cyclical nature of anti-Semitism in nineteenth-century Polish society, which peaked during times of political instability and economic downturns, is referred to by a character from Boleslaw Prus's classic Polish novel, The Doll (1890): "I began to notice that the people we formerly called 'Poles of the Mosaic confession' we now called 'Jews.'" Eventually, tensions between Poles and Russians, whether Czarist or socialist, would be most deeply felt in eastern Poland, especially near the border.

Nineteenth-century Ludvipol would have been a frontier town

by the standards of Poles living to the west in Lublin, Krakow, or Warsaw, as well as Russians in stately Kiev, about 160 miles east of Ludvipol. A clue to urbanites' view of the region comes from a scene in The Doll in which a man who wears old, unfashionable clothes to a performance at Warsaw's Grand Theatre is greeted by titters and whispers that he must be "some squire from Volhynia."

But as the town built its economy on land-based industries, by the mid-nineteenth century Ludvipol was thriving. Community records show 286 Jews were living in Ludvipol in 1847. In that year there was a paper factory in the town as well as two Jewish pharmacies, ten Jewish stores, a number of Jewish craftsmen, and a local branch of the national Association of Jewish Craftsmen. The town also had a Jewish inn that was frequented by lumber merchants and other travelers.

Pogroms terrorized Jews early in the 1880s in other parts of what is now the Ukraine, but there is little evidence of pogroms in Ludvipol at that time. By the end of the nineteenth century, Ludvipol's population had increased to 1,428. Most of the residents — 1,210 — were Jews. As their numbers grew, Jewish culture flourished. The town had five synagogues, a rabbi, and three kosher butchers during this period. It also benefited from a network of Jewish cultural institutions in the surrounding region, such as a rabbinical seminary and a Hebrew printing press in Zhitomir, eighty miles to the southeast, about halfway to Kiev.

Ludvipol's population continued to grow with the brisk trade that developed along the Slusch River. Logs from the region were sent down the Prypet River to the Bug and Vistula rivers and finally to the port of Gdynia on the Baltic Sea. Sales of cattle and horses flourished in Ludvipol, and businesses large and small made money from the sale of secondary agricultural products, such as goose down, sunflower and other seeds that were pressed for oil, hog bristles, livestock feed, and fertilizer. Only thirty-five miles away was the larger town of Rovno (population forty thousand by 1931), with a busy railroad junction.

Into this region, with its rural economy and modest but live-ly Jewish cultural institutions, World War I and the Bolshevik Revolution exploded brutally. The war heightened tensions be-tween Poles and Russians, and brought a short-lived grab for inde-pendence by the Ukrainians. There were harsh repercussions for Jews. Between 1917 and 1919, fifty thousand Jews in the area were murdered by the forces of Simon Petlura, who tried unsuccessfully to establish an independent Ukrainian republic. Marauding bands of fighters who took cover in the large forests around Ludvipol ha-rassed the townspeople during the war and afterward. This period of anarchy and lawlessness made life particularly harsh for the Jews. Without governmental infrastructure, criminals tormented Jews without fear of punishment. Peasants frequented Ludvipol's only tavern and drank until they lost consciousness or became rowdy and broke glass bottles all over town. Efriem Kozuel re-called, in the Yizkor book, an incident when a group of non-Jews came to Ludvipol on Shabbat and forced two youngsters, Benjamin and Abraham Zabodnik, to "dance" on a sheet of metal over a fire, while pistols were fired above their heads. The community paid each of the thugs fifteen rubles to stop.

Although the partition of Poland ended in 1918, its eastern border (including Rovno and Ludvipol) continued to be subjected to frequent battles and changes in government. Ludvipol changed hands five times in less than two years during this period. In quick succession, it was occupied and governed by the Ukraine (Petlura), Bolshevik Russia, Poland, and then Bolshevik Russia again. In September 1920, Poland, whose people were mostly Roman Catholic, regained control along its eastern border, but compli-cated political and social hostilities continued. The Russians never took their envious eyes off the border, with its Ukrainian, Russian Orthodox population. Meanwhile, a significant number of Jews, es-pecially idealistic Zionists, embraced socialism. Photographs from this era show parades of Zionist youth groups marching with so-cialist youth groups. The association made Poles, who were deeply threatened by communist Russia, see them as Russian sympathizers; their fears were aggravated when Russia attempted (unsuccessfully) to push through Poland into Germany.

To counter ethnic Ukrainian dominance in Volhynia, the Polish government attempted to strengthen the Polish presence in the area and encouraged Poles to relocate there, with government loans for land and businesses. The "Swój do swego" (Polish for "Stick to your own") movement was an organized attempt to coerce Poles into using only Polish businesses and services.

At the same time, the end of the partition meant new borders, and the new borders separated Jews in Volhynia from their traditional centers of learning and trade. Cultural, family, social, and economic ties were severed when Kiev, Kharkov, and Odessa (now in Russia) were replaced by Vilna and Grodno, largely unfamiliar to Ludvipol's inhabitants. Families were split, as they found themselves living in different countries. Transportation came to a standstill, and constantly changing currencies wreaked havoc on the value of money, especially paper money. Food became scarce, and people hoarded it toward worse times ahead. Commerce and trade all but stopped. In addition, two major disasters struck Ludvipol. In 1918, a fire destroyed much of the town, with numerous families losing everything. A typhus epidemic followed, reducing the population drastically.

With Eastern Europe's economy in decline, international Jewish organizations came to the rescue. The People's Relief Committee to Aid Jews in Europe and Palestine reminded Jews that they are responsible for one another and that, quoting the *Mishna* (the written version of Jewish oral laws), "to save one person is to save the world." The American Jewish Joint Distribution Committee (JDC or "the Joint"), established just a few years earlier to distribute the funds raised by Jewish organizations, sent money, supplies, and volunteers to Ludvipol. It reported in June 1920 that conditions were deplorable and getting worse by the day. The committee's report said that Ludvipol's Jewish community was "unique" in its particularly large number of orphans, about 25 percent of its children, including 15 with no home. Although a public kitchen in Ludvipol was providing food for 175 youngsters in June, the committee's December report indicated that it was no longer operating. In June, three Jewish schools taught 195 students, but by December, only one was open, with an enrollment of 125. Different paper currencies accompanied every change in government, roads and bridges were not repaired, the infrastructure was failing, and trade had come to a standstill.[8]

In 1922, the JDC took upon itself the task of building and repairing public baths to improve the deplorable conditions in communities throughout Volhynia. Directing the projects was an American doctor, Jacob J. Golub. As director of the JDC's medical service program in Poland, Dr. Golub traveled widely in Volhynia and reported that medical conditions were tragically inadequate and that the Jewish population required extensive assistance. The committee devoted hundreds of thousands of dollars for bath houses in Volhynia, as well as clinics for the cure of favus (a skin disease), and public health education programs. Dr. Golub worked closely with the Polish government to stop the spread of epidemic diseases and created a Jewish organization, TOZ, to conduct most of the activities of the Medical Sanitary Department in Poland.[9]

In the 1920s Jews were the third largest national group in Volhynia, after Ukrainians (68 percent) and Poles (16 percent). Jews represented about 11 percent of the population in 1921 and 10 percent in 1931; that year, there were 207,792 Jews in Volhynia out of a total population of 2,077,769. This mirrored the ratio of Jews to Poles and other ethnic groups elsewhere in Poland, where Jews made up about 10 percent of a total population of 32,000,000. Among Polish Jews, roughly 90 percent identified Yiddish or Hebrew as their native language (in nine out of ten cases, Yiddish); in Volhynia, the percentage was considerably higher at 98.9 percent. Most Jews in Ludvipol also spoke Polish and Ukrainian.

Ludvipol right after the 1918 fire (JDC archive)

Bath house in Ludvipol, repaired by the JDC, in about 1922 (JDC archive)

253

Beset by these problems, including cyclical anti-Semitism, a history of conscription into the Czar's army, fires, typhus, political instability, lawlessness, and a devastated economy, the lure of emigration was irresistible. The less security and wealth someone had, the more sense it made to break free and take his chances in the *Goldene Medina*, the "golden land" of America, where the streets were paved with gold and from which so much help had come. Sholom Aleichem wrote, "America is where all the unhappy souls go."[10]

Meanwhile, the anti-Semitic Endecja movement was gaining adherents throughout Poland. The instability of the country's borders on both the east and the west caused a "defensive nationalism" to emerge, and loyalty to the nation of Poland became extremely important. The question of whether Jews were primarily loyal to Poland or were a nation apart was debated in the context of a newly re-invigorated anti-Semitism. The question was particularly emotional in Volhynia because of its still-large Ukrainian population and its proximity to Russia.

Small towns were fighting their way back to normalcy and struggling to rebuild their economic bases after World War I when the Great Depression hit at the end of the 1920s. Hard times sharpened economic competition. Jews, who controlled a high percentage of Poland's manufacturing and other industries, were the target of jealousy and suspicion. Jewish firms not only employed more than 40 percent of the Polish labor force but were heavily represented in commerce and the professions; a 1931 survey of professionals bitterly concluded that more than half of Poland's doctors and a third of its lawyers were Jewish. "As everywhere in Europe, widespread joblessness and poverty stoked extremist and fanatical tendencies. In Poland, these tendencies were given additional impetus by old prejudices and new statistical realities."[11]

With Polish society under stress from the Depression and ominous signs of military buildup in Germany, outspoken anti-Semitism was condoned to a degree that would have been shocking in more prosperous and tolerant times. The Polish government passed laws severely restricting Jews in business, forcing once-comfortable merchants and professionals to join an overabundance of shoe-makers, tailors, and carpenters or to peddle food and commodities between villages.

Several survivors from Ludvipol, including Mordechai Velman and Pesach Kachenstern, indicated that there were pogroms in the vicinity during the early 1930s.[12] Nevertheless, it was a decade of relative stability in Ludvipol, which now had a population of about two thousand Jews and one hundred non-Jews. A new school opened under the sponsorship of the Tarbut network, followed by a trade school. A public library held well-attended lectures and discussions, and numerous cultural groups flourished. The town regularly sent delegates to international Zionist congresses, and Zionist youth movements prepared young people for immigration to *Eretz Yisrael* (the Land of Israel), then a British mandate. In addition, a Polish army base near the town created a market for many services, including photography for personal use and for identification documents.

In 1939, with German invasion imminent, there was a brief period of feverish growth in Volhynia, as thousands of Jews fled east from the cities of western Poland. For several months, the refugees fed business and enriched culture in the region, but the short-lived bubble of excitement burst when Volhynia was invaded by Russia and found itself trapped.

Fiercely loved by diverse peoples, fiercely coveted by great powers, Volhynia had seen many wars over the centuries, but had survived them all. Each time, peace had brought population growth, industry, and culture. At the time of Hitler's attack on Poland in September 1939, many families who had lived there for generations remained optimistic. They could not imagine the genocide to come. They could not foresee that when this war ended, nearly all these families would have been murdered and the cradle of their memories would be irrecoverable.

1. Eva Hoffman, Shtetl: The Life and Death of a Small Town and the World of Polish Jews, p. 30
2. Adam Zamoyski, The Polish Way, p. 106
3. Hoffman, Ibid., p. 42
4. Hoffman, Ibid., p. 42
5. Devora Gorin Wiseman, in Ludvipol's Yizkor book
6. Zamoyski, Ibid., p. 344
7. Hoffman, Ibid., p. 112
8. Joint Distribution Committee, Archives, Volhynia 1919 and 1920
9. Joint Distribution Committee, Archives. Dr. Jacob J. Golub's relationship to the Golub family in Ludvipol is not known. During the eighteen-month period in which he lived in Rovno and traveled to every Jewish community in the region, he saw "at close range the impact of virulent typhus and the economic problems of [Jewish] refugees." In 1922, Dr. Golub directed the construction or repair of twenty-eight bath houses, including at least one in Ludvipol. A letter of recommendation, dated May 29, 1924, from Bernard Flexner, then-chairman of the Joint Distribution Committee's Committee on Medical Affairs, to Norris A. Miller in Boston, refers to Dr. Golub as "a man of splendid character personally, and of loyalty to the work that he may at any time be engaged in. He has demonstrated executive ability above the average, and I think you will have no fault to find as to his knowledge of public health." Later, in 1947, Dr. Golub directed a medical mission to study the health needs of Europe's surviving Jews in eight European countries. In 1948, he was director of the Hospital for Joint Disease in New York and chairman of the JDC's Committee on Health.
10. Julia and Frances Butwin, "Get Thee Out," Favorite Tales of Sholom Aleichem, p. 648
11. Hoffman, Ibid., p. 171
12. Ludvipol's Yizkor book

The Family Business

Despite the Depression and growing anti-Semitism, at the time of Aharon's childhood, Ludvipol was lively, even idyllic. The town was small enough for people to say that when a carriage entered Ludvipol, the heads of the horses stuck out on one end of town and the wheels of the carriage on the other.

Ludvipol was surrounded by natural beauty. On one side were the waters of the Slusch River and on the other, a branch of the Slusch formed two creeks, the Smorodinka and Habel. Near the center of town was a third creek, the Kolchik. A dam on the Smorodinka Creek guided water to a mill pond, a section of which was kept clear of vegetation and served as a recreational spot where the children practiced swimming and the adults exercised and enjoyed the sun. The men bathed there on Friday afternoons before Shabbat. Sometimes they bathed in the Slusch River, and sometimes they hauled drinking and cleaning water from the Slusch; only rarely did they haul water from the big river in early or late winter, when the ice might suddenly crack and they might slide under it to their doom. For a spring hike or picnic, the favorite destination was a beautiful park east of the Slusch, nestled among towering trees near the ruins of the ancient castle. Beyond the park lay a meadow and then the vast forest.

Most of the houses were neat, one-story homes; larger houses of two stories stood at the corners of the town. Most of the three hundred or so families who lived in them were traditional families with neither too much nor too little.

Ludvipol's council had decided, in the early 1930s, to spruce up the town: The main streets and the marketplace were paved, which decreased the amount of unsightly and inconvenient mud. This made it easier to drive a car into town — the county supervisor was one of the few who did. The wide wooden sidewalks were replaced with brick walkways, although they were too narrow and only accommodated two people abreast. Lovely new plantings of trees and grasses graced the main street, and everyone was ordered to improve and decorate the fronts of their houses.

Businesses in town included a blacksmith, wagon maker, two rope weavers, several small flour mills, at least one oil mill, Baruch Golub's grain and lumber mill, and numerous shops. Ludvipol survivor Pesach Kleinman remembered watching blindfolded workhorses plod in circles at the Shemesh family's oil mill, where the children were permitted by Shechna Shemesh to dip their own bread into the delicious hot oil.

The center of life on weekdays was the marketplace, a round area with stalls in the center and shops, including two sweet shops, lining two sides. The iron-rimmed wheels of farmers' carts sounded like machine guns, tak! tak! tak! as they passed over the cobblestones. Arje Katz, a Ludvipol *landtzman* (Yiddish for someone from your own town) and childhood friend of Aharon, fondly recalled carp and *shlion*, a tasty reddish fish that his family bought at the market from local farmers who moonlighted as fishermen when it was too cold to work in the fields.

Statistics from 1920 indicate that 78 percent of Ludvipol's total population of 2,145 was Jewish (1,680) and that nearby Selishtch, too, was mostly Jewish, with 847 Jews in a town of 1,272.[1] Ludvipol and Selishtch each had a Polish church, both of whose leaders were "good people who watched out for the best interests of the Jews," said Katz. At least two local Gentile families were singled out by survivors as being both wealthy and kind: Vasily Menchikow, who let Jews pasture their cows on his land, and Moraviow, who lived with his wife and children near the town hall.

Larger than the church, and the biggest place in town, according to Arje Katz, was Baruch Golub's huge mill. "The Golubs were top people in town, very well known by everyone and very well respected," said Katz. Although the mill supplied electricity for battery-operated radios, people relied mostly on the moon and oil lamps at night.

Yona Blueshtein (Raber) remembered that on long winter nights, young people would go for a horse-driven sleigh ride and the silence of the night would be broken by the tinkling of sleigh bells. On summer nights, the town's inhabitants packed the streets and walked to the bridges, over the Smorodinka and Habel creeks that linked Ludvipol with Little Selishtch.

Asher Gurfinkel noted, "On benches that stood in front of many of these houses, we organized youth unions, we conducted [Zionist] meetings, we loved first love.... On many, many summer nights, we sat on the porch, wondering and dreaming about our world and future."[2] On those same benches, their parents and grandparents sat and read the weekly newspaper or discussed politics, the economy, and the local community.

"Since I started to know people, I knew Arieh," said Pesach Kleinman, whose grandparents lived next door to the Golub family and shared a garden with them. "I spent a lot of time at Arieh's house and playing in the garden together, especially after I became an orphan when I was nine. We built houses out of beanpoles, with leaves and twigs for a roof, the same way children everywhere play. We dug up carrots, picked tomatoes, and cracked sunflower seeds. I especially remember the blossoms of the potatoes. When a bud sprouts, you cut the potato into two and plant both pieces, and a few weeks later, there are blossoms," he said, "and I remember picking cherries, holding the ends of my shirt to catch them, and occasionally swiping apples from other people's yards, and drinking delicious warm milk and sweet cream from my grandmother's cow, which I watched her milk every day."

Pesach Kleinman also loved spending time at Gittel Golub's light-filled photography studio. Baruch Golub undertook to train Kleinman's cousin, a young woman from town, Yona Tuchman (formerly Tibel Kleinman), in photography and she became an assistant at the busy studio. Photographs were especially in demand for newlyweds, bar mitzvah boys, babies, and family groups. In addition to maintaining the photography studio, Gittel managed the family and household beautifully. "Gittel was a nice woman, a *balabusta* (Yiddish for a good homemaker)," said Tuchman.

1. Joint Distribution Committee, archives
2. Ludvipol Yizkor book

Jewish Life

People in Ludvipol were traditional "but not fanatic like they were in Galicia," said Arje Katz, "where they were Hasidim and only attended *yeshivas* [religious schools]." According to Katz, most people went to the mikvah and steam baths every week, the women on Thursday afternoons, the men on Friday afternoons and Saturday mornings. Some poor people, such as Joseph the shoemaker and Isaac the shoemaker, lived with their families in the same building as the mikvah and steam bath; they helped run the facilities and were partially supported by the community.

Ludvipol thrived on discussion and debate, and every weekend Tailor Street became a gathering place for speeches by *shlichim* (emissaries) from Eretz Yisrael, visiting rabbis, and religious orators. On election days, non-Jewish peasants would come and try to strong-arm Jews to vote for certain Sejm (Polish parliament) candidates, and it was on Tailor Street that the czar was formally blessed when Ludvipol was under Russian rule, and the president of Poland when it was part of Poland.

In many homes, the man of the household made Kiddush while the mother lit the Shabbat candles. Havdalah (traditional ceremony for the end of Shabbat) was observed on Saturday nights. Spices were passed around, the prayers were said, and the braided havdalah candle was lit, although it was not necessarily passed around because of fear of starting a fire.

According to Shmuel Shafir, Ludvipol's Jews observed all the fasts, major and minor. For instance, the fast of Tzom Gedalia (Gedalia was an ancient leader of the Jews) was observed the day after Rosh Ha'Shana. Another fast was Shiva Asar b'Tammuz, beginning the three-week mourning that culminates on Tisha b'Av, the ninth day of Av, between late July and mid-August, when the Babylonians destroyed the first temple and the Romans burned the second; on this day, the Book of Lamentations was read. In fact, said Leon Rubinstein, who grew up in nearby Koretz, "It seemed as if the older people would look for any excuse to fast."

On Pesach, it was traditional for rabbis to collect charity from every house so that every Jew could observe the holiday. Many families participated in making matzah. "We would all go and help make the matzah, mixing the dough, rolling it out, and making the holes," said Arje Katz. "We brought our own boxes to put them in."

"Passover then was very much the same as today," said Katz, "with the same prayers, the same books, the same meal." While most families held seders on the first and second days, others held them the first and last days. The seder began as soon as the men and boys returned from shul and candles could be lit. "We used Hebrew haggadahs, with Yiddish translations, and said the same exact prayers we say today, the same prayers that have been said for generations and generations. And the seder plate had the same charoset, parsley, salt water, egg, roasted lamb bone, and other traditional foods as today," Katz said. He added, "For the meal, the family ate the same gefilte fish with horseradish, chicken soup with matzah balls (we preferred them soft), and *mandels* (small dumpling-like balls of matzah meal and oil), carrots, the best meat dish the housewife could afford, a vegetable, and then for dessert, stewed prunes or other fruit, and cakes made from matzah meal. Families sang the same songs they sing today." Those include "Avodim Hayinu" ("We Were Slaves"); "Dayenu" ("It Would Have Been Enough"); "MaNishtanu" ("Why Is This Night Different?"); and "Chad Gadya" ("One Goat"). The seder took four or five hours, and children were expected to participate fully, and to be quiet and respectful the entire time, according to Katz, except during the search for the hidden afikomen matzah, which was always found by the youngest child. The seder always ended with "Next year in Jerusalem!"

Rubinstein said that his father, who baked the family's bread every Thursday, used to bake fewer loaves the week before Passover so that there would be less waste when the house was rid of *chametz* (leavened bread).

The forty-nine days of Omer were counted from the second

day of Passover, the time of sowing grains in Israel, to the time of harvesting grains in Israel, with a prayer and principle, such as *chesed* (grace, love) or *g'vurah* (respect, severity) for each day. People would focus on these principles during prayers and try to put them into practice as they went about their daily lives. For four weeks, joyous activities were curtailed, but they resumed on the thirty-third day, the holiday of Lag b'Omer.

On Shavuot, some people stayed up all night discussing religious texts, dairy foods were eaten, and children wore white.

"In sum," said Katz, "the Jewish holidays in Ludvipol were complete. Perfect. And nothing was missing. We did everything."

Then, as now, there were differing viewpoints about the importance of observance and the meaning of holiness. To illustrate this, Katz told a version of a familiar Hasidic story, claiming that it took place in Ludvipol.

"One time, all the people came for Kol Nidre, and the rabbi didn't start the prayers. The people wondered why he didn't start the prayers. Then a poor boy came in and whistled loudly. At that moment, the rabbi said, 'Now, we can start. He has opened the gates to God.' This boy was an orphan and had been raised in a village of gentiles. Realizing he was a Jew, some Jewish people had encouraged him to come to shul, but the boy did not know how to behave, so he whistled. Although he did not know the proper way to do things, he was completely sincere, with his entire heart."

The Zionist Dream

For hundreds of years prior to the opening of Tarbut Schools, Jewish boys in Eastern Europe started their studies at the age of three in a *cheder* (room, in Yiddish), which depended on the personality and viewpoint of its individual rabbi or *melamed* (teacher, in Yiddish). The teacher sat at a table, surrounded by his young students, and read aloud from the Torah, first in Hebrew and then in Yiddish. In unison, the boys would repeat what he said, word-for-word. It is a common saying that the main teaching aids at the cheders were the *teitl* (wooden pointer, in Yiddish), with which the melamed pointed to the letters and words, and the lash or cane.

Most boys finished their studies at the cheder at age seven. Some went on to study at the synagogue, and others went to the local Polish schools until the age of fourteen. In the 1920s, Ludvipol's boys were still being educated in traditional cheders, although some had added modern subjects such as mathematics, geography, and literature to their curriculum. By the mid-1930s, however, most boys — and girls — were students at the Tarbut School, which offered a modern Zionist education.

Those who did not go to the Tarbut School, but to the Polish school in Selishtch, walked two miles to school. Nachum Feldman recalled that in autumn and spring, they sank up to their knees in thick mud, and in the wintertime, they sank into deep snow. Others described the Jewish students walking in groups for protection from their Ukrainian classmates, who would ambush them on their way home from school, throwing stones and attacking them with clubs as they walked through Selishtch. Feldman wrote, "We were always on the alert for it. Whenever we left school, each one of us collected stones of all sizes and put them in our schoolbags and pockets, so that if we got attacked, we would have something to hit them back with."

Sometimes the Jewish children sent a patrol ahead to find out where the Ukrainian students were hiding. Then they had to decide whether to take a different route back to Ludvipol or surprise the Ukrainians with fists and stones. "Every time we were able to surprise the enemy and attacked them, we knew we would have quiet times ahead for several weeks before they decided to attack us again," said Feldman.

He recalled that the teachers, all of whom were Polish, were especially harsh with the Jewish students. "I remember since I was in the first grade of school that the principal used to smack us with a ruler for the slightest delay or other violation. And while he was hitting us, he used to curse us saying things like 'dirty Jew, dog's blood (in Polish, *psiakrew*).' We naively thought that this was part of the educational methodology and that we couldn't be educated without it."

This situation was not unique to Ludvipol. Leon Rubinstein, who attended a local Polish school in Koretz and was tutored at home in Hebrew, remembered being made to stand while the Polish and Ukrainian students made the sign of the cross. "There were probably only six of us Jews there, and they looked at us like we were strangers," he said.

Because Jewish students were treated poorly at Polish schools in general, many Jewish families stopped sending their children to them during the early 1930s. With Zionism sweeping through Eastern Europe, the institutional anti-Semitism of the Polish schools, and the traditional priority given to education by Jews, it was not long before the new Zionist school movements, Tarbut and Yavneh, became very popular. In addition to their high standards, they prepared young people for aliyah. Before long, about one-third of all Jewish students in Poland attended one of these schools. The percentage was even higher in Volhynia, with more than two-thirds of Jewish students attending the new schools.

The first Hebrew kindergarten in Ludvipol was established in 1927 by Chaia Zamir, who grew up in the nearby town of Mezrichi and studied in Rovno. She taught the children Hebrew, using songs that emphasized Jews' long-held dreams of reestablishing a homeland. Only a few of these children survived the Holocaust, but Zamir survived and immigrated to Israel.

The Tarbut School began a few years later, meeting at first in local homes, with three teachers and two grades. Soon, young graduates of the teachers' college in Vilna joined the staff. Ludvipol and other Jewish communities in the area, large and small, cooperated to establish the school. Within a very short time, the school offered seven grades and almost all of the Jewish students in Ludvipol and the nearby villages attended it. The school graduated four classes during its nine years of existence.

Tarbut became the center of cultural life for both children and adults, who took classes on Saturdays. There were parties for the community on Jewish and Polish holidays. Numerous fund-raising campaigns raised money for local and international Jewish organizations. Visiting lecturers spoke on topical issues, especially Palestine and the situation of Polish Jewry. The school had its own orchestra, chorus, and actors. "One play that we performed on Polish Independence Day, November 11, excited even the anti-Semites in town," recalled Yona Blueshtein (Raber) in the *Yizkor* book.

The first principal of the school, Arie Morik, began a Hebrew immersion program. Despite the fact that none of the teachers were fluent in Hebrew at the time, it quickly became the main language spoken by all of the students, as well as the teachers and administrators. Polish was still taught as a second language, mostly for the purpose of commerce.

Zionism was not new to the town. After the devastating fire of 1918 and subsequent typhus epidemic, international Jewish organizations like the Joint Distribution Committee had not only sent volunteers, food, money, clothes, and blankets, but given the people of Ludvipol hope for a better future and an end to the Diaspora. They had instilled the dream of making aliyah to Eretz Yisrael, and laid the groundwork for Zionism in Ludvipol.

In 1920, Leibel Rozenberg founded the town's first Zionist youth movement, HaShomer HaTzair. This group emphasized self-empowerment and secular texts. Although some older people were dubious about where this would lead, they eventually supported the movement. Members of HaShomer HaTzair were divided by age: *B'nai Midbar* (Children of the Desert) was for younger members and *HaTzofim* (The Scouts) for older members. On Saturday afternoons, the older group met outside town at the mountainside property of Basily Menchikow. At dusk, the enthusiastic teenagers lit a fire for warmth and light, and finally returned home, singing all the way, when the moon was high. On holidays, the HaShomer HaTzair children spent all day in the forest, cooking, debating, and competing in athletic events.

The forest gradually became a meeting center for other youth movements as well. Shmuel Shafir recalled, in testimony at Yad Vashem, "The instructors used to read to us from books and pamphlets they received from Palestine. It was before the Russian occupation. I remember singing, dancing, hiking, a lot of hiking."

Nor was Ludvipol alone in its embrace of Zionism. Throughout Poland, there was intense interest in the movement. In the early 1930s HaShomer HaTzair had thousands of members in sixty-eight groups and five *hachshara* (rigorous training) camps, preparing youngsters for aliyah. Dror HeChalutz had a membership of 4,310 in seventy groups and nine hachshara programs.[1] The youths who completed their training and immigrated to Palestine served as a personal example to those left behind.

In the mid-1930s, the Polish authorities began to restrict Zionist youth movements across the country. Certain movements were authorized and allowed to operate, but others were outlawed. HaShomer HaTzair was declared a "leftist social movement hosting elements hostile to the Polish government." After it was banned, many of Ludvipol's youths met secretly on the banks of the Slusch River near Hovkov. There, they sang *HaTikva* (the Hope), which later became the national anthem of Israel, and swore allegiance to the movement and the flag of Eretz Yisrael. Their three-finger salute symbolized one nation, one language, and one land. After these children were discovered by the Polish police and their parents were threatened with arrest, many of them switched to *HeChalutz HaTzair* (The Young Pioneer), a youth movement that was authorized by the Polish government.

Another movement, Gordonia, came to town not long after HaShomer HaTzair and became the second largest youth group. Gordonia was named after Aaron David Gordon, a Russian Zionist who immigrated to Eretz Yisrael, where he became a labor worker and inspired generations of Labor Zionists. Sometime during the 1930s, Gordonia established a kibbutz with several dozen members, mainly from local towns, near Ludvipol. The Gordonia kibbutzniks were easy to spot because they wore high yellow boots and leather coats, and because they chopped wood and did other physical work that was outside traditional Jewish occupations; some Jews hesitated to buy their products, perhaps because they thought it strange for young Jews to be chopping and selling wood and perhaps because the kibbutzniks were competing with peasants who had been supplying the firewood to the Jews of the town for centuries.

Beitar was named for Josef Trumpeldor, who emigrated to Palestine in 1912 and organized the Jewish Legion, first against Turkey and later in self-defense against Arabs. In 1920, he was killed during an Arab attack on Jews in Tel Chai. His dying words, *"Tov lamut be'ad artzaynu,"* (it is good to die for our country) became a Zionist slogan.

Other Zionist youth movements in town included *Hatchia* (the Zionist Education and National Revival movement), *HeChalutz* (The Pioneer), *HaOved* (The Worker), and *HaNo'ar HaOved* (The Working Youth). All these youth groups competed energetically in sports tournaments and fund-raising efforts; membership was usually based upon friendships rather than ideological distinctions.

The primary focus for all the youth groups was Eretz Yisrael. Young people in Ludvipol exchanged letters with young people who had already made aliyah and learned Israeli songs and dances. The movements collected libraries of Hebrew books and sponsored wide-ranging discussion groups about literature, music, theater, politics, and Israel.

Jewish political life in the 1920s was "a spectacle of bewildering abundance and variety" with parties and factions covering every inch of the political spectrum, and all of them represented even in the smallest *shtetlach* (small Jewish towns).[2] The Zionist movement itself included dozens of competing splinter groups in an "extravagant pluralism [that] bespoke the ebullient self-confidence of Polish Jewry, even in the face of growing anti-Semitism."[3]

Every four years, when elected delegates from the international Zionist congress gathered from all over the world, Zionist energies in Ludvipol intensified. One could hardly go anywhere in town without hearing Hebrew pioneer songs. In records archived at Beth Hatefutsoth, votes for the Sixteenth Zionist Congress (1929) from Ludvipol were discounted for an unknown reason, but in 1933, Ludvipol voters cast 153 votes for the slate of the Eretz Yisrael Labor Party and fifty-four for the Mizrahi Party.

Meanwhile, Poland's government after the First World War was working "to accord the new state a distinctly Polish national character, while consolidating its economic and cultural standing."[4] While Ukrainians and Byelorussians lived in clearly defined areas, Jews were scattered throughout the country in thousands of small settlements, as well as a handful of cities. In 1931, Poland's economy was based on agriculture, but only a small minority of Jews (4 percent) were farmers. Far more were involved in commerce, management, trade, and crafts, and about 42 percent in industries such as lumber, textiles, clothing, and food. Jews were also heavily represented in the professions open to them, especially law, medicine, social welfare, journalism, and publishing. They were rarely able to obtain government jobs, however, because the authorities were strict about maintaining the state's Polish national character.[5]

Between 1934 and 1939, as relationships in the country between Jews, Poles, and Ukrainians deteriorated, new taxes on Jews and Jewish businesses, as well as other restrictive economic policies, caused more Jewish businesses to close. Jewish merchants, managers of estates and businesses, and craftsmen were targeted by Poles and Ukrainians as unwanted and "nonproductive" — and, even worse, the cause of Polish and Ukrainian poverty.

This was the culmination of generations of church-sanctioned propaganda blaming the Jews for the rest of the population's troubles. Besides the large number of traders, merchants, leaseholders and managers of mills, taverns, and estates, the major dealers in grains, cattle, horses, and other domestic animals, and the money lenders were Jews. It was easy to blame unpleasant business transactions on them as a group, and anti-Semitism spread from Germany in the east and the Ukraine in the west.

In 1935, the most powerful figure in Polish politics since 1918, Jósef Pilsudski, died. Pilsudski had championed a relatively liberal attitude toward Jews, but with his death the anti-Semitic Endecja movement was embraced by formerly moderate leaders and the wealthy class. The Catholic Church contributed significantly to the reactionary climate, publishing Jew-baiting literature and allowing anti-Semitic sermons. Vicious propaganda was published by Polish schools and newspapers, and pamphlets that portrayed Jews as harmful to Poland's economic interests, corruptors of moral health, and agents of communism were everywhere. Because of well-established links with Russia and socialism, "for the self-professed anti-Semites, the Jew was no longer only the Other, but the internal enemy, the serpent within."[6]

As increasingly violent pogroms ravaged Eastern Europe, the Polish movement "Don't buy from the Jew and don't sell to the Jew" or "Ours to Ours" spread, with Polish merchant and trade cooperatives initiating and physically enforcing boycotts of Jewish businesses. The Polish prime minister announced that the government endorsed "economic struggle *by all means* (*owszem*), but to do harm, no," which was widely interpreted to sanction economically motivated violence.[7] Among the laws passed to restrict Jewish business, kosher slaughter was outlawed by the Sejm in March 1938, although this was not strictly enforced.

As Nazi propaganda circulated, the movement to bar Jews from Polish universities gained adherents and to force those already matriculating to sit separately at "ghetto benches." Some liberal Poles joined Jewish students who refused to go to the benches and, in protest, stood up during lectures, and a small number of intellectuals resigned from their posts in protest of anti-Semitic academic policies, but Jewish enrollment and matriculation dropped dramatically.

During these years in Ludvipol, Jewish homes and towns were set on fire by local Ukrainians, according to Arje Katz. Katz said that family members would try to save their precious belongings from burning by throwing them out of the windows and doors. The villagers who set the fires knew this, and waited outside to seize and steal the belongings.

After a particularly disastrous series of fires set by Ukrainian thugs, a group of young Jews set up security patrols. Then they decided to fight fire with fire. "Our houses were wood and so were theirs, but their roofs were straw, which is very easy to burn up," said Katz. "The young men burned an entire Ukrainian village down, and after that there were no more fires, although there were still some drunken brawls."

A wave of Jewish flight ensued, especially to Palestine, Argentina, and Canada. The Polish government obligingly printed special exit visas for Jews willing to leave Poland to the Polish.

1. Shmuel Spector, The Holocaust of Volhynian Jews, 1941–1944
2. Eva Hoffman, Shtetl: The Life and Death of a Small Town and the World of Polish Jews, p. 175
3. Hoffman, Ibid., pp. 175–176
4. Leni Yahil, The Holocaust: The Fate of European Jewry, p. 187
5. Yahil, Ibid., p. 187
6. Hoffman, Ibid., p. 192
7. Hoffman, Ibid., pp. 195-196

271

Our Two-year Reprieve

On August 23, 1939, Russia and Nazi Germany signed the Molotov–Ribbentrop non-aggression pact, with a clause providing for the partition of Poland, home to 3.5 million Jews, between Germany and Russia in the event of war. Then, on September 1, 1939, Germany attacked Poland from the west; Russia attacked from the east a few weeks later, on September 17. By September 18, the Polish government had fled to Romania (it later moved to London) and eastern Poland, including Ludvipol, fell under the control of Russia.

Just before and after these invasions, thousands of refugees, many of them Jewish, flowed into Volhynia from western Poland. The influx slowed by November and stopped by the end of the year. Ludvipol at that time had a Jewish population of 2,000 and a Gentile population of 150.[1] The town did its best to "adopt" the refugees and find suitable work for them. Naftali Feder (who later was a member of the Israeli Knesset) was hired as a biology teacher at the Tarbut School. Another refugee found work at a photography studio, presumably Gittel Golub's. The refugees confirmed rumors that in the west, the Germans were instituting anti-Semitic policies and forcing Jews into ghettos.

Meanwhile, as one of the first towns occupied by Russia, Ludvipol was in the throes of mass confusion. Many of its families found themselves split apart with some members on one side of the border and some on the other. Pesach Kleinman's aunt, for instance, never saw her parents again.

In Ludvipol and elsewhere, Jewish and Polish reactions to the occupation differed significantly. Notes Eva Hoffman, "To the Poles [in the village of Bransk], the Russians were a traditional enemy, hated nearly as much as the Germans. To the Jews, the Red Army was seen, first and foremost, as an army of liberation from the much worse German menace. In addition, a segment of the Jewish population felt an ideological affinity with the Soviets [and] a sizable portion of the Jewish community welcomed the Soviet soldiers with flowers, banners, and expressions of joy. To the Poles, this was a distressing and an alienating spectacle."[2] Ideological affinities with the Soviets, however, were far less compelling for the youths of Ludvipol than their dreams of a homeland.[3]

On June 22, 1941, almost two years after the Soviet occupation of Ludvipol began, German soldiers swarmed through Poland to launch an attack on the Soviet Union, and the Red Army began its hasty retreat. A map showing the front between Russia and Germany indicates that fighting took place within a few kilometers of Ludvipol. Despite warnings, the Soviet army was inadequately prepared and flight was its only choice. At the same time, Germany was instituting the first phase of its genocide of Jews. The German *Einsatzgruppen*, mobile death squads, followed the German army into small towns similar in size to Ludvipol and systematically executed their Jewish inhabitants. During the next six months, it is estimated that one million Jews were killed in Poland.

The Russians were making their preparations to abandon Ludvipol and the commissar apparently urged the Jews there to flee with them to Russia and not expose themselves to the Nazis. Entire families as well as some groups of young people, especially those who had a strong connection with some of the Russians, fled eastward into the interior of the Soviet Union. "Two or three days before the Germans came into our town," Shmuel Shafir said, "I escaped to Russia with my brother Isser." Those who fled into the Soviet area included Arje Katz, Belle Katz, Bernard (Bell) Raber, Nachum Feldman, Tzvi Katz, Jacob Allerhand, Naftali Feder, Harold Feld (a teacher in the Tarbut School), Hershel Tzvi, and Yona Blueshtein (Raber).

Arje Katz said he had been drafted into the Russian army the week of Germany's attack on the Soviet Union, but never had to serve because of the confusion of the times. He left for the Soviet Union as soon as the border, about thirty kilometers away, reopened. "I was lucky," he said. "I traveled by train from Gorodnisa, about twenty kilometers from Ludvipol, and the border had just opened. From there, I went to Stalingrad, the Urals, Siberia, all over. My parents stayed home with my sisters." One sister intended to leave for Russia, too, but missed her opportunity because she was working in the forest.

Those who stayed were on their own and hoped for the best. Many of them did not want to leave their homes and community to become refugees. Many thought that the Russian army would regroup and return. Optimists reflected on past times and believed that the years ahead would be no worse than similar periods of war and anti-Semitism, or periods of illness and natural disasters, and that they would survive. Leon Rubinstein remembered his father's ruminations, as the family observed Jewish refugees fleeing Germany and western Poland. His father shook his head and asked, "How do you pick up and move a family with seven children?"

Katz recollected an odd incident that shows how complicated the times were. "There was a very rich little village, which was really just one extended family, called Outka, and the people there were very good friends to the Jews. Frequently, when an Outkan came on market day, he stayed at our house. We often exchanged presents. Well, because of the war we couldn't keep our cow, so we tried to give it to this wealthy family. They were too afraid to take the cow because they might be seen as too friendly with us somehow. We couldn't slaughter the cow because of complications with the shochet, either. We didn't know what to do with the cow. We ended up giving it away to someone else."

Meanwhile, Ukrainian sentiment against Jews was intensifying, and Ukrainian nationalists claimed that their primary goal was the creation of a "normal" Ukraine, with a completely Ukrainian population. The editor of a Ukrainian newspaper at the time wrote, "All the elements residing in our cities, whether Jews or Poles who were brought there, must disappear."[4] According to former Ludvipol resident Bitya Akerman, "Here in Ludvipol we did not feel the anti-Semitism of the big cities, but the Ukrainians who ate challahs from our tables were the first ones to attack us."[5]

1. Beth Hatefutsoth archives
2. Eva Hoffman, Shtetl: The Life and Death of a Small Town and the World of Polish Jews, p. 212
3. Nachum Feldman, Yizkor book
4. Ulas Samchuk, "We Shall Conquer the Cities," Volhyn, 1941
5. Bitya Akerman, Yizkor book

II. The War

On the Day of my Bar Mitzvah

By noon of the first day of German occupation, Jews in Ludvipol were dragged out of their homes and rounded up in the center of town by the Ukrainians. An unknown number of Jewish women were raped by German soldiers, including four women from the Gandelman family.[1] Ukrainian villagers immediately began to terrorize their Jewish neighbors, storming Jewish houses, attacking their inhabitants, and stealing anything they desired. "The sequence of events quickly fell into the pattern of a pogrom," reported Baruch Guttman in Ludvipol's *Yizkor* book. Afraid for their lives, Jews locked themselves in their homes and hid their daughters in attics. Some fled to nearby villages, and their homes were plundered by local Ukrainians. Several days later, the Germans issued an order that they must return to Ludvipol on penalty of execution.

In September 1941, a local *Gebietskommissariat* (government) was established for the area, which was part of the Reichskommissariat Ukraine and commanded by Erich Koch from Rovno. The regional governor was named Guenther, approximately fifty years old, tall, heavyset, light with blond hair and a mustache. The head of the local Gebietskommissariat, based in Ludvipol, was Franz Norgall.[2]

As soon as he arrived, Commissar Norgall ordered the arrest of at least eight Jews, including Akiva Zaltzman, Akiva Vasserman, Szejle Welman and two of his brothers, Yacob Berman, Eliezer Fineman, Lea or Sara Alt, and perhaps Dawid Grud, who were accused of having belonged to the Communist party. They were tak-

276

en to a sandy area behind the church and shot next to a ditch that had been dug in advance. Shaulik Valman and Naftalk'e Valman were also killed that day.

Elsewhere in Volhynia, similar horrors were under way. The killings took place on the largest scale in Lutsk, Dubno, Rovno, and Ostrog, where thousands were murdered in the first days of German occupation. It is estimated that in the first wave of slaughter in the province, fifteen thousand Jews, 6 percent of the Jewish population, were murdered. The early victims were often local public figures, well-educated people, and rabbis, in accordance with the German goal of eliminating Jewish leadership as soon as possible.

Local Ukrainians created lists from which victims were chosen, served as informants, and were often co-perpetrators of the violence.[3] In his 1993 eulogy for the Jews of Ludvipol, Arje Katz bitterly recalled abuses perpetrated by the Ukrainian villagers. For instance, he said, there was "a Jewish man named Yankel Schmirgold, the son of Mikhle, who lived with his family in a home near Lazar Shitchik, a Ukrainian, and his family. One day, Lazar Shitchik and his sons dragged Yankel Schmirgold and his six-year-old son to the Shitchik vegetable garden. Once there, they killed both Schmirgold and his young child and buried them there in the garden." After that, the Shitchiks returned to Schmirgold's house and looted it, he said.

Similarly, Katz said, the Ukrainian brothers Kirilo and Andrei Abramchik attacked the young grandchildren of their neighbor, Yehezkel Eisenman; Eisenman owned the local vegetable oil factory and shared a house with his daughter Sara, son-in-law Shechna Shemesh, and grandchildren Yosef, age thirteen, and Avraham, age eleven. "The Abramchik brothers attacked and threatened the children with pitchforks, demanding that they tell where their parents' money was hidden. Neither child panicked. They remained calm, repeated a private password for dangerous situations, and sprang straight ahead, like arrows from a bow, to the field behind their house. Then they ran north towards the River Slusch. Fortunately, it was after sunset and they managed to disappear in the darkness, running a winding path into the green grain, and then over the River Slusch at the one and only crossing point. Apparently, the brothers fled to a Mazurian village, where they sought shelter and were protected," he said.

A few weeks after the entire Jewish population of Ludvipol was forced into the newly erected ghetto, the Germans conducted an *aktion* (German selection, deportation, or mass murder) in nearby Rovno. Between November 7 and November 8, 1941, approximately twenty-one thousand Jews (80 percent of the city's Jewish population) were marched six kilometers, to a pine grove at Sosenski, and shot dead.[4] Communications to and from the ghetto had been severed, however, and it appears that Ludvipol's Jews did not know about the event.

"Taking advantage" of the Jewish workforce was one of dual Nazi goals, the other being its annihilation. As Obergruppenführer Friedrich Wilhelm Kruger advised other German administrators, "By means of police coercion, for the first time many Jews have been induced to engage in fruitful labor in the service of the community."[5] Forced labor was a prelude to their eventual death from hunger, thirst, illness, and exhaustion. Most of Ludvipol's Jews over the age of eleven were ordered to work on the road between Admovka and Brezno, although some were put to work at a sawmill in Chmielowka, some in agriculture, some in the forest cutting lumber, and some digging peat.

Certain Gentile residents, between eighteen and forty-five years old, were also forced to work for the Germans. Unlike the Jews, however, these workers were not controlled by armed guards who were prepared to shoot them at the slightest provocation. They were paid and allowed to keep their pay, whereas Jews were paid on the whim of the Germans and Ukrainians and had to exchange their wages for rations and a place at the soup kitchen.

The German mayor, former schoolteacher Hering, set up a local

Judenrat that included Mottel Etsztein, Joseph Gluzmann, Barder the baker, Yenia Gachpinboim (the president) and Kalman Valman (the deputy).[6] According to Shmuel Shafir, "They were not bad people. They were appointed because they were relatively well-to-do and were well known in the community. Like everyone else in Ludvipol except the few who managed to escape, they were all killed by the Nazis on the day of the mass murders." Josef Gitterman later testified, according to documents at the Ludwigsburg archives, that Norgall personally escorted the Judenrat members to the military barracks on the morning of the mass murders and watched their execution.

The Judenrat was responsible for promptly enforcing orders and "requests" from Hering and Norgall. On risk of beatings and death, they provided Jewish forced laborers for projects, brought Jewish girls to the Germans, and collected money, goods, and bribes from the Jewish community. On a whim or in return for the promise of a temporary pass, for instance, Hering would demand gold and valuables. On some occasions, he would casually mention an item that he coveted, such as someone's gold watch or silverware, and the Judenrat would have to deliver it. Only the smallest items of jewelry could be hidden. The collections happened regularly, although one collection that came to be known as Golden Night stands out. On April 14, 1942, the Jews were forced to pay Norgall all of their remaining valuables, "a ransom in gold, silver, and merchandise."[7] Although Judenrat members were occasionally successful in bribing the Ukrainians, the pressures on them as they tried to stay alive and at the same time do their best for the community were intense and destructive.

Commissar Norgall went once or twice daily to monitor the road construction work, and harass or murder the workers. On one such visit, he saw Leibel "Trotsky" Keck relieving himself in the bushes instead of working, and shot him dead, then ordered the laborers to bury him beneath the road.[8] Work continued that day as if nothing had happened. "The workers were afraid to even glance at their murdered friend because the bloodthirsty eyes of the murderer were still looking for his next victim, and every one of those present saw himself as the next candidate. The Nazi killer used to patrol the work site daily. His only purpose was to shoot and kill, and he always found one reason or another to kill a Jew."[9]

Keck was the first, but not the last, Jewish slave laborer to be buried under that road. Being unable to lift a heavy stone, stretching for too long, or being too far from the road were reasons enough to be killed.

Survivors' testimony in Ludwigsburg and Yad Vashem refer to other atrocities perpetrated by Commissar Norgall and his underlings Glanz and Spiegel. Norgall would barge into Jewish houses and order a thorough search for scraps of food; if even a crumb was discovered, a family member, perhaps a child, parent, or grandparent, would be executed on the spot in front of the rest of the family.

One time in June 1942, when those confined to the ghetto were dying from starvation, the Judenrat requested permission for a group to go into the woods and collect berries. Norgall permitted it, but when the Jews emerged from the woods with their pails, the precious berries were taken from them and they were beaten with iron bars. Those who cried out were struck fifty times, those who did not cry out were struck twenty-five times.[10]

There were numerous citations of people who were murdered by Norgall for possessing bits of food. In the summer of 1942, Golda Goldin was inspected by the Ukrainian police on her way back to the ghetto after work and was found to be hiding food. Norgall and Glanz ordered her to be arrested and taken to the police station. The next day her body, beaten to death and perhaps drowned, was found on the fence outside the police station.[11]

Berel Kogut, a laborer found by Norgall to be hiding five potatoes in his pocket, was ordered to lie on the ground and then shot four times by Norgall. After the first two bullets, Kogut begged the commissar to spare his life. Jews nearby were ordered to bury the body and remove all traces of the murder.[12]

Joseph Keck, arrested on Norgall's orders for possession of food, was brought to the police station. The next day, the Judenrat was ordered to remove and bury his corpse.[13]

A Jewish cobbler whose last name was Zimech, found to possess a few potatoes, was shot and killed by Norgall.[14]

Norgall murdered Scheindel Alt when a small amount of food was discovered during an inspection of forced laborers.[15]

Norgall was also a known rapist who demanded that the Council of Jews deliver young girls to his quarters. The girls he ordered to his quarters included thirteen-year-old Zelda Guttman, fourteen-year-old Schendel Fela, and sixteen-year-old Sara Schindel. During the forced march to the *kasharan* (former barracks of the Polish army) during the liquidation, he pulled fourteen-year-old Chana Raber out of the column, forced her to stay in his quarters for eight days, and then murdered her.[16]

One of Norgall's deputies, either Spiegel or Glanz, ordered a pair of pants from the tailor Itzik Kaftan in May and shot him when they were delivered. The Judenrat was told to provide four Jews to bring his body from the police building into the ghetto.[17]

The testimonies of survivors include this partial catalog of Norgall's atrocities:

He murdered a retarded youth, Jakub Finkielman, for being in the ghetto instead of going out with a labor crew.

He shot and killed a mentally disturbed man of about thirty-five, Jakub Kogan, for being outside the ghetto (on the bridge over the Smorodinka Creek) without a pass.

He caught Ajzik Wajsberg and his son Cemach on the bridge over the River Slusch, after they had slipped out of the ghetto and begged for bread in the village of Chubkow, and had them shot in the barracks.

He caught and shot two Jewish women, and a Jewish girl from Cholopy, who were returning from forced labor, but had gone to the village of Janiow to beg for bread. The women died but the girl managed to drag herself to the ghetto.

He murdered Aisik and Zimech Weissberg, Etel Charssen, Moshe Funt, and Godel Jarmolaj.

He murdered seventeen-year-old Efraim Goldin, who had worked for him until that moment.[18]

One survivor said, "He amused himself as a sharpshooter, using Jews as targets."[19]

In addition, assisted by Glanz, Spiegel, and Ukrainian police, Norgall murdered approximately one hundred Gypsy families who had been brought to the barracks and confined there for two weeks.[20]

Little is known about Norgall. Some survivors remembered him as Leon Nordel, others as Norgler, but archivists at Yad Vashem in Jerusalem and Zentrale Stelle in Ludwigsburg, Germany identify him as Franz Norgall. Mention is made in the archival materials of a son who stated for the record that his father, Franz Norgall, was the commissar in Ludvipol. He was also identified by Josef Gutermann, Judah Raber, and Josef Waldmann from a photograph.

Norgall was born on May 30, 1898 in Boettchersdorft and was of average build, with dark brownish skin, greenish eyes, and a long scar on one cheek, and wore a brown uniform with a swastika on the arm. After the liquidation of the Jews of Ludvipol, he is said to have been wounded during a skirmish with partisans, and walked with a limp henceforth. In 1938, he was a second lieutenant for the SA Sturmfuehrer, party member number 342,751, and lived at 58 Neuhoefer Street, Heilsberg, East Prussia.

Norgall was investigated and tried by the Nazi Party's own Supreme Court the following year for excesses, including severe mistreatment, multiple murders, and moral transgressions, related to Kristallnacht, November 9, 1938. He was tried in the Nazi Party Court and found responsible for entering the Heilsberg apartment of a Jewish couple named Seelig and murdering both of them, "motivated by hatred of Jews" but contrary to Nazi orders. The court's proceedings say that he had acted out of "excessive anti-Semitism" and had "violated Nazi discipline." For the violation, the court issued a warning and banned him from public office for three years.[21]

A 1964 report in the German archives says that, after the war, a gardener in Schacht-Audorf/Schlewsig-Holstein was "identical to Norgall." Malka Gitterman, according to testimony by her husband Joseph Gitterman, saw Norgall at a train station in Liebnitz, or Gras, Austria, in 1945. She shouted an alarm and tried to catch him, but he managed to lose himself in the crowd.

Norgall reportedly died in an accidental fall from a trailer in Schacht-Audorf/Schlewsig-Holstein in 1946 and, because he was said to be dead, the investigation into his abuses during the Holocaust was discontinued. In 1964, Norgall's wife was reported to be residing in Wuppertal-Eberfeld, Friedrich-Ebert-Str. 478.[22]

Little is known about Glanz, other than that his first name was probably George, he was between thirty and forty years old during his tenure in Ludvipol, and he wore a green military uniform. The last time he was positively identified was January 1944 in Holliwien (renamed Golowin), near Kostopol. Nothing seems to be known about Spiegel's history before or after the war.[23]

Hearing rumors that the mass murder of the Jews in Ludvipol was already being organized, a group of young people, led by David Zuker and Israel Dobina, tried to organize an escape from the ghetto. Community members discouraged them, fearing German reprisals and hoping that the rumors were false, but several young people went ahead and jumped over the ghetto fence. In one version of the story, a non-Jew learned of the plan and disclosed it to the Germans. Most of the youths were captured and executed, but Dobina managed to escape.

There are numerous conflicting versions of Dobina's story. According to Baruch Guttman's account at Yad Vashem, Dobina visited Ludvipol in 1939, when he was a young activist at a HaShomer HaTzair hachshara near Chernichov. He went to Ludvipol to see his uncle, Barder the baker, and was at a flour mill when several

Ukrainians arrived to grind their grain; one of the Ukrainians re-marked that the Germans would enter the town soon, and that he would murder the mill's owner and take over the mill then. Dobina angrily picked up a pole and hit the Ukrainian, who dropped to the floor unconscious. Dobina then returned to his hachshara.

Two years later, when the Germans occupied Ludvipol, Dobina was again near Ludvipol, this time chopping timber in the forest with other young people. In the woods, he encountered Russian partisans, with grenades and other weapons, who said that more partisans and weapons would be parachuted in soon. Later, per-haps after escaping from the ghetto, he and David Zuker went to look for these partisans. They encountered a man who appeared to be a partisan and told him about the atrocities Norgall had per-petrated, as well as his routines and patterns of travel between Ludvipol and Kostopol. That man was later caught by the Germans and revealed details of the conversation.

Dobina and Zuker went into hiding in the attic of the tailors' shul, but Norgall ordered the Judenrat to surrender them immedi-ately or five hundred of Ludvipol's Jews would be executed the next morning. One of Dobina's childhood friends, Joseph Gluzmann, told Dobina about the order, and Dobina without hesitation turned himself in. He and Zuker were taken first to the local gendarmerie, where they were interrogated and tortured, and then to Kostopol, where they were further interrogated and tortured. When two German soldiers dragged them into the woods to be murdered, Dobina asked to be granted a last wish: permission to remove his shoes before being executed. He was granted permission, tied the shoes together, and swung them hard into the face of one guard. He and Zuker ran, but Zuker was shot and killed by a guard; Dobina escaped and joined the Ukrainian partisans.

In another version, Dobina and Zuker escaped en route to Gestapo offices in Kostopol, attacking the Ukrainian police escorts, grabbing their weapons, and fleeing into the forest. Zuker was found dead in the forest and Dobina was never heard from again.[24]

Another story from survivors' testimony is consistent with Guttman's. During the winter of 1943, two partisans arrived in Fifale asking for food. Mikolitzik, a Polish villager, asked where they were from and one of them said he was from Ludvipol. Mikolitzik took him to the woods, where he was helping some Ludvipol survivors. When they approached the hiding spot, he shouted, "Drink l'chaim, Ludvipol brothers!" People immediately recognized him as Israel Dobina. That night, as they sat around a fire sharing their stories, Dobina said he had joined the Ukrainian partisans.

Several survivors cited Dobina's death by public execution, and some said he was denounced by a Ukrainian peasant who joined the partisans and claimed that Dobina had taken a pair of boots from him during an attack on his village. Dobina was tried, found guilty, and executed by the Ukrainian partisans.

Perhaps the most detailed and credible account of Zuker and Dobina is told by Boris Edelman, who connects them with the activities of his own father and brother.

"On the road construction to Brezno in 1942, my father was put in charge of a road crew of about sixty girls. One day, the German commissar, a very bad person, went to watch the people work. He was riding my father's big, beautiful horse, the nicest in the area, and sat on a little hill watching. Some of the teenagers — my father knew every one of them — had to take a rest, and pee. When my father let them stop working for five minutes, the commissar rushed down on my father's horse. I was a kid, working with the Gentile engineers, holding the tape while they measured, and I was standing there. The commissar could see that the engineers liked me and asked me to hold the horse for him. The horse knew me, of course, and when I touched the horse, the commissar said, 'Why are you touching my horse? I'm going to shoot you.' Then for some reason he went over to my father and made him lie down there, and put his foot on my father's neck, and took out his gun, and put it against the side of my father's head. And then he pulled the trigger, but the gun refused to go off. He said, 'God wants you to live still, your time is not up.' My father got up and the commissar beat him a little, then came and took the horse and pushed me a bit. Oh, my father was carrying so much hate for him and planned to kill him.

"He got together with a group of Ukrainians and two Jews, one of whom had lived with Aharon's family (David Zuker] and Israel Dobina, who had been beaten up by the Germans a lot. The commissar had seen the wife [Manya] of one of the Jewish guys [David Zuker] and said, 'Go and take a bath' and then he had taken her and...raped her. The husband was very upset and talked to my father, and together they planned to kill him. My father and the two guys and a Ukrainian got some guns and made their plan to attack the commissar in a couple of days, when he was going to leave town to transport some supplies. But the Ukrainian man was captured by other Ukrainians, and gave away the names of the Jews involved in the plan. The Germans went to pick [Zuker and Dobnia] up, handcuffed them, and were taking them to Kostopol.

"My father saw two Germans coming towards him and was certain that they were going to pick him up, too. But the Ukrainian had not remembered his name or something — at any rate, he had not identified him. The two other Jews signaled to my father, 'Don't worry. They don't know about you.' The Germans took the guys behind the jail and said, 'Dig a grave with these two shovels,' and I guess they said something like, 'Take off your shoes.' Dobina grabbed the shoes and hit one of the Germans in the face, then grabbed the gun and ran. His friend from Aharon's family place [David Zuker] was running, too, and the other German shot him. But Dobina ran away. After that, he organized a group of fifteen or twenty people — Polish,

Ukrainians, anyone — and attacked the Germans and captured wagons and ammunition from them. Then he joined the Medwiedow partisans in the woods. Those were the Russian partisans that my brother, my uncle Alter Tiktin, and my cousin Samuel Tiktin were with. These Russians had come in by parachutes in the beginning. It was a big organization, thousands of people.

"Dobina had a group of people under him who used to do things like put mines under the trains and blow them up. At some point, as I understand it, Dobina had gone into a village and, because his boots were torn and he was almost barefoot, had said to a guy with new boots, 'Let's change shoes,' but later, that man had joined the partisans. He recognized Dobina and reported to an officer that Dobina had once stolen his shoes, and they took Dobina and executed him. My brother Alex was working in the kitchen there and he saw this.

"Not long after, my brother saw Dobina's accuser stealing meat from the kitchen. He wrapped it in parachute material and hid it in the woods, and then, when his parents came to visit him on Sundays, gave them the meat. My brother told the partisans, 'This man is stealing the meat from the kitchen and is wrapping it up in parachute material and giving it to his parents.' The partisans watched him one Sunday, and saw what he did, and hanged him from a tree."

Community members' fears that a rebellion or planned escape was doomed to failure, since the Jews had no weapons and were suffering from malnutrition and disease, and that it would provoke severe reprisals, were realistic. Elsewhere, resisters' families, neighbors, and sometimes entire communities were murdered after an attempted escape or rebellion or the discovery of plans for one. The community paid the price for the act of an individual or group, which was a German tactic to control people that worked equally well in large and small communities, in ghettos, and in concentration camps. Resistance in Jewish communities was effectively stifled, say scholars, by the threat of this kind of collective punishment.[25]

At the same time, many people in Ludvipol did not believe the extent of the Nazi atrocities or that the regime's goal was to annihilate the millions of Jews in Europe. Older people who had lived with anti-Semitism all of their lives and heard stories from countless previous generations were particularly unable to believe the worst. They tried to adjust to the difficult times and focus on staying alive until it got better. They could not conceive the magnitude of the situation.

The psychology of denial in Jewish communities at the time was complex. There was optimism and faith, supported by clandestine radio reports of German battle losses that encouraged the belief that the war would soon end with an Allied victory. In the meantime, the first responsibility of the living was to survive. As the Yiddish saying goes, "As long as one limb stirs, thoughts of the grave are deferred." It is thought that numerous escape attempts were made but not documented because no witnesses lived to tell about them.

It took a huge effort simply to stay alive, and the weakened physical condition of the Jews was another factor in their seeming passivity. Malnutrition and starvation, overwork and exhaustion, disease, loss, and shock precluded clear planning — even if they had had access to weapons against the well-supplied Germans and Ukrainians — and the capability to implement such plans.

In the analysis of scholar Leni Yahil, four active responses were possible for the Jews of Poland: self-defense, flight to the forest, finding refuge somewhere nearby, or attempting to qualify as a productive laborer needed for Germany's war machine. Of these, the best option for survival appeared to be qualifying as a "productive laborer," which protected a relatively large number of Jews for a relatively long amount of time. In fact, the German state itself was undecided whether to murder all Jews outright or work them to death. The most important document a Jew could possess was the *schein*, a work permit stating that the holder was required by the German authorities. After a deportation, people were told that only those who were a burden on the ghetto had been taken away and, often, that it was the last deportation; it was reasonable to believe that the Germans would continue to exploit the Jews to build much-needed roads, weapons, and equipment.[26]

A massive uprising was out of the question for most ghetto dwellers, given their isolation, illness, and lack of weapons. Escape to the forest meant near-certain death: Although a handful of people found refuge with rural villagers or partisans, it is believed that tens of thousands of Jews perished in the forests. Those who survived were usually physically fit youths between fifteen and thirty years of age who had received some prior training in survival skills. They had to be able to survive on very little food and water, under harsh conditions and extreme temperatures, to have a good sense of local orientation, an iron will, and, "the kind of luck ... without which, no one could get away."[27]

1. Yad Vashem, File TR.11/101, Police of Israel inquiry into Nazi crimes in ghettos Kostopol and Ludvipol, German; Ludwigsburg, Germany archives, State Court Administration, 1964. As part of the research for this book, the entire file of testimony at these hearings was translated into English.
2. Ludwigsburg archives, Ibid.
3. Shmuel Spector, The Holocaust of Volhynian Jews
4. Leni Yahil, The Holocaust: The Fate of European Jewry, p. 162
5. Yahil, Ibid.
6. Ludwigsburg archives testimony of Josef Pikowsky, indicating that Hering collaborated with the Germans before their occupation of Ludvipol, and that he was thin, of medium height, and about forty-five years old in 1941
7. Yad Vashem, Ibid; Wiesenthal Institute archives
8. Ludwigsburg archives, testimony of Joseph Waldman
9. Ludwigsburg archives, testimony of Baruch Guttman
10. Ludwigsburg archives, testimony of Josef Gitterman, based on conversations with a local Mazurian, Mazure Kowalczyk, who said he had witnessed the killings, and had been forced by the Germans to help close the three mass graves
11. Ludwigsburg archives, Gitterman
12. Ludwigsburg archives, Guttman
13. Ludwigsburg archives, Gitterman
14. Ludwigsburg archives, Guttman

15. Ludwigsburg archives, testimony of Judah Raber
16. Ludwigsburg archives, Gitterman
17. Ludwigsburg archives, Guttman
18. Ludwigsburg archives, assorted testimonies
19. Ludwigsburg archives, Pikowsky
20. Ludwigsburg archives, Gitterman
21. www.history-of-the-holocaust.org, "Report of Chief Nazi Party Judge on Kristallnacht"
22. Ludwigsburg archives, Raber
23. Ludwigsburg archives, Raber
24. Ludwigsburg archives, Raber
25. Yahil, Ibid., p. 171, 462
26. Yahil, Ibid., p. 462, 553
27. Yahil, Ibid., p. 553

The Mass Murders and Our Escape Into the Forest

In the fall of 1941, mass murders of Jews were initiated in Volhynia as part of the first phase of Germany's Final Solution of the Jewish Question in Europe, but they stopped between December and August. The reasons for the temporary halt are not clear. It is known that Jewish slave labor was needed for the German war machine, and it is conjectured, even by well-known Jewish scholars, that Germany was having trouble finding murderers to conduct the up-close mass shootings, which resumed in mid August 1942; 17,500 Jews in Lutsk, home to Jews since at least the eleventh century, were marched out of town and shot alongside pits that served as mass graves. But again, the inhabitants of the Ludvipol ghetto were aware neither of the extent of the killings nor of their temporary halt.[1] When Norgall informed the Judenrat that unproductive Jews would be killed, the community worked even harder and made sure that their children accompanied them to work every day.

On Sunday, August 23, 1942, Norgall met with non-Jewish leaders of the villages near Ludvipol and told them that the Jews were not sufficiently productive and were not contributing enough to the German war effort: They would all be killed soon. Some villagers managed to sneak word of the Nazi plan into the ghetto, but the warning was perceived as unreliable and was not believed.

The night of Monday, August 24 there was an especially strict curfew. Early the next morning (Yud Bet Elul in the Hebrew year), German soldiers and about 120 Ukrainian police surrounded the ghetto. The Jews were told that their labor was no longer needed and they were forbidden from leaving their homes. A half-hour later, they were ordered into the ghetto square.

Commissar Norgall stood in the square and said the soldiers would be taking them to the barracks, where their record books would be examined to ascertain their productivity. They were marched out of the ghetto in groups to the edge of town and over the River Slusch to the kasharan, about one kilometer away. Norgall rode ahead on horseback. Some people collapsed along the way and were beaten with rifle butts; healthier people were ordered to carry those who had fallen. Ukrainian and Polish villagers stood along the way and watched, and at least one survivor recalled that some laughed and mocked them. "This thing depressed our souls to death," Judah Raber wrote in the *Yizkor* book. "If anyone thought he could escape, he changed his mind in the face of his Christian friends' and acquaintances' behavior."[2]

Some recalled that several mass graves had already been dug in the woods near the kasharan; others recalled digging their own graves, with help from Poles and Ukrainians, some of whom had been forced into labor as punishment for helping Jews. Some survivors recalled standing next to the graves that day and sleeping there that night. Others said they spent the day and night at the kasharan, in a square surrounded by a tall wooden fence. They were given some food, to fool them into thinking they would be safe, until Norgall announced, "Tomorrow morning at five am you will all be killed." He added that the children would be given a last piece of bread. Everyone was screaming and crying.[3] A daytime escape was planned by some of the young people at the kasharan, but others convinced them to wait at least until dark in order to prevent detection and retaliation. They are said to have abandoned the plan, but some managed to scramble over the fence that night, assisted by friends and neighbors who offered their backs to climb upon. The escapees ran into the forest. About sixty-five of the Jews held captive near the ditches also attempted an escape into the woods that night, and several survived the guards' gunfire.[4]

The mass murder began at seven in the morning and lasted all day. It was August 26, 1942 (Yud Gimmel Elul). "At the beginning of the executions, the commissar came to the site, stepped up to the members of the council of Jews, shook their hands, and said to them, 'I have promised you that you would not be shot by me. I keep my word and put you into the hands of the Gestapo.' This was a cynical leave-taking by the commissar from his collaborators in the council of Jews."[5]

At the site, Norgall shook hands and said goodbye to the naked victims as they walked onto planks set over the graves. They were executed by SS soldiers, some of whom were drunk, in groups of twenty-five. First, the children. Then, the women. Lastly, the men.[6] At day's end, the dead and injured were covered with earth. Fifteen hundred of Ludvipol's Jews were murdered that day at the mass grave.

Those who had hiding places inside the ghetto sealed themselves in at the first announcement to assemble in the square. The Germans and Ukrainians made thorough searches of every house and yard first thing in the morning, and marched those they found to the mass graves, where they were executed. The searches continued for several days, during which time about 150 more people were discovered. Most of these people were killed on the spot or brought to the ghetto square and executed there.

One woman, Sofia Szteinman, wrote in testimony that she decided in desperation to try to escape. "I made a break for it just outside of town and the barracks, wrenching myself from the hands of my nieces and nephews. I ran down a slope and fell into a clump of tall flowers under the window of a Ukrainian cottage. The Ukrainian woman heard the noise, opened her window, saw me, and cried out to the police, alerting them to the presence of a Jew. Fortunately, the people walking on the highway were shouting, wailing, and lamenting so loudly that the police did not hear. I crawled out of the flowers and ran to the rear of the house, where I found open fields and a privy. I quickly concealed myself in the privy, but the Ukrainian woman ran to the privy, opened the door, and resumed her shouting for the police. This time they heard. One of them ran up and began hitting me around the head and face with a carbine — afterward I had ten scars on my head from the blows and eight of my teeth fell out — and I begged him to just kill me, not to torture me. He indicated that he did not want to waste a bullet on me. Deputy Spiegel was nearby and ordered me to get up, then beat me around the face with his fists and kicked me. He was a big fat German. When I was barely breathing, he ordered me to run to the commissariat, where he would kill me." Yenia Gachpinboim, president of the Judenrat, was at the commissariat and convinced Spiegel to let Szteinman go to the kasharan with him and die with her husband.

She did not join the line of people heading to the barracks, however. Instead, she went to her house, which she noted was filled with goose feathers from pillows ripped apart when rampaging Ukrainians searched for hidden valuables; and then to a nearby potato field, where she covered herself with a bloodstained bedspread and stayed motionless. "People walked near me, but no one noticed I was alive. Others were led to the field and shot, to fall dead on me. I lay in a pool of blood. The Ukrainians began to dig gigantic long pits and said they would pile the Jewish corpses in there. After a while, carts filled with bodies began to arrive and the bodies were thrown into the pits. I lay there watching. I felt that at any moment I would lose my wits. The Ukrainians began to collect the corpses around and on top of me but, fortunately, they became tired and decided to put off the rest of their work until the next day." That night, she said, she crawled away to the home of Piotr Lamoski, a friendly Pole with whom her daughter had been hiding.

In Koretz, too, large pits for Jewish prisoners were dug outside of town. Earlier, some of Koretz's Jews had learned that the Germans were preparing for their mass murder and had organized an escape, but few people were willing or able to join. Moshe Gildenman, about forty years old and chairman of the Artisans Association at the time, later described "the apathy — the feeling that nothing mattered anymore — that afflicted people as a consequence of the first aktion.... People found it hard to make decisions, to take initiative, or to launch themselves into the unknown in the forests...." Several focused on the importance of the

Jewish workforce to Germany and continued to believe that only the "unproductive" Jews would be exterminated. After all, if the Jewish forced laborers were executed, their work would have to be done by Germans who were badly needed on the war front. Others feared that they would die in the forests anyway, and gave up. Another said that, having already lost his wife and three children, life had no more value for him and he would stay in the ghetto and await the end. There was also a widespread and realistic fear that those left behind would be tortured by the Germans and that anyone trying to escape would "bring down a catastrophe on our heads. When they find that you have gone to the partisans, they might, Heaven forbid, kill all the Jews in the ghetto. Don't dare to do it!" Some of them knew that ten innocent bystanders were shot in Lvov in retaliation for one person's escape, in addition to some or all of his relatives, who were publicly hanged.[7]

Then, on Shavuot, the town's entire population of about 2,200 Jews was executed. Leon Rubinstein's father, who had connections with the Polish police because of his bicycle and lock business, had put his energy into finding safe houses for his wife and children, but was unprepared for the suddenness of the round-up. "While the Germans were banging on the doors, [my father] succeeded in hiding my mother and most of the family, but not himself, one of my brothers, one of my sisters, and me. We were taken out to be killed," Rubinstein said. His father told him, "Run!" and somehow he escaped; he conjectured that his escape was possible because the German soldiers were preoccupied with murdering a woman nearby. Rubinstein's father escaped, too, but his sister and brother did not. The day after the mass murder, Gestapo officers told Koretz's survivors, "The aktion is over. Tomorrow morning, all remaining Jews must report to their places of work. Jews who were in hiding can return to the ghetto. They are no longer in danger."[8]

Rubinstein and his father slipped back home under cover of darkness to look for the rest of the family. One of Leon's sisters, Hyala, about eleven years old, and one of his brothers had been murdered. Rubinstein's father was able to make a passport for the daughter who survived. "He took the passport of a friend from an adjacent town, who had passed away, and carefully added my sister's photograph to it, and melted wax on top to make it look right. He insisted that she go to the Russian border, which she did. She survived," Leon explained. His father made arrangements for him to hide in a friend's house. He himself kept moving, looking for hiding places and quick exits wherever he went.

Moshe Furshpan, a ten-year-old boy from Ludvipol, stayed in the heated hut with the family that did not make room for Aharon as his feet froze. Furshpan had escaped the liquidation of the Jewish community of Ludvipol because he had been warned about it. "My parents," he explained, "had arranged for me to be taken care of by a Gentile man who was a good friend of theirs, and I'd take his cow to pasture every day. That morning, the farmer brought me some food out in the field and said, 'Don't go home! Go to the forest or they will kill you!'" Furshpan's entire family was killed that day, but he survived.

In the forest, he found a woman from Ludvipol who had also escaped with two of her children. He stayed with them for about a week, after which she brought him to another Ludvipol family hiding in the forest. This was the Grosspish family, two children and their parents. He had not known them before the war, although they knew who he was. The father's nickname, Furshpan recalled, was Diodia. He stayed with this family for the duration of the war.

Discussing his life in the woods with the Grosspish family, Furshpan said, "I was like a nothing, worthless, just a child. They could use me. I was very polite in manner and did what they told me to do, sort of like paying my way. I had to do a lot of things to stay with them, unbelievable things like going by myself into the forest at night and to villages to beg for food and bring it back to them. The villagers would give me (a little kid) bread or potatoes. I had no one else to protect me, but I wasn't considered part of the family and never felt like part of their family — honestly, I don't know what I was to them. The situation was that they told me to do this, do that, behave like this or that. I had to stay with someone because by myself I wouldn't survive.... I couldn't say they were good people or bad people. I wasn't looking for 'nice' people. I was only interested in surviving, and they were the people I could stay with."

Although Furshpan was a Tarbut School student, he did not recall being acquainted with Aharon before the war. He remembered Aharon hiding with the Grosspish family for a while and that "he already had frozen feet." Asked how he felt about that, he said, "It's hard to explain my life. I was just a child, and mixed up at that time, but I remember that Aharon was left alone in the forest. We had to leave the area because the Germans were not far away, and were going into the forest and killing a lot of Jews.... I remember they gave Aharon a place that was a hole in the ground with branches for a roof."

Later, after the Russian partisans took over the area, Furshpan became separated from the Grosspish family. He said, "The next time I saw Aharon, he was with his uncle and aunt, the Edelmans, on the other side of the river. I happened to meet them in the village, when his aunt was cleaning his feet. It was terrible. I remembered them from home and they told me we had been close neighbors. I was very sick, and was going from family to family. I was falling on my face from illness when I went to the Edelmans. They did not have room for me. It was a situation where you cannot blame anyone — everyone had to help himself. But then someone else I went to said OK and helped me, and after about ten days, I could walk again. I stayed over the winter with a family who knew my parents, especially my father. I worked for them in their house, doing whatever they asked me to do. My parents, maybe, were like angels above me and gave me the right directions."

---

1. Leni Yahil, The Holocaust: The Fate of European Jewry
2. Ludvipol Yizkor book, reported by Judah Raber
3. Ludvipol Yizkor book, Ibid.
4. Ludvipol Yizkor book, various accounts
5. Ludwigsburg archives, testimony of Josef Pikowsky
6. Ludwigsburg archives, testimony of Josef Gitterman, based on conversations with Mazure Kowalczyk
7. Yahil, Ibid., p. 267, from Sefer Koretz, ed. Eliesar Launo (Tel Aviv, 1959)
8. Yahil, Ibid., p. 266

Rescued

Between three hundred and four hundred of Ludvipol's Jews survived the liquidation and escaped into the forests, but fewer than half survived until the end of the war.[1] Throughout Volhynia, thousands suffered from exposure and frostbite, and were unable to keep a step ahead of the police and bandits. Those who were sick, old, or wounded perished. Aharon Golub was a rare exception.

At first, immediately after the liquidation and while the weather was still moderate, people were able to sleep outdoors in the woods, in farmers' outbuildings, or in improvised shacks built of tree branches, and could forage for food in the fields, gardens, and orchards. Winter, however, brought serious new problems, including an increased risk of discovery. Because their footprints could be easily followed after a fresh snowfall, survivors learned to cover their tracks by dragging branches behind them, or stayed in one place until snow started falling to cover their tracks. The winter of 1943–1944 was particularly harsh, many survivors recalled. That winter, recalled Mordechai Ben Shecna, a survivor from Ludvipol, "the snow fell on the Ukrainian forests mercilessly and constantly, covering the blood-soaked soil with hard white cover.... Even now, when I'm writing down my memories, I'm chilled to remember the freezing cold that surrounded us."[2]

Thankfully, some villagers helped the Jews, especially in isolated rural villages. According to one survivor, a Ukrainian couple who helped him and other Ludvipol Jews was financially supported by Russian partisans. The survivors were taken to a group in the forest, called Niedzwiedzki (after its leader, Stanislaw Niedzwiedzki) of about one hundred Russian partisans and ten Jews. About twenty others stayed in the woods near Levaches, a Polish village in partisan territory. "The [Polish] farmers did not betray them, even under threat from the Germans, despite the fact that they often suffered severely as a consequence."[3] A Polish farmer named Mikolaj Kurjeta and his family helped about fifty Jews in the area from 1942 until the end of the war in 1944, according to Kurjeta's own deposition, which was signed by a number of the survivors. Kurjeta said he had been born and raised in the forest outside of Piplo and had become a farmer in a particularly isolated spot near Ludvipol; he lived there with his wife and six children. He was friendly and on good business terms with Jews from Ludvipol, Koretz, and other local towns.

The day before the liquidation of the Ludvipol ghetto, ten Jewish acquaintances from Ludvipol, including Pesko Kechzor, his son Lowa, Lowa's wife, Wierny Awrum, Awrum's wife and two children, and Aba Guttman, escaped and fled to his farm and were hidden in a loft. After a few days, other Jews from the vicinity straggled in. Despite the danger of discovery, he aided them all. His thought was, "If I die, then I'll be dead." In other words, death would be the same whether he helped a lot of people or just a few. When the group grew to twenty or so, he gave them spades, axes, and other tools and helped them make hiding places in the woods. Some of those who were ill, and mothers with young children, stayed in his house. He and his family brought the hidden Jews food and clothing, and warned them whenever search parties or police were near. When they had to find new places, he assisted them. His family also hid a small child whose mother went to join a partisan group. The skilled refugees went to the Kurjeta house when it seemed safe and worked together making sheepskin rugs, blankets, and coats, which he sold to partisans and villagers. Once, he brought them a little honey on Rosh Ha'Shana. "They saw the honey, began saying something among themselves, and then started to cry," he said. "They explained that there's a Jewish custom to serve honey on New Year's Day, and this honey reminded them of the time they lived like everyone else." Although neighbors and relatives were aware of the Jews there, no one informed on them.

Poles were more likely to assist Jewish refugees than Ukrainians were. Arje Katz said, "Certain villagers, called Mazurim, were good to us. They were neither Ukrainian nor Polish, nor were they a partisan group. They were a different kind of Christian. They lived in our area, had their farms there, and helped the Jews hide in the forest. They brought them food and saved their lives in any way they could."

The Mazurian villages, he said, were isolated in the thickest forests and swampy areas beyond the River Slusch, where there was also significant Russian partisan activity. In his eulogy, Katz praised the inhabitants of the Mazurian villages, specifically Piplo, Levaches, Namilia, Matchulanka, Stara-Uta, Strij, Mishakova, Lushakova, Borovay, Mokreh, Zavoloche, Nova-Uta, Kozarnik, and Smolarnia, for their assistance.

Others, including Aharon Golub's childhood friend, Itzak Gurfinkel, also singled out Mazurian villagers for their generous help. He explained that Mazurians were "mixed in with the Polish and Ukrainians, and their villages were deep in the forest in very isolated places where Germans did not go.... On one side of the river were Ukrainians, and on the other side were Mazurians. They had been given land a long time ago by Poland and some of them were in the Polish army. Namilia, Strij, and Lushakova were Mazurian villages, and possibly Nova-Uta." He remembered Matchulanka and Stara-Uta as Ukrainian villages.

The Mazurians appear to be a "people apart" and are listed as a separate entity in Poland's census report in 1900. Their religion is Protestant, not Catholic like most Poles, and their speech is a separate dialect, a combination of Polish and German. At various times in history, they were mistreated by both national groups, but seem to have suffered the worst deprivations during decades of Prussian occupation. Krystyna Jaworowska, a retired Smith College astronomy professor from Poland, said she spent time as a young person in the Mazurian area of Poland near Byelorussia. She compared the Mazurians in Poland to the Cajuns in the United States, who were also ostracized from the mainstream and also survived in harsh, isolated swamplands. Both groups developed unusual survival skills and maintained their own traditions. It is possible that the Mazurians went to Volhynia (and Byelorussia) from Mazuria, a region near the Baltic Sea with as many as thirty thousand glacial lakes. Absentee aristocrats with large tracts of thickly forested land are believed to have allowed the Mazurians to settle on their land and help themselves to the berries, mushrooms, maple syrup, meat, hides, and wood there, as well as graze their animals. Over generations, they traded at local marketplaces and formed stable, long-term relationships with local Jews.

Katz credited Mazurians with teaching the Jewish refugees various survival skills, such as how to dig trenches, fox-holes, and bunkers to hide in and how to protect themselves against wolves and other feral animals, as well as providing food, clothing, and footwear, and serving as guides through the area. Furthermore, he reported that they kept vigilant watch for bandits and murderers, and warned the Jews whenever the Ukrainians were combing the area.

Jews who fled into the forests had some factors working in their favor. Generations of Jewish travelers throughout Volhynia had accumulated some familiarity with the topography, paths, and conditions. It stood the Jews in good stead to know which farms and villages were likely to be friendly, and which ones housed thugs or collaborators. Local Jews had established extensive networks during their long years in commerce, the trades, and crafts. Some of these connections assisted them now, despite the dangers. And young people were better prepared than they would have been in previous generations, thanks to the self-sufficiency training they received in the Zionist movements, to fight for survival in the forest.

Most of the survivors stayed in barns, sheds, and attics, surviving on a crust of bread, an occasional potato, or nothing at all. They wandered from place to place, often under cover of darkness, sleeping in shifts. It was rarely safe to stay for more than a few days in any one hiding place; they had to find new hiding places every few days to avoid detection. Besides being caught up in anti-Semitic fervor, and fearing for their own safety if they were to protect Jews in any way, the villagers had economic incentives to discover and turn them in. An account by physician Jakob Wallah in *Sefer Koretz*, says that "announcements were posted in the streets [of Koretz] stating that any person who brought the head of a Jew to the Commandant would receive a kilogram of salt. The Ukrainian murderers fanned out through the forests to hunt Jews. They murdered them, cut off their heads, and brought them to the Commandant. It was terrible to see the murderers walking the streets of the town clasping the severed heads of Jews."[4] Poles were particularly sought out by the murderers now that the Germans and Ukrainians being in power. In Ukrainian villages, the rallying cry "Death to the Lakhiv" (Poles, in Ukrainian) was frequently heard.

Fugitives survived in small camps, sometimes under the protection of Russian partisans. One such camp east of Ludvipol was protected by a united group of Polish and Soviet partisans, the Dzierzynski Battalion, and appears to have sheltered some one hundred Jews. There were several smaller camps outside Pavursk, Ratno, and Olyka. According to Judah Raber, the Edelmans and Aharon Golub lived in one of these camps.

Polish and Ukrainian partisan groups had first begun organizing clandestine nationalist operations during the Soviet occupation; the Soviet partisan movement (Naumo partisans, named after their leader) began later, in the autumn of 1942, well after the Russian retreat from Poland.

The Polish partisans of the Home Army (Armia Krajowa, in Polish) were trying to reestablish Poland as an independent country with its prewar border in the east. They supported self-defense units in Polish villages but kept a fairly low profile.

Ukrainian partisan groups (Ukrainian Resistance Army), on the other hand, were comprised of the worst anti-Semitic rabble whose mission, besides the establishment of a Ukrainian state sometime in the distant future, was to hunt down and murder Jews. Well-organized and stronger than the Soviet partisans at first, the Ukrainian partisans for a time controlled much of central, western, and southern Volhynia. In the spring of 1943, after the liquidation of most of Volhynia's Jews, they turned their attention to the hated Lakhiv, and Polish refugees fled into the woods. Small villages of Polish bunkers and huts sprang up. At that point, and later, when Russian partisans were parachuted in large numbers into the forests, German movement in the forests of eastern Poland decreased significantly; no longer did they move freely around the villages and forests of Volhynia, although they still controlled the cities and towns.

Jews hiding in the forests and villages were shot by all three types of partisans, especially extremist Ukrainian and Polish groups (Narodowe Sily Zbrojne). Sometimes they were killed in crossfire, sometimes because they were Jewish, and sometimes because it was safer to kill strangers than risk betrayal or ambush. All three groups waged relentless war against each other, with animosities especially deep between the Poles and Ukrainians. In the countryside, they burned each other's villages and killed their inhabitants.

There are no reliable figures on the number of Jews who were murdered by partisans in the forests, nor the number of Jews sheltered by them. "Even at the peak of…the partisan movement, those Jews hiding in the forests could not feel secure, as quite a number of partisan leaders were infected with Jew-hatred. Despite claims of discipline and strict supervision, lower-rank partisan leaders were given considerable leeway and could act arbitrarily."[5]

There were Jewish fighters among the Russian and Polish partisans; some of the Russian partisan commanders who were parachuted into the area were Jewish. Nevertheless, Jews who wanted to join the partisans routinely had to provide gifts of weapons as a condition for acceptance, a requirement that did not apply to non-Jews. Even after relinquishing their weapons, Jews were not necessarily accepted. One group of Ludvipol survivors who joined Soviet partisans were abandoned in the forest during a trek to the Pinsk swamps.

As many as sixteen hundred Volhynian Jews survived in the

woods long enough to join Soviet partisans. By the end of 1943, about 10 percent of these partisans were Jews.[6] Some scholars believe that as many as twenty thousand Jewish partisans were fighting in the woods of Eastern Europe.[7]

Alter and Samuel Tiktin, who had escaped into the woods during the liquidation of the Ludvipol ghetto, joined the Russian Karilow partisans. After the liquidation, they led a successful Karilow attack on the German and Ukrainian forces in Ludvipol, killing two Ukrainian policemen and wounding Commissar Norgall; Norgall escaped and returned, later, to burn the town to ashes.[8] It was as a result of his wound that Norgall limped from then on.[9]

Alex (Shalom) Edelman joined the Naumo partisans and was active in direct combat with Germans and in destroying German trains on their way to the Russian front. He knew no fear and fought even after he was wounded.[10]

Many of the Jews in the forests were unfit for combat. What they needed from the partisans was shelter and food. Family camps were set up and maintained by some partisan units, and those who found shelter there tried to make themselves useful by tending the wounded, growing vegetables, cooking, sewing, and repairing tools and weapons. Their presence increased the partisans' need for supplies, including food, from local farmers and fueled not only anti-Semitism but hostility toward the partisan groups. Additionally, the mobility of the partisans was impaired by children and old people in the family camps.

Over time, conditions improved slightly. Although still in hiding, some Jews had enough to eat and were able to start working at trades and set up small-scale commerce. Some were able to help the families of Polish refugees who had previously assisted them.

Other Survivors' Stories

Pesach Kleinman was one of the Ludvipol Jews who, like Aharon Golub, survived the Holocaust by living in the forest. Just prior to the liquidation, his father had somehow succeeded in moving his family out of the ghetto to their grandfather's house, which was less heavily guarded and from which he was able to find work in the nearby villages. Even so, he could not sustain his family on the food he could bring in, and so he arranged for Pesach, who was fourteen years old, and another son, fifteen-year-old Mordechai, to work as shepherds for two Polish families. "My life with the Polish villagers was easy. I got food, clothes, and good treatment from my employer as well as the rest of the villagers, even though they all knew I was Jewish," Kleinman said.[11]

One day, his Polish employer told him that the Jews had not shown up for labor on the road from Admovka to Brezno, and that there was a rumor that they were to be executed soon. Pesach stayed with his employer, but his brother crossed the river to take refuge in the woods. For a time, the employer and his family kept Pesach supplied with food as well as news that "made my head spin," he said. "I thought about everything — my family, my friends, the life in town, school, hiking, swimming in the river, the celebrations of the holidays."

Eventually, though, the farmer no longer felt he could shelter Pesach, and the boy took refuge with some Polish shepherds in the high pastures. One day, as he was sitting with the shepherds, a group of Ukrainian policemen approached. "I was sure someone had informed," he recalled. "One of the shepherds pulled himself together and yelled at me, 'Piatro [Peter, in Polish, not a Jewish name]! Go see where the sheep have run to!' and I ran away." After that narrow escape, he looked for another location and crossed the river into unfamiliar woods and fields. First he stayed in the village of Namilia and then in Smolarnia. It was in Smolarnia where, after about two weeks, he met some friends from Ludvipol — Itzak Gurfinkel, and a woman named Natka and her daughter Chaia. He wandered in the woods with Gurfinkel until they met others from Ludvipol, who informed him that his father and uncle were still alive.

"While in the woods, I got sick with typhus. I didn't eat, I didn't drink. We were living in holes in the ground and I almost died," he remembered. "Everybody had fled away, fearing that the Germans were nearby. I was on my own." At some point, shepherds surrounded his hiding place, an underground bunker made of wood, and were about to set it on fire, but he managed to call out to them and, instead of burning the shelter down, they gave him bread and left. Kleinman started to crawl away. "I knew there was a path Jews used, but I couldn't crawl more than a mile. Suddenly I heard voices coming and I realized I needed to prepare myself to die." He was wrong. It was his father, coming to bury him with a group of friends. They carried him away and he recovered. "I have no words to describe that meeting," he said. They told him that his mother, grandmother, and sister had been murdered while looking for escape routes from town.

Pesach, his father, and his uncle continued to live in the woods, changing locations often for two years. They constantly lacked one necessity, he said: salt. They needed salt in order to preserve the meat they found, killed, or stole. When the partisans came from inner Russia, they traded them homemade wine for salt. In the summer, he recalled, they gathered black berries, red berries, carrots, potatoes, and mushrooms. Winters were harder. "We wore one filthy cloth on top of the other. We had millions of lice. We used to walk to the villagers' houses and ask for food. They gave us from their mouth a piece of bread, or a hot doughnut from the oven." Mordechai joined the partisans and survived the war.[12]

Judah Raber spent the early part of the war with Chava and Usher Edelman, he wrote in the *Yizkor* book. He and his wife, Devorah, were being sheltered by a Christian friend, Adaska Shzigedla, when Usher arrived one night and urged the Rabers to join what remained of his family in the woods. They agreed and Shzigedla gave them food and directions to his potato field.[13]

In the woods, they met Chava Edelman with her two sons and two daughters, "girls beautiful like gold," as Raber described them. Polish neighbors led the group deep into the woods of Levaches to a place that seemed safe, and they built a campsite there. Two sisters from Ludvipol, Rachel and Cipa, joined them and some local shepherds brought food for them almost every day. However, one of the most dedicated shepherds, by the name of Branwizcky, told them one day that their presence had become well known in the village, and he was afraid that they would be discovered and killed. His own brother, he feared, would inform on them — and he and the other shepherds would be shot. They stayed a few more days, with the shepherds faithfully bringing supplies, but after some kind of altercation or heated verbal exchange with a villager (it might have involved pistols Edelman had obtained for himself and his older son Alex), the group decided to leave as soon as possible.

Usher, Alex, and Boris Edelman, Judah Raber, and Rachel left to find a suitable place. A few hours later, the search group heard loud gunshots, so loud that Raber thought that he was the quarry. As feared, Branwizcky's brother (or someone else) had informed on them to the Ukrainian police.

Chava Edelman was the only one who escaped the attack. Despite hours of torture, Devorah Raber did not reveal who had been helping them. After murdering the women and children, the Ukrainian murderers took bread from the campsite and brought it to the closest village, Namilia; they broke into people's homes there and compared the bread from the campsite to the bread at each household, in order to catch and punish anyone who had helped by bringing food to the hidden Jews.

Judah Raber and the other survivors returned to the site of the massacre as soon as it seemed safe, and quickly buried their dead and marked the spot for a decent burial later, a desire they were never able to fulfill.

While he was in the woods with the Edelman group, wrote Judah Raber in the *Yizkor* book, his feet became very slightly frost-bitten, and when they were warned that Germans would soon be hunting goats nearby, he was almost left behind. However, when his feet were rubbed with salt, he was able to walk. Chava Edelman set him by the warm oven at the forest keeper's hut for a few hours, and then he proceeded with her on foot to Mokreh, which was controlled by the Naumo Russian partisans. There, he was sheltered by a villager during his convalescence.

With the winter rain, ice, and cold, they went deeper into the woods and eventually came across a group of survivors from Ludvipol and Koretz, including relatives of Chava Edelman, Alter Tiktin and his twenty-year-old son, Samuel. In all, there were about twenty people. They dug a bunker together, but it was too small for all of them, so ten people left. These ten people were never heard from again. The others traded their remaining possessions for food from friendly villagers and built an oven for heat, cooking, and hygiene.[14]

Itzak Gurfinkel said that in the woods, the survivors would meet up, separate, and then meet up again. When they left Ludvipol, he recalled, "Aharon's legs were fine. Then, when we met again in the Ukrainian forests between the Mazurian villages and the River Slusch, Aharon could not walk. It was just a fact — we did not have time for feelings like pity or fear.... In the forest, we dug into the ground to stay warm. Sometimes, we made a fire and sat near it; we had matches. But usually, we did not make fires because we did not want to be seen. We foraged for potatoes and roasted them. We went to villages, asked for food, and took what we could when we had the opportunity. Everyone was afraid. We were afraid the villagers would give us away to the Germans, but the villagers were afraid the Jewish partisans would seek retribution if they informed on us. I was with the Medwiedow Russian partisans, and so were a lot of other Jews. We went from place to place, traveling at night and sleeping during the day. When the partisans stopped, we stopped. We tried not to have anything to do with the Polish partisans because they were anti-Semitic."

Leon Rubinstein survived the war by hiding in the home of an unlikely friend, a young Ukrainian partisan. Even though the Ukrainian partisans hated the Jews, these two were old friends. "He was about a year older than me and was in charge of the household because his father was fighting in the Russian army. His mother did not want to take me in, but he was in charge and made her," he said. "The Ukrainian partisan's home was a small isolated farm with two cows, two horses, and two pigs. The house consisted of a kitchen that served as a bedroom, and a small bedroom that was about six feet by six feet. The floors were dirt with a clay mixture spread on top which made the floor hard enough to sweep, and there was a cast iron woodstove in the house. His mother was afraid I would be discovered. I had two hiding places. One was a hole in the floor of the barn, underneath the cows and manure. The other was a hole in the ground of a potato patch. They would come once a night to see me."

Rubinstein stayed there for three years. About six months after the Russians had liberated the area, they came to look for his friend because of his membership in the Ukrainian partisans. They found Rubinstein instead, still hiding in the hole in the field. Rubinstein immediately knew they were not Germans. "They took me, fed me, gave me a machine gun, a Russian uniform, and kept me with them. I was very fortunate. It was about 1944 and I was fourteen years old." He stayed with the Red Army and went with them to Rovno.

1. Yad Vashem archives
2. Ludvipol Yizkor book
3. Leni Yahil, The Holocaust, p. 268
4. Yahil, Ibid., p. 268
5. Yahil, Ibid., p. 488
6. Martin Gilbert, The Holocaust: A History of the Jews of Europe During the Second World War
7. Yahil, Ibid., p. 489
8. Baruch Guttman, Yad Vashem testimony
9. Archival materials, Ludwigsburg, Germany
10. Ludvipol Yizkor book
11. Ludvipol Yizkor book
12. After the war, Kleinman's brother moved to Israel; in 1979, he was murdered by Palestinian terrorists.
13. Ludvipol Yizkor book
14. Ludvipol Yizkor book. After the area was liberated, Raber went to Matchulanka and worked at the same company as Usher Edelman. When he was ordered to a labor camp by an anti-Semitic Ukrainian manager, however, he fled. Later, he remarried and moved to Israel.

For Us, The War Ends

On January 10, 1944, Ludvipol was liberated by the Red Army, although it was mostly ashes, and a civilian administration was quickly established in Matchulanka, about twelve kilometers away. The Edelmans moved to Matchulanka, where Usher became an insurance services manager. Almost four weeks later, on February 4, 1944, the city of Rovno was liberated by the Red Army, with assistance from Vasily Begma's partisan forces. The liberation of the rest of Volhynia followed during the next five months.

While there were less than a few dozen Jewish survivors in the city of Rovno itself, Jews emerged from the forests and small towns and congregated there. Between forty and seventy-two Jews returned to Ludvipol after the war, but when they found it had been burned down, most went on to Rovno, where they were given permission to establish a religious community and a distribution center at a synagogue for refugees. Usher was involved in supplying food and clothing to survivors, and took Rubinstein to the center later for some clothes.[1] Jews were supposed to register at the Russian militia office but, afraid that they would be drafted into the army or sent away to find employment, few did so.

Alex Edelman joined a battalion of the NKVD (Narodnyi Komissariat Vnutrennykh Del, People's Commissariat for Internal Affairs), a special unit of the Russian army and the predecessor of the KGB whose mission was to track down Ukrainian collaborators and Poles considered "unreformable enemies" of communist Russia, and kill them or surrender them to the Russian government. Among Jewish survivors, they were called "brothers for revenge." Alex is thought to have led a Red Army group into the Ukrainian village of Marna, near the site where his sisters were murdered, and to have participated in burning the village and killing its residents.[2]

Alter and Samuel Tiktin, who were in the Russian army, were also said to be involved in NKVD activities. Alter is believed to have been the leader of a large group of partisans for a time. He was killed in battle near Rovno, according to some stories; other people have said that he was publicly executed by fellow partisans for reasons unknown. Samuel, who was part of a special unit that fought on Polish soil, lost his left arm clearing a mine and received special decorations for his actions as a partisan and soldier.[3]

Other Ludvipol survivors who joined the NKVD include Haim Shlifer and Ben Shecna. Shlifer, one of Shmuel Shafir's older brothers, was born in 1911 in the Ukrainian village of Selishtch; the family later moved to Ludvipol, where their father, Rabbi Yeshaiyo Dov Shlifer, was a chazzan (cantor, in Hebrew). A local organizer for Beitar, Haim married Hannah Babtzuk in 1938. They had one daughter. According to Shmuel and another surviving brother, Isser, Haim witnessed the murder of his wife, daughter, and other brothers by Germans or Ukrainians and was determined to avenge their deaths. During or after the liquidation, he fled into the woods and joined the Medwiedow partisans, then moved to Mezhirichi and joined the NKVD. While with the NKVD, he and Ben Shecna took part in numerous operations against Nazis and local collaborators. When the Russians were unwilling to track down perpetrators who had killed Jews, which happened frequently, these two operated with an independent group of Jewish survivors; Shlifer was said to be the head, hands, and legs of the group. One of his most famous deeds was the capture of a man, known as "Truchon" or "Combat," who, as a senior commander of the Ukrainian Bandera partisans, had murdered a large number of Jews. After the war, Truchon was known to have gone into hiding in the village of Lipka. Sixty armed cavalrymen from the Red Army accompanied Shecna and Shlifer to the outskirts of the village. When the villagers opened fire, the soldiers wanted to withdraw, but Shlifer insisted on entering and fighting until the Bandera leader was captured and handed over to the authorities; Truchon admitted to numerous atrocities and was hung with thirteen other murderers. Shlifer continued his pursuit of Nazi killers and collaborators until the tenth of Tevet, 1945 (December 14), when he was ambushed and killed by Ukrainians on his way to an action in Skitzin, near Mezrichi. He was buried in Mezrichi with thirty-seven other partisans, the only Jew in the group.

Leon Rubinstein and Aharon met in March or April of 1945, a month or two before the war ended and after Rubinstein's Russian protectors had been killed on missions, leaving the boy to fend for himself. Rubinstein recalled, "I was walking on a street in Rovno, probably by myself, wearing a Russian uniform and carrying a machine gun when Aharon saw me and looked me over. An open-minded fellow, he started a conversation with me in Russian and, once he realized that I was Jewish, he took me home to introduce me to his aunt and uncle."

When they arrived at the modest apartment in a crowded refugee building, he said, "Chava was cooking soup with herring, potatoes, and perhaps some onion. Salt and spices were hard to find, and the herring was enough to make the soup taste good. In the Russian army, our diet had been mostly horrible tasting dried potatoes, sliced about an eighth of an inch thick, and canned foods. Nothing was fresh; even the cheese was canned. Food was terribly scarce and there was no bread and no milk. We ate a lot of sardines, canned cheese, and dried potatoes. Chava's bowl of soup was wonderful." In the apartment, there was a broken sewing machine which Rubinstein recalled trying to fix. He was introduced to someone there who had papers for himself and his missing daughter to leave Poland for "somewhere else, perhaps England," and was desperately searching for the girl. He eventually let Rubinstein travel with him and use her papers, perhaps persuaded by Usher Edelman. "This man — I never knew his name, which was not unusual because many people preferred anonymity — and I traveled together by train," said Rubinstein, "but sat in different corners so that we wouldn't look suspicious. After a full day and night we arrived at Bitom. We went to the address the man had been given, but it was after midnight and the people wouldn't let us in, so we slept in the hallway. The next morning, we parted ways and the people there brought me to an orphanage in Bitom. A couple of years later, I bumped into the man I had traveled with and learned that he never found his daughter."

Bitom is a mining city in Eastern Upper Silesia, Poland, contiguous with the larger city of Katowice and in an area viewed by the Nazis as a vital resource because of rich coal deposits and a highly developed industrial base. Although Bitom's Jewish men were compelled to perform forced labor and Jewish property there was confiscated as early as 1939, ghettos were not created until relatively late — 1943, three years after the Warsaw ghetto was erected and two years after the ghetto in Ludvipol.[4] Food rations were significantly better than elsewhere and Jewish movement less restricted as well. In early 1940, factories in Eastern Upper Silesia supplying shoes, clothing, and other basics for the German army employed more than six thousand Jews who were designated as essential to the German war effort and spared deportation; thousands of other Jews there did forced labor on roads and other infrastructure projects.

In 1942, the Germans began deporting local Jews to Auschwitz, just fifteen minutes by car from Bitom today. In August, more than twelve thousand Jews from the area were transported. Tens of thousands still had work permits, however, and the Jewish survival rate there was about 50 percent higher than elsewhere in Poland at that time. In June 1943, the final liquidation of Jews began in the Bitom area with the deportation of more than thirty thousand Jewish residents to death camps. Some members of Dror attempted an act of resistance, firing on Germans from hidden bunkers and killing or wounding at least two SS officers. Ironically, the last Jews from Eastern Upper Silesia were sent to Auschwitz the same month that Ludvipol was liberated, January 1944. After the war, Bitom was returned to Poland in compensation for territory in the Ukraine.

1. When Rubinstein went back to Rovno in 1991, the synagogue was still there.
2. Baruch Guttman, Yad Vashem testimony
3. Samuel Tiktin later studied in Kiev, and then taught English in Rovno for many years. Ben and Cindy Golub visited him and his family in 1988 and helped them make aliyah to Israel in about 1991. Aharon visited Samuel, his wife Ida, daughter and son-in-law Larissa and Simeon Ehrlich, and grandchildren Eugene and Ilana in Israel. He died of cancer in 1994.
4. Israel Gutman and Isreal Gutnamm, editors, *Encyclopedia of the Holocaust*

Ludvipol and the Holocaust: A Chronology

1938 November 9, 10. During the Kristallnacht pogroms, Ludvipol's future commissar, Franz Norgall, breaks into an apartment in Heilsburg, Germany and murders a sleeping couple; he is later singled out by the Nazi Party's Supreme Court for excessive anti-Semitism and violations of Nazi Party discipline. Concentration camps at Dachau, Buchenwald, and Sachsenhausen are expanded by Jewish slave laborers deported from Austria and elsewhere. By November, over thirty thousand Jews, many of them exiled from their own countries and not allowed into any other country, are rounded up and incarcerated there.

1939 Thousands of Jewish refugees flee from western Poland into the eastern parts of the country, and some of them passing through or settling in Ludvipol. They warn the residents about the brutality and anti-Semitism of the Nazis.

August 23	Germany and Russia sign the Molotov–Ribbentrop Non-Aggression Pact.
September 1	Germany attacks Poland, which has 3,500,000 Jews.
September 3	Britain and France declare war on Germany.
September 10	The Polish forces retreat to the outskirts of Lvov to try to regroup. Canada declares war on Germany.
September 17	Russia abandons its neutrality, attacks Poland from the east, and occupies Ludvipol and neighboring towns.
September 18	The Polish government flees to Romania. Poland is occupied by Germans in the west and Russians in the east.
November 1	The entire western Ukraine (population 41,900,000) is annexed by Russia.
December 12	Hans Frank, the Nazi officer in charge of German-occupied Poland, orders Jews to wear armbands with the Star of David. Restrictions on Jewish

movement, communication, business, and more, increase.

1940 Jewish businesses and property in Ludvipol are confiscated by the Bolsheviks and their previous owners face deportation, as the town is reorganized by the Communists. Zionism is seen as a threat to Russia, Hebrew is outlawed, and a Russian curriculum is instituted in all schools. Nevertheless, Jews in Russian-occupied Poland are relatively safe compared to those in German-occupied Poland, where they are forced into ghettos, starved, murdered, and deported to concentration and slave labor camps.

February 10   Two new wings of the extremist anti-Semitic Ukrainian nationalist group, Organization of Ukrainian Nationalists (OUN) form under the leadership of Andrew Melnyk and Stepan Bandera.

November   In Warsaw, about 140,000 resident and refugee Jews are forced into the newly constructed ghetto and sealed off.

1941 In June, Germany attacks Russia and invades Russian-occupied Poland. Russia immediately retreats, abandoning Ludvipol; by November 30, over 3,800,000 Russian soldiers surrender. In early July, Ludvipol is taken over by Germans. By early October, a ghetto has been erected and the Jews are forced into isolation behind its walls. Between June and December, an estimated 1,000,000 European Jews are killed by Einsatzgruppen, mobile German death squads, in the first phase of the genocide of Jews.

June 22   Germany attacks Russia, which becomes a de facto ally of Poland. The Russian soldiers and administrators flee Ludvipol within days, accompanied voluntarily by many Jews who fear the approaching Germans. Before they leave, the

	Russians set fire to some establishments in town so that they cannot be utilized by the Nazis and Ukrainian collaborators. The Russian NKVD organization kills over 19,000 Ukrainian nationalists imprisoned in Lvov and elsewhere in the western Ukraine.
June 28	Germans occupy Rovno, home to about 25,000 Jews and the administrative center for the region.
June 30	Germans occupy Lvov, home to about 200,000 Jews, including 100,000 recent refugees from western areas. Over the next four days, they murder about 4,000 of these Jews. Ukrainian nationalists declare a Ukrainian state.
July 7	Germans occupy Ludvipol. Arbitrary murders and atrocities begin immediately led by Einsatzgruppen units C and D.
July 9	Germany's promises to support a Ukrainian national state are undermined by its arrests of Stepan Bandera and other Ukrainian nationalist leaders, who are deported to Sachsenhausen prison camp in Germany.
July 16– *September 1*	Germany divides its eastern occupied territories into two commissariats: Reichskommissariat Ostland and Reichskommissariat Ukraine, which includes Volhynia. Rovno is named the capital and Erich Koch (1896–1986) its highest level commissar. Gebietskommissarz (government) headquarters are established in Kostopol. Commissar Franz Norgall is in charge of the Ludvipol area, assisted by deputies Glanz and Spiegel.
September	Ukrainian nationalist guerrillas begin military operations against Russia and Germany.
September 26	Russia surrenders Kiev after a fierce battle involving 665,000 Russian troops.

September 29   German Einsatzgruppen murder 33,771 Jews in
Kiev (Babi Yar).

October 1   Norgall orders all Jews in Ludvipol and surrounding villages to wear the Star of David.

October 12   The western Ukraine is incorporated into the
General Government of Germany.

October 14   On Simchat Torah, the Jews in Ludvipol and surrounding villages are forced to move into the
ghetto. Movement, communication with both the
outside world as well as other ghetto dwellers,
and possession of food other than rations are
outlawed. People are beaten, tortured, or murdered for infractions, including those committed
by family members and neighbors.

November 7–8   In Rovno, 21,000 Jews are forced into a pine
grove and shot by death squads alongside pits
dug in advance.

November 8–   Jews from Lvov and surrounding villages are
December 15   forced into a ghetto.

December 7   Pearl Harbor is bombed; the United States de-
clares war on Japan and Germany.

1942 Germans step up their deportations of Jews to death
camps, where they are systematically murdered; an estimated 2,700,000 Jews are murdered by the Nazis in 1942.
Thousands of Jews from Lvov are deported to Belzec and
Auschwitz death camps as well as to slave labor camps.
In Ludvipol, Jews are raped, starved, worked to death, and
shot for infractions of orders. Then, in October they are
marched to the forest on the other side of the Slusch River
and executed. A handful succeed in escaping.

January 20   The Final Solution to the Jewish Question, the
murder of every Jew and annihilation of the entire European Jewish population, is approved at

	Germany's Wannsee Conference.
April 14	In ransom for their lives, Ludvipol's Jews bring Commissar Norgall all of their remaining gold, silver, and merchandise.
July 13	The Jews of Rovno who survived the first mass murder (about 5,000) are forced into the forest and shot by death squads, alongside pits dug in advance.
July 22	Between July 22 and the end of the year, over 300,000 Jews from the Warsaw ghetto are sent to death camps and murdered.
August 20–23	The Jews of Lutsk (Lodz) (about 17,000) are forced into the forest and shot by death squads alongside pits dug in advance.
August 25	The Jews of Ludvipol (about 2,000) are forced into the forest and held overnight either in the barracks or forest. At least 60 people attempt to escape under the cover of darkness, and some succeed.
August 26 *(Elul 12)*	The Jews of Ludvipol are shot in the forest by death squads alongside pits dug in advance.
August 26–27	In Ludvipol, Germans and Ukrainians hunt down and murder nearly everyone who evaded the mass murders. Many of the victims are buried in two mass graves in the town.
November	The tide of war begins to turn against the Germans.

1943 Jews who escaped the mass murders in Ludvipol and else-where struggle to survive despite extreme temperatures and no food or shelter in the vast forests of Volhynia. A worse enemy than nature are people. In addition to the German Nazis, the people in the woods have to avoid discovery by anti-Semitic villagers anxious for a reward, as well as collaborators, informers, and bandits. In addition, certain partisan groups are extremely anti-Semitic. A significant number of Russian partisans, some of them Jewish, are parachuted into the area and provide food and shelter to many refugees. Germany, encountering increasing resistance from its allies and puppet states, abandons the exploitation of Jewish slave labor in favor of immediate and total annihilation of Jews in death camps. Ghettos are cleared out and their residents deported to highly efficient death camps. Jewish activists continue to organize acts of resistance, despite brutal conditions and a lack of weapons.

January 31   German troops in Stalingrad surrender.

June 1 and 2   In Lvov, when an act of armed resistance fails, the entire Jewish population is rounded up and murdered.

July 5–   Russians capture Kursk in the northeast and Kiev,
November 6   the Ukrainian capital.

1944 Germany loses the war in the Ukraine. Russia occupies Odessa, Ludvipol, Rovno, Lutsk, and Lvov. Jewish survivors from Ludvipol and elsewhere flock to Matchulanka and Rovno, and desperately try to find lost family members.

January 10   Ludvipol is liberated by the Soviet army, but has already been destroyed by fire.

February 5   Rovno is liberated by the Soviet army and a Russian partisan unit led by Major General Vasily Begma. Lutsk (Lodz) is liberated. Survivors from Ludvipol search for news of their families and begin to gather in Matchulanka and Rovno, where they establish a distribution center for food and clothing.

June 22   Stalin and Russia's NKVD leaders secretly propose that all Ukrainians who survived the German occupation in the Ukraine be exiled to Siberia.

July 22   Lvov is liberated by the Soviet army and the underground Polish army.

July–August   Zionists work tirelessly to find and assist survivors. They attempt to illegally get Jews into Palestine through Hungary and by sea but fail as Britain steps up its militant guard against Jewish immigration. A repatriation program for Polish nationals tempts some Jews to stay in Poland, despite continuing anti-Semitism.

October 14   German occupation of Ukraine ends after 1,871 days.

1945 The war in Europe ends. Thousands of traumatized and orphaned Jews make their way to Displaced Persons camps in Germany, Austria, and Italy. Few are willing to risk staying in Europe. Some stay, but mask their Jewish identity and pass as Christians. Despite atrocious conditions in the Displaced Persons camps, life reaffirms itself with a Jewish population explosion. A U.S. presidential advisor urges Britain to allow homeless Jewish refugees into its Middle Eastern mandate immediately, but Britain refuses to do so.

February 4–11 At the Yalta Conference in Crimea (Ukraine), Roosevelt, Churchill, and Stalin plan post-war Europe, with western Poland in the Russian zone of influence and Volhynia in the Ukraine.

April 30   Hitler commits suicide in Berlin.

May 8   The war in Europe ends (VE Day).

July 4   Forty-two Jewish survivors who repatriated to their hometown, Kielce, Poland, are murdered by Christian neighbors.

July 5   Britain and the United States recognize the Russian provisional government as the legal authority in Poland.

Legal Papers for Palestine

At the end of World War II, the Allied powers found that millions of people had been left homeless; more than six million were quickly repatriated, but one million Jews who had survived were homeless. Few of them were willing to return to the places of their betrayal and the murders of their families. "Having been subjected to widespread anti-Semitism on the part of their Christian neighbors both before and during the Holocaust, [they] wanted only to begin new lives in countries that were not haunted by bitter memories."[1] About three hundred thousand Jews filtered into Displaced Persons camps in Germany, Austria, and Italy. Earl G. Harrison, sent by U.S. President Harry S Truman to investigate the American-zone camps in Germany in the summer of 1945, found that conditions, especially for Jews, were shockingly bad and blamed the United States military. (Conditions in the camps run by England and France were no better, however.) Clothed in the same disease-laden rags they had arrived in, sometimes even the striped "pajamas" of the death camps, Jews were behind barbed wire and under armed guard in former concentration camps, and were forced to share tight quarters with Nazi perpetrators. They slept on tiny wooden shelves and were denied adequate food and medical treatment. The DPs had no homes, no communities to return to, no means to feed and clothe themselves, and many spirits were broken beyond repair.[2] Harrison strongly recommended that the only solution to the problem of Holocaust survivors' homelessness was relocation to the British mandate of Palestine, and he urged the United States to pressure Britain to issue 100,000 entry permits immediately.

Zionist and non-Zionist groups, including Agudah Israel, Poalei Agudah Israel, Jewish Brigade soldiers, the Jewish Agency, and the Palestine Jewish community were active in the DP camps, and a handful of Jewish organizations, principally the Joint Distribution Committee (JDC) and the World Jewish Congress, took up the cause of the DPs. The JDC alone helped one out of every two Jewish survivors in Europe, and in 1946, the American Jewish community contributed $102 million to their cause. By 1947, over two thousand doctors, nurses, teachers, and social workers were working with Holocaust survivors in the DP camps, and tons of supplies were donated and distributed. The Bricha organization was helping survivors from all over Eastern Europe make the journey to the DP camps, often on foot for hundreds of miles, and Aliyah Bet was arranging passage, usually illegally, to Palestine. The rest of the world was relatively indifferent to their condition but the Sh'erit HaPletah (saving remnant, in Hebrew) proved amazingly resilient, embracing life with new schools, new friendships, and new families.[3]

Moshe Trosman, originally from a small town in Volhynia called Rokitno, was about fourteen years old when he met Aharon in Bitom. He lived with his brother Issaschar and mother Eita; to support themselves, they sold fabrics Issaschar got in Berlin and milk jugs brought in from the countryside. "Aharon had a warm house then, with an uncle and aunt who took care of him nicely," Trosman recalled. Whenever possible, he and Aharon played games and talked about aliyah to Eretz Yisrael. Both boys wanted to join Dror, a Zionist youth movement that was gathering surviving Jewish orphans from their hidden places, including some who had been sheltered during the war by non-Jewish families, for aliyah to Israel. Shlichim from Eretz Yisrael took care of the children.

Trosman and Aharon visited the Dror orphanage in Bitom, where they saw the children studying and dancing enthusiastically. Aharon was clear that he wanted to be part of the group and immigrate to Eretz Yisrael. Trosman, on the other hand, stayed with his mother and brother, and embarked on a difficult journey into Germany, where he learned that Aharon and the Dror Bitom group was in nearby Landsberg, and decided to join, too. "It is hard to explain," he said, "but our only dream was to immigrate to Israel. We didn't join those who dreamed about America or Canada."

Sisters Behira Zakay and Chana Haklay, Arie Medlinger, and

Shmuel Peleg, all of whom joined the Dror group, were found wandering around Bitom and elsewhere by Youth Movement members and brought to the orphanage in December. Behira Zakay recalled being picked up by Natke Gold and Uta Greik, both of whom were about seventeen years old and had been Dror members before the war. When they were released from a labor camp, they started working for Dror. "We came because they told us that we could immigrate to Israel with these children," said Zakay. About seventy children, mostly orphans, stayed in three or four rooms, sleeping on mattresses on the floor. Chana Haklay recalled that their meals were served on enamel plates, which she took offense at: "I had the feeling only dogs get food on such plates." Two Jews from the Russian army, Leon Rubinstein and Yasha [last name not recorded], immigrated to Israel with them.

Arie Medlinger, the youngest of the children who later went to Kibbutz Yagur and were subsequently known as the Dror group, survived the war with his mother, posing as a Polish family, first outside the Warsaw ghetto and later in the town of Kielce. Two weeks before the Russian army liberated Kielce, his mother died of typhus and was buried under her Polish pseudonym, Maria Jabobska. (Many years later, Medlinger found her grave and gave her a Jewish burial at Kibbutz Yagur under her real name, Rosa.) Medlinger was considered too young to go to Israel, but a young woman at the Dror orphanage, Haviva Rosenberg, agreed to take him. "Ever since I had been a child and heard about hachsharas training people for life on a new settlement," he said, "I'd wanted to live in a country that was only for Jews. It was winter. I collected my belongings in a blanket, threw them out of the window, and [Haviva] took me."

They all remembered being smuggled with the other Dror children, early in 1946, across the Polish border into Czechoslovakia and posing as Greek refugees returning to Greece. They spoke in Hebrew, not Polish, but Peleg recalled that "the Poles knew who we were and said, 'You are Jewish! Don't pretend!'" Many Polish Jews received Greek papers, and the frontier patrols mistook Hebrew for Greek and let them through. "After a time, Greek authorities, unaware that such a large 'Greek' colony existed in Poland, wondered why none of these people reached Greece."[4] The Czechs, Peleg recalled, "let us ride for free on the train and electric cable cars. 'The poor kids,' they said. One woman gave us a needle and strings." "They gave us their seats in the cable cars because we didn't reach the bars," added Zakay. Then they made the illegal border crossing at night into Germany. "It was a hard walk in deep snow," Peleg remembered, "and extremely hard for Aharon because of his legs."

A few of the other children — called "pure Poles" because they came from cosmopolitan Polish cities like Lvov, Warsaw, and Lutsk — were already educated, and leaders sprang up. Aharon was a natural leader to whom the other children turned for guidance. He was more knowledgeable, active, and mature, as well as slightly older than the others, said some. According to Trosman, he was the group's "spiritual" leader and "used to answer questions that no one else knew the answers to." "While we had reached only third grade," said Peleg, "Aharon had finished at least six grades and could already speak and write in both Hebrew and Yiddish." In a sense he was the guardian of the children, and negotiated with the instructors on their behalf. Haklay, too, recalled Aharon as the group's leader. He was "very smart, with an ability to express himself and communicate well with everyone," she said.

The DP camp in Landsberg had been a German military compound and was eventually the second largest DP camp in the American zone, with mostly Russian, Latvian, and Lithuanian survivors. Its newspaper, the *Landsberg Lager Cajtung* (Landsberg Camp Newspaper; later, the *Jidisze Cajtung*, or Jewish Newspaper), was one of the best in the American zone; its educational system, preschool through college, was extensive; and it offered many cultural activities to revive the spirits of the people. The children settled into an unused school and began studies that included general education, Hebrew, the history and geography of Eretz Yisrael, and physical exercise. As Trosman pointed out, "Some children had been in hiding for six years, and only in Landsberg did they start to get a preliminary education. Some of them had to be taught things like how to eat properly."

Trosman remembered that in 1946, a delegation arrived at the DP camp to register forty of the children for legal immigration to Palestine. He had gone to a movie, however, and so was not registered with his friends. Aharon and thirty-nine others were given legal papers to enter Palestine.

Near Marseilles, the children probably stayed in Grand Arenas, a former military camp that was the main transit camp in the area for Jewish survivors immigrating to Palestine. (This and other camps near Marseilles later sheltered the Jewish refugees from the boat *Exodus*, as well as Egyptian Jews in 1956, Moroccan and Tunisian Jews in 1961, and Algerian Jews in 1962.)[5]

From Marseilles, as many as fifteen hundred Jewish children from youth movements including Dror, HaShomer HaTzair, and Mizrahi boarded a ship, the *Champollion*, for Palestine. Moshe Furshpan, the boy who had been with Aharon when his feet froze, was one of the children on the *Champollion*. After the war, he had stayed in the village of Levaches ("They treated me so nicely and gave me food, clothes, and shoes, and invited me to stay in the village," he said), but he was desperate to find his family. A Levaches villager named Ludwig took him to Koretz twice in hopes of finding news of his family, telling him, "Over here are some Jews, and if you go and find somebody and want to stay with them, OK, but if you don't find anybody and have nowhere to stay, come back here and I'll take you home." On the second trip to Koretz, Furshpan found a family to stay with for a couple of days, then hitchhiked to Rovno with another child. "That's where I met Aharon again, and other people from Ludvipol. Then someone took me to Lublin and an orphanage for Jewish children there accepted me." The orphanage relocated to East Germany, Furshpan said, after which "someone from Israel was looking around for kids to emigrate to Israel, and took us — we were maybe sixty or one hundred children. The manager called me in one day and told me I was too young to emigrate, that I should stay, but others said, 'Come with us.' For some reason, they took us back to Poland briefly, and then I was on the same boat as Aharon Golub, the *Champollion*, which left from France. I remember being part of a group of about one hundred kids. The delegates who brought us out from the orphanage grouped us and I went to Kibbutz Kfar Menachem."

Named after Jean-François Champollion, an early nineteenth-century French Egyptologist who discovered the meaning of Egyptian hieroglyphs, the *Champollion* was initially launched in 1921 for travel between Egypt and Syria, with a maximum capacity of 450 passengers. In 1934, it was renovated and enlarged, and from November 1942 until the end of the war it was used for troop transports around Algiers. When the Dror children embarked, it was 168 meters long with a gross capacity of 136,000 tons.

Behira Zakay remembered it as "a heavily armored warship." The children settled in on the third level, while about 400 French soldiers were on the first level. Rubinstein recalled that the children, crowded together with three or four on a hammock, were told not to speak to each other. "I was scared to death on the ship," he said. The soldiers disembarked in Bizerte, he recalled, and were replaced by a group of Jewish refugee children; the British arrested the children and took them off the boat at the next stop but they reboarded shortly afterward. The boat arrived in Haifa on April 26, 1946.

---

1. Menachem Z. Rosensaft, in *Life Reborn: Jewish Displaced Persons 1945–1951*
2. Michael Schneider, in *Life Reborn*
3. Rositta Ehrlich Kenigsberg and Romana Strochlitz Primus, in *Life Reborn*
4. Leonard Dinnerstein, *America and the Survivors of the Holocaust*, pp. 110–111
5. www.crif-marseilleprovence.com/histoire/juifsprovence.htm;
   http://motlc.wiesenthal.org/text/x15/xm1579.html;
   www.yadvashem.org/exhibitions

III. A New Beginning

A Brief History of Mandated Palestine and Kibbutz Yagur

Between 1880 and 1914, about sixty thousand Jews fled their homes in Russia, Galicia, Romania, Poland, and other Eastern European countries and immigrated to Palestine, most of them settling in the cities of Haifa, Jerusalem, Jaffa, and Hebron. During this period, the Zionist movement was catching the imagination of Jews throughout Russia and Europe; the first kibbutz in Palestine, Degania, was established in 1910.

Seven years later, Britain won a victory over the Ottoman Empire in the Middle East and announced, in the Balfour Declaration, that it would set aside 11,000 square miles of its 1,184,000-square-mile Mandate for a Jewish national home. The declaration was ambiguous, however. At the same time that it favored the establishment of a "national homeland" for the Jewish people in Palestine, and said that it would use its best efforts to facilitate such a homeland, Britain imposed severe new limitations on Jewish immigration to the Mandate and assured Arabs that they would take preference over Jews; nothing would be done that might infringe on existing, non-Jewish communities.

Between 1917 and 1920, during which period 100,000 Jews in Russia and Eastern Europe were murdered in pogroms, large numbers of Jews made aliyah to Palestine. 10,000 immigrated in 1919 and 1920, and 27,000 more fled there during the next three years. The Arab response was immediate. On March 1, 1920, Arabs attacked and killed eight Jews, including the founder of HeChalutz, Josef Trumpeldor. What followed became a pattern. Britain restricted Jewish immigration (to 16,500 a year) and otherwise ignored the violence. Jews organized a self-defense force, the Haganah. Arab leaders incited a three-day riot against Jews and their property in Jerusalem. Britain continued to largely ignore Arab riots, but sentenced proponents of Jewish self-defense, such as Vladimir Jabotinsky and several colleagues, to long terms in prison.[1]

In May 1921, after Arab actions left forty-seven Jews and forty-eight Arabs dead, Britain was faced with the need to maintain friendly relations with oil-producing Arab countries and therefore suspended *all* Jewish immigration to the Mandate. However, it lifted the ban in July. Arab attacks shut down seven kibbutzim, but in Jerusalem's Old City, they were stopped by the new self-defense force, the Haganah.

The following year, when the Mandate's population was 750,000, including 83,000 Jews, Britain published a White Paper (the term for British regulations relating to its mandate in Palestine) that promised Arabs that it would *never* permit Jewish immigration to exceed the economic capacity of Palestine to absorb them. Britain continued its policy of imprisoning Jews who organized defense units and announced a strongly pro-Arab interpretation of the Balfour Declaration. The British Colonial Secretary of the time, Winston Churchill, also decreased the size of the proposed Jewish home territory, promised that Jewish immigrants would never be allowed to become a burden on Arabs and that political undesirables would always be denied entry. The Jewish community reluctantly accepted the order, but it was rejected by the Arabs. Frequent outbreaks of violent attacks on Jews continued, but Jewish action remained limited to self-defense.

Over the next decade, while anti-Semitism spread in Europe, about 75,000 Jews managed to slip into Palestine and Arab leaders loudly proclaimed from the pulpit that Jews had sinister designs against Arabs and Arab holy places. The oratory was effective, and in August 1929, a four-day period of violence began in Jerusalem and spread to Haifa, Hebron, and elsewhere, with more than 133

331

Jewish civilians killed. The British did little or nothing to quell the violence and continued to arrest Jews who tried to organize Jewish self-defense.

Amid the increasing violence, there was a flight of Arab moderates from the Mandate, with thirty thousand upper- and middle-class citizens and their families leaving the country and creating a vacuum of moderate Arab leadership. By 1936, with nearly one-third of the population now Jewish, the Mufti of Jerusalem, Haj Amin Muhammad al Husseini (an ally of Hitler, Mussolini, and the Nazi military in subsequent years), incited crowds in Haifa by telling them that the goal of Jews was to expel all Arabs. He also demanded that Britain outlaw Jewish immigration and make it illegal for Jews to purchase land. A three-month long campaign of bus bombings and other lethal attacks on Jewish civilians followed. The Haj's followers also destroyed thousands of acres of Jewish trees, vineyards, and crops. A proposal by the League of Nations' Peel Commission to establish separate Jewish and Arab states, with Jerusalem under British control, was opposed by both Arabs and Jews.

The next year, Jews began to take proactive measures to prevent Arab attacks. Special Night Squads were organized by a British officer, Orde Wingate, to patrol the oil pipeline between Haifa and Iraq and identify terrorists. These Night Squads used the element of surprise and intimate knowledge of the countryside, as well as intelligence and reconnaissance.[2] The squads proved to be an apt training ground for Jewish soldiers and leaders, however, and Britain transferred Wingate out of the country.

After his removal, the Haganah set up its own proactive strike force, Fosh (also called *Plugot Sadeh*), commanded by Yitzchak Sadeh. Sadeh was a familiar face at Kibbutz Yagur, where Aharon and the Dror group would settle eight years later.

In May 1939, another White Paper restricted Jewish immigration to ten thousand a year for five years, after which the British high commissioner would be permitted to add twenty-five thousand over the next five years. After 1944, no Jews would be permitted entry without prior approval from Arab leaders. In addition, any obligation of Britain to facilitate a Jewish national homeland would end. The White Paper has been seen, in retrospect, as a message to Hitler that Britain would distance itself from Jewish rights.

As Jews tried to flee from the Nazis, Britain tightened its blockade around Palestine. Jewish refugees were arrested and sent back to Europe or delivered to detention camps on Cyprus in the Mediterranean and Mauritius in the Indian Ocean. In 1940, Britain forced thirty thousand Jewish refugees to return to Europe. The Haganah stepped up its pressure on Britain to allow Jewish refugees to enter Palestine. Sometimes, these efforts were ill-advised; it tried to blow a small hole in the hull of the *Patria*, an old boat carrying 1,900 illegal Jewish refugees from the port at Haifa to the detention camp on Mauritius by British order, but the ship sank, killing 240 of the refugees and a number of British guards. Britain responded by further tightening its military blockade, but as many as 90,000 Jews managed to enter that year.

Haganah leaders David Ben-Gurion and Eliyahu Golomb, another familiar face at Yagur, disbanded Fosh and had its papers destroyed, theoretically because they could not reconcile themselves to the existence of a unified strike force devoted to a charismatic commander — Sadeh — over whom they had no control.[3] Shortly after, however, Sadeh became the leader of a new organization, *Poum* (*Plugot Meyuchadot*, special companies), whose goal was to develop Jewish intelligence resources and special operations.

In 1941, the Haganah and *Yishuv* (the Jewish community of Palestine), with permission from England, started all-out efforts to organize a coordinated Jewish fighting force, the *Palmach* (acronym of *Plugot Machats* - shock, or strike, companies), to fight Germany and the Axis powers if the European war came to Palestine. But the Palmach also aimed at defending Jews in the Mandate against attacks. Again, Sadeh was the leader, and he chose his former associates in Poum, Fosh, and the Special Night Squads to be commanders. Palmach's earliest recruits, 427 men and 7 women, began proactive, coordinated defense of Jewish settlements. The Palmach mounted patrols from the Lebanese border to the outskirts of Tel Aviv and conducted nighttime raids to intercept bandits. By 1943, the Palmach had 1,000 highly trained troops. Many of these soldiers had served in the British armed forces as part of the Jewish (Star of David) Brigade, active on the front in 1944 and 1945.

Kibbutz Yagur

Nine Russian immigrants, eight men and one woman, established Kibbutz Yagur in 1922. In Russia, they had belonged to the Russian Zionist organization, Poalei Zion, and in Palestine joined *Achva* (Hebrew for fraternity), founded in 1910 in the first Zionist town in Palestine, Petach Tikva. Both organizations worked for a "muscular" Judaism that emphasized physical work and strength, rather than textual study and prayer. Most of the men in Achva had trained and served in the Hebrew Battalion of the British Army during World War I and believed that Diaspora Jews must learn to be self-sustaining on the land and capable of defending themselves.

At that time, finding employment in Palestine was difficult for Jews because the workforce was controlled by Arabs. Nor did Jewish immigrants adapt readily to the climate and culture. Achva's immediate goals were to help Jews get jobs, purchase and develop land in Palestine, and establish a utopian society based on pooled resources and cooperative living.

In March 1922, the group that later founded Yagur settled briefly in the south of Palestine near Tel Arad, but difficult conditions forced them to abandon their plan of creating a kibbutz there. They toured swampland in the Zevulun Valley, near Haifa and Mount Carmel, though it was considered unsuitable for farming and dangerously isolated from other Jewish settlements. This, in fact, was the land on which they settled. The group's leader, Yoel Bergman, looked at the lush vegetation on Mount Carmel and announced, "Don't you see? This is a wonderful place! It's just like

Switzerland!"[4]

A private investor had purchased land in the area, once called Shomria but later renamed Emek Zevulun, and was willing to allot part of it to the group. It was thought, however, that they had little chance of surviving. Indeed, the Zionist institutions were so outraged that they threatened to sanction the group if it grew to more than twenty-five families.

A Dr. Kliger of Haifa's health department wrote to the Settlement Department in Jerusalem, "This site is the most dangerous one that you could have chosen. We have no idea what is the reason that induced you to choose this place of all places and in general we are surprised you chose any spot without first consulting with the Institute, whose duty is the anti-malaria work in the Hebrew settlements."[5] The Settlement Department responded with a statement about the scarcity of acreage available for Jewish settlement in the Mandate. Two other groups tried to buy land in the Shomria area, *Tchelet Lavan* (Blue and White) and *Chafetz Chaim* (Desiring Life), but both eventually withdrew their petitions.

While they waited for Achva to settle the land purchase, the founding members lived on acreage leased by the owner of a nearby cement factory. One rainy day toward the end of 1922, with little more than a pair of mules from a kibbutz in Sharon, and calling themselves the Laugh Group because their supplies were a joke, the group spent its entire treasury of 10 lire on a barrel of salted fish, and began building its *meshek* (small farm or settlement). At first, they named it Yahazor, after a nearby Arab village, Yajoor; later, they changed it to Yagur.

Members dug irrigation channels, planted eucalyptus trees, and tried to establish fields. The first plowing was done behind a set of railroad tracks, where they sowed wheat and barley by hand. One member, Noach Yaguri, went to the Galilee and returned with a cow, and the group procured a few skinny chickens. But the soil was poor — and the water was very dirty. Engineers sent by Zionist institutions found that it would cost a prohibitive three thousand lire to drain the swamp, wrote Yaguri in the *Yagur Book*. "Only savages can settle in such a place," Zionist leader Menachem Oshiskin commented when he visited a year later in 1923.[6]

Poverty and hardship were accompanied by disease. Several of Yagur's founding members, including Bergman, contracted fever and died. The others, after much debate, concluded that in order to succeed, Yagur would need a diversified economic base and a larger number of contributing members. They joined HaKibbutz HaMeuchad, a group that would help buy additional land and send new members. They developed a line of dairy products, established a can manufacturing plant, and found outside employment, mostly in the port of Haifa and the cement factory, around which had grown the town of Nesher.

Draining the marshes and trying to turn over the soil was backbreaking work. During the rains, the soil flooded. During the dry weather, it was too hard-packed and dry to cultivate — a plow blade could barely slice into it. But they managed to plant wheat, barley, and hay by hand. They also built a wall that somehow protected the water from contamination.

By 1933, the fields had started to bloom and Yagur had several hundred members. A popular joke at the time, recorded for posterity in the *Yagur Book*, is that a police officer arrived on the scene after a traffic accident and asked one of the drivers where he was from. "Yagur," he was told. The other driver promptly exclaimed, "I'm also from Yagur!" The officer added, "So am I!"

By then, Yagur had experienced at least one Arab attack. In the rioting that began in Jerusalem on August 23, 1929 and spread throughout the country, seven of the 133 Jewish victims were killed in nearby Hadar HaCarmel. Bandits armed with clubs, iron bars, and axes gathered in Yajoor and attacked the kibbutz, but Yagur members defended the settlement successfully with only seven rifles, a few defective guns, and a small stock of ammunition; it was thought that the chance appearance of a British airplane overhead frightened the attackers. It was a turning point for Yagur's members. They realized they had only themselves to rely on for security. Wasting no time, they erected a fence with guard posts around the kibbutz and began to recruit for the Haganah underground. On weekends and evenings, men and women, boys and girls secretly practiced combat skills and defense tactics.

Like the other Jews in Palestine, they had few weapons and almost no ammunition. The Haganah, however, was using its connections in Europe to smuggle weapons and ammunition into the Mandate. According to Abraham Shapira, who joined the kibbutz in the 1930s, many of these weapons were stolen from European armies. At first, he wrote, it was mostly pistols, smuggled inside tourists' suitcases, packages, and cement barrels; later, it included rifles, machine guns, and submachine guns hidden in steamrollers, lathes, and tractor wheels.

At Yagur, bunkers were built into double-walled houses and cellars were dug for hiding weapons and ammunition. When the British sealed off the port of Jaffa, until then the main port of entry for smuggled weapons, Haifa took its place and nearby Yagur became the largest arms warehouse for the Haganah. Meanwhile, Arab leader Fawzi al Qawukji was organizing local combat units, and on April 5, 1931, the units waylaid three Yagur members and murdered them. Eventually, some members of Yagur volunteered to protect smaller settlements in the Mandate, possibly with support from the Special Night Squads or Fosh.

Thus, Yagur's members were involved in numerous activities: developing combat skills; helping in the defense of other settlements; nurturing the land and increasing Yagur's agricultural yield; creating a manufacturing plant; doing outside paid work; and hiding arms for the Haganah. Also, during World War II, they joined the Star of David (Jewish) Brigade, and several members were killed in service, including one who died parachuting into Nazi-occupied Italy.

And there was more: As part of the Jewish Resistance movement, Yagur members were helping to bring legal and illegal Jewish refugees to Palestine and get them settled. On October 10, 1945, members of Yagur and nearby kibbutzim liberated 208 Holocaust survivors being held indefinitely by the British in a center at nearby Atlit. The escapees were ambushed by British police at a dry creek bed near Atlit, but a Jewish officer in the British police force secretly helped Yagur members rescue them, according to A. Rakabi in the *Yagur Book*. Miriam Shachar recalled the same incident: "We went to meet them near the Carmel mountain and led them quickly and quietly to Yagur, where we exchanged clothes with them and told them to throw away their identification cards and declare themselves 'Jews from Eretz Yisrael.'" That day, hundreds of illegal immigrants took their first steps as free people in the Promised Land, thanks to the fast work of Yagur members.

Yagur had a significant influence on the new nation, and many leaders were associated with it. Among its many visitors was Eliyahu Golomb, who immigrated to Palestine in 1909 from Volkovysky, Byelorussia. He organized agricultural training programs in Kibbutz Degania Alef from its inception, and when World War I broke out, he urged Jews to create an independent Jewish defense force rather than enlist in the Turkish army. By 1918, he had founded the Jewish Legion. Then Golomb helped organize the Haganah underground. Between 1922 and 1924, he was in Europe arranging for arms shipments for the Haganah and mobilizing the fledgling pioneer youth movement. Believing firmly that the British should be ousted from Eretz Yisrael, he helped initiate the use of field units (Fosh) during Arab riots in Palestine. Later, he helped found the Palmach.

Yitzchak Tabenkin, whose first wife lived at Yagur, was a prominent labor movement leader in Israel and one of the principal thinkers and main voices of the kibbutz movement. Born in 1887 in Byelorussia, he attended a traditional cheder and then received a secular education. Tabenkin helped bring the Poalei Zion movement to Poland and, later, establish agricultural settlements closely associated with the Dror movement in Eretz Yisrael. He immigrated there in 1911 and, like Golomb, worked in agriculture. He joined HaShomer HaTzair and in 1921 helped found Kibbutz Ein Harod, which became the center for HaKibbutz HaMeuchad. A strong populist and advocate of kibbutz living, he helped found the *Achdut HaAvodah* (United Labor Party), Mapai, and Mapam movements. After the War of Independence, he was an esteemed member of the Knesset, where he spoke out on behalf of labor and the kibbutzim. Until his death in the early 1970s, he continued to make impassioned speeches and publish papers on those subjects. His son, Josef Tabenkin, was a leader in the Palmach during the War of Independence, serving as the brigade commander of the Harel Brigade (also called the Tenth Armored Brigade), to which many Yagur members belonged.

Yitzchak Sadeh was also a familiar face at Yagur. A charismatic and colorful figure, Sadeh was born in Russia in 1891, arrived in Palestine in 1932 and "seemed to have spent the years 1914 to 1919 successively fighting for the Czar, serving in the St. Petersburg police, and doing hatchet jobs for various White and Red organizations."[7] He has been described as a former circus wrestler, foreman of a rock quarry, art dealer, journalist, and doctor of philosophy and, later, a hopeless administrator and born leader.[8]

Sadeh was involved in several early efforts to organize Jewish self-defense and active resistance to Arab attacks, coordinated resistance to the British as acting chief of the Haganah general staff, and later took part in numerous important operations during the War of Independence, including the battle for Jerusalem and Operation Horev. With two exceptions, he trained all of the later chiefs of staff of the Israeli Defense Force (IDF) and many of its generals, including Moshe Dayan, Yigal Yadin, and Yigal Allon, in Fosh or the Palmach. In the Palmach, they called him *HaZaken*, the Old Man. Sadeh was also in charge of Poum, which during World War II occasionally cooperated with the British to supply skilled personnel for commando raids against Axis forces. It also gathered intelligence and conducted special operations, operated a police force, smuggled arms, photographed targets, located Arab terrorists and Jewish informers — and attacked British boats preventing refugees from landing in Palestine. Furthermore, it helped build the Haganah, and some of its members went on to create the Mossad, Israel's intelligence agency.

Sadeh left military service when the Palmach disbanded after the War of Independence, and until his death in Tel Aviv three years later he wrote essays, stories, and plays, sometimes under the pen name Y. Noded. He was also an active supporter of sports, and the competition slogan, *"Alafim v'lo alufim"* ("Thousands, but not champions") is attributed to him. The first track race in Israel, *HaKafat Har Tavor* (Around Mount Tavor), started as a memorial to him. Two kibbutzim in the Negev, Nir Yitzhak and Mash'abei Sadeh, are named after him.

Israel Bar Yehuda, who joined Yagur in 1930 as an Achva member, later became a member of parliament and the minister of the interior in the new State of Israel's government, playing an important role as a representative of Achdut HaAvodah to the government. Bar Yehuda was instrumental in establishing an early yardstick for who was officially Jewish. Recognizing that many European Jews immigrated with Gentile spouses and children, and wanting to "spare these mixed couples complications and embarrassment," he believed that officials should simplify matters by recording information as it was supplied by new immigrants. "Any person declaring in good faith that he is a Jew shall be registered as a Jew, and no additional proof shall be required," he proposed. This was highly controversial and ultimately a compromise was reached; a person who claimed Jewish ethnicity could not simultaneously be a member of another religious group, such as Christian or Moslem. Bar Yehuda also promoted separation between religious law and civil law.[9]

Moshe Carmel also lived in Yagur. Carmel was a respected leader and the top commander of the northern front during the

War of Independence. Carmel had made aliyah to Palestine from Minsk, Poland, in 1924. After the war, he became Israel's minister of transportation.

Uzi Gal, another member of Kibbutz Yagur, invented the Uzi submachine gun, which has been used widely by the armies of Israel, the Netherlands, and other European countries. In 1976, he retired from Israel's government-owned weapons-manufacturing company, Israeli Military Industries, and moved to Philadelphia to pursue medical treatment for his daughter.

1. Howard M. Sachar, A History of Israel from the Rise of Zionism to Our Time, pp. 300–301
2. Martin Van Creveld, The Sword and the Olive: A Critical History of the Israeli Defense Force, pp. 39–40
3. Van Creveld, Ibid., p. 42
4. Zeev Aner, Kibbutzim Stories
5. Yagur Book: Forty Years for Aliyah to the Soil
6. Yagur Book
7. Van Creveld, Ibid., p. 40
8. Larry Collins and Dominique Lapierre, O Jerusalem!, p. 36
9. Sachar, Ibid., pp. 604–605

New Life in Our Ancient Land

Shmuel Peleg recalled that when the group arrived, there was a celebratory mood — "half of Haifa was on the docks." Before going to Kibbutz Yagur, the new immigrants were taken to Atlit refugee camp, where they were sprayed with DDT against parasites and lice, as was customary. Children from religious backgrounds were sent to religious communities, while those from secular backgrounds were placed by the youth movements to which they belonged. Because Dror was affiliated with Achdut HaAvodah, one of the most influential Zionist organizations, the Dror children were sent to Kibbutz Yagur, as youth leader Zvi Zahira had promised them when they were still in Bitom.

Behira Zakay remembered a heartwarming reception at Yagur. "The Yagur members were crying...crying," she said. "We were the first survivor group to arrive. We were thirteen or fourteen years old, although we looked not more than ten or eleven. They showered us and dressed us with Eretz Yisrael clothes — khaki shorts and T-shirts. For the first time, we exposed our white legs. While we were eating, they started to surround us and asked us, in Yiddish and Polish, 'Who are you?' 'Where do you come from?' 'Do you know this and that?' There was great excitement." Her sister, Chana Haklay, remembered that the Yagur members were carrying red flags for May Day.

An article dated May 3, 1946 in the *Yagur Journal* reported the arrival as follows:

"We were blessed to receive among us young new immigrants, a group of children, survivors of our people who survived in Poland in Gentiles' houses and in the camps and who came here now via France on the boat *Champollion*. Only late in the evening, the night of May 1st, the kibbutz was given permission to take the group to Yagur the next day, and when the May meeting was over, the secretary, the education committee, the school committee, teachers and educators sat until late after midnight to discuss the urgent arrangements. As to the question of whether to accept the children, there was no objection...and few arguments were held regarding the first place to settle them.... Shoshana Goldman, who worked in the kibbutz as a youth leader, was nominated as instructor.

"In excitement, the public waited the next day for the arrival of the children. In the dining room, the tables were set to celebrate the event. The members' patience was stretched, since they were told the children would arrive by noon, but only at 4:30 pm did they arrive from Atlit. While they were dining, a crowd of members and children surrounded the newcomers. In the evening, a reception was conducted on the lawn, with songs and plays with our children, and after dinner our children still sat with them to sing together.

"The group consists of thirty-two children (eight of them arrived only yesterday): eighteen boys and fourteen girls. Their age range is fourteen to fifteen, but four of them are eleven. The origin of all of them is Poland. Their house mother is Shindel Globerman.

"Let us pray that we will succeed in erasing from their hearts the disasters they have already seen in their short and hard lives and to educate them to be beneficial links in the project of building the nation and its land. Let us pray that soon we will receive many more like them. Thus, let us bless them...."

Fifteen-year-old Moshe Trosman, who had not gotten legal papers to enter Palestine, was detained as an illegal refugee on Cyprus. There were two sections there, he said, each with hundreds of refugees crowded into rudimentary tin huts. After learning that his brother, a Haganah commander, and sister-in-law were in the other section, he arranged for friends to stuff his bed in the morning and eat his rations, and he sneaked into his brother's camp. Later, his sister-in-law made a jute bag large enough for him to climb into, and practiced carrying it in a way that would not arouse suspicion. Trosman was small for his age, due to years of near starvation, so he climbed into the sack, and the three escaped by boat to Palestine. At Atlit, he asked to be reunited with the Dror group. "It was a big warm meeting with Aharon," remembered Trosman.

"We had been really good friends from the moment we met each other."

In 1946, there were twenty-six thousand Displaced Persons in the cramped British internment camps at Cyprus, which "were made as forbidding as possible to discourage would-be immigrants."[1] Thousands of refugees all over Europe and Israel were trying to find their lost family members and listened to the radio program *Who Recognizes, Who Knows?* every day, hoping against hope to hear news of relatives and friends who might have survived. Presumably, this was the case at Yagur, too, with adults and children huddled around the radio.

Despite their traumas or because of them, the children at Yagur barely talked about their families or personal lives. "Everybody thought that his experiences were his own private problem," said Chana Haklay. "It was only later, when the Eichmann trial made it legitimate to talk, that we opened up, and we only spoke then to prove that we did not go 'like cattle to the butcher.'"

"We had tolerance for others," added Behira Zakay, "when some of us were wetting in bed or shouting at nights...sometimes years after we had come. The war taught us to be tolerant." Rubinstein said, "At the kibbutz, nobody talked about how things really were for us. Nobody asked about the families we had lost. It was not encouraged. I had nightmares...and still have them. Until today, they never stop."

Ezra Sherman, who was acquainted with the Dror group in Germany, had immigrated to Palestine illegally with his older brother and then rejoined the group in Yagur. He said, "Most of us were left by ourselves now. We had survived in the forest or in a village. It was a trauma for a boy of fifteen. We didn't talk about it, even between us. Somebody might ask you something, and you would answer here or there, but you would never, never sit down and tell your story. I didn't talk about it until the last ten or fifteen years. We were busy with ourselves. I was less than fifteen years old but I was thinking like a man of thirty-five."

Rubinstein remembered sharing the last room on the second floor of the building with Kalman Offir, Ezra Sherman, and Mordecai Aviv, and said that it was difficult for the refugee children to adapt to their new lives. Some of them were from radically different cultural backgrounds, although they were all Jews. "Mordecai, for instance, was an orphan from Egypt with kinky hair — we'd never seen that before — and he spoke French and Arabic while we spoke Yiddish," said Rubinstein. "The two cultures, Egyptian and Eastern European, didn't mix. We used to gang up on him in our spare time, and do things like put toilet paper between his toes when he was asleep, or mount a balloon filled with water on the door so that it burst on him when he came in. Looking back, it was very cruel."

Some of the Dror children also felt that they were not fully welcomed as part of their adoptive families by the sabra children: "They disapproved of us," Shmuel Peleg said. Chana Haklay and Behira Zakay said that the only children who welcomed them fully were the Teheran children, so-called because they had been smuggled out of Europe via Teheran; they had been at Yagur since 1943. She said, "Everyone who was on the fringe of the society, who wasn't accepted by the *b'nei meshek* (kibbutz natives) became our friends. We lived almost in two different societies."

By the end of World War II, three Jewish groups were prepared to fight for their freedom from Britain. The largest and most moderate was the Haganah, which was socialist in philosophy and acted as the military branch of the Jewish Agency. The two other groups, the Irgun (Etzel) and Lechi, were smaller, more radical, and operated underground. At times, the internal animosity between the three resulted in raids on each other's sites, with kidnappings and interrogations of each other's members.

Lechi had split off from Etzel due to a philosophical disagreement. In December 1941, the British had refused to allow a boat carrying 769 Jewish refugees, the *Struma,* to land in Palestine and like hundreds of other boats carrying illegal Jewish refugees, forced it out to sea. The *Struma* sank near Istanbul and hundreds of refugees, including 250 women and 70 children on board, drowned. Etzel members who wanted to avenge their deaths founded Lechi (an acronym for *Lochame Cherut Israel*, Israel's Freedom Fighters), which was also known as the Stern Gang after leader Avraham Yair Stern.

Shortly after the end of World War II, the Haganah, Etzel, and Lechi formed the United Front of the Revolt, with the Haganah handling most of the organizational work and Etzel and Lechi handling most of the actions. All three groups were united in their commitment never to target women and children.

In mid-June 1946, the Jewish resistance attacked and destroyed ten of the Mandate's eleven bridges across its borders, virtually cutting off all traffic in and out, including the Arab Legion's access from Transjordan. Abraham Shapira recalled that the British commander in Palestine sent an urgent letter to London saying he needed at least two additional divisions of soldiers to fight the Haganah, Lechi, and Etzel. In response, they were told, "Make a list, go into the kibbutzim, and arrest those people." The British had until then "refrained from striking back at Jewish sabotage with quite the harshness they had demonstrated in their repression of Kenyan or Malaysian rebels; they were by no means impervious to the tragedy of European Jewry. But the destruction of the bridges ended the last of [their] restraints."[2]

British authorities reacted on June 29 with Operation Agatha, later referred to as Black Sabbath or Black Saturday, a two-week, country-wide sweep for Jewish leaders and weapons. The British had gotten their hands on a list of Palmach members, but it was written in a code they were unable to decipher and, thanks to a warning from the Haganah's intelligence service, many of the listed men and women were able to hide within the civilian population. The British found and arrested nearly three thousand organizers, and held most of them at a camp in Latrun, twenty miles west of Jerusalem. They subjected about 200,000 Jews to invasive searches, and were so thorough in their search for weapons that they broke and inspected the casts of patients in hospitals. Settlements suspected of hiding Palmach members, arms, or *shlichim* (messengers and emissaries) were treated with particular harshness.

The entire country was in turmoil but the search was particularly extensive at Yagur, where the British suspected a hidden arsenal of illegal weapons and the presence of key underground leaders.

Thousands of soldiers, called in Hebrew *kalaniot* (anemones) "because of their red berets and black hearts," besieged Yagur and occupied it for seven days. The day before, a British officer secretly informed the kibbutz's leaders about the upcoming occupation, and they asked the Dror children to help protect the kibbutz. Speaking in Yiddish, they explained that the British were going to try to take over the kibbutz the following day. The Dror children could help, they said, by joining the sabras and other children along the kibbutz fence at four am, and standing with their arms crossed in non-violent resistance.

"We woke up and saw all the Carmel Mountain covered with soldiers," Peleg recalled, "and we went to the fence. We could hear the armored vehicles surround the kibbutz." A delegation of British officers asked permission to enter and identify the male kibbutz members, and were refused "because it was the Sabbath." The soldiers dragged away tractors and other large pieces of machinery the kibbutz had set up to block their way and lobbed tear gas to make the children give up their positions along the fence. According to Peleg, "An officer stood on an armored vehicle with his hand up in the air. And we, who were used to the Germans, thought that once he takes his hand down, they will finish us." The children left the fence and joined the majority of the kibbutz members. Upon a signal from the officer, the troops turned on strong jets of water and oil, forcing them all into the dining room. There, soldiers with machine guns guarded every window. "People were soaked with oil," recalled Haklay, "and in our innocence, we were sure they were going to kill us."

The army gave the crowd ten minutes to surrender themselves, leave the building, and be identified. It was a long ten minutes, during which tension ran high, but no one budged. A *Yagur Book* account by Rakabi recalls that when the Dror children were told to retreat to the kitchen for safety, they refused, and shouted *"Mit aleman!"* ("Together with everyone!" in Yiddish). Then everyone started to sing HaTikva, the Israeli national anthem. "It was the first time we'd heard such a big crowd singing HaTikva in public, freely," recalled Haklay proudly.

Once the British realized that Kibbutz Yagur's members would not leave the dining room voluntarily, they threw tear-gas canisters and oil through the doors and windows. Some people collapsed in near-suffocation. Others were wounded by glass from the broken windows. In the chaos, children were screaming and some fled, but the staunch resistance continued. Chaim T. described the nightmare in the *Yagur Book* as follows: "Only little air for breathing was left.... One of the teenagers [had] survived only yesterday from Nazi extermination camp...and the scene reminded her of gas chambers.... [She] got into a state of shock and started to scream hysterical, heart-wrenching screams. Her eyes were wide and enraged as a frightened animal's. Her instructor hugged her and tried to calm her down, but there was no way to control her. Once outside she broke away from her instructor and jumped upon the soldiers, hitting them with tight fists, spitting straight in their faces and screaming at them, 'You are Nazis! Dogs! Murderers!'"

As the soldiers forced them onto trucks to take them away, Haklay remembered, "We spat on them and threw salt into their eyes." They were taken to Jelamy, a nearby police station where Eichmann was later held during his trial, and locked into holding pens, one for the women and children, one for the young men, and one for the old men. That night, the children, as well as most of the women and old men, were taken back to Yagur, where they were kept under heavy guard for nearly a week. The younger men were jailed.

In the Yagur Book, a fourth grader wrote this poem:

Soldiers came with tanks and guns,
They searched, destroyed rooms,
They also arrested children, they arrested members,
We are sad but we are not crying.

Using metal detectors and destroying buildings, crops, and even graves, the British soldiers searched for and found most of the weapons hidden at Yagur. According to one account, they seized 500 guns, 96 small mortars, 12 large mortars, and 500,000 bullets. Another account puts it at 325 rifles, 100 mortars, 10,000 hand grenades, and several hundred thousand rounds of ammunition. Either way, it was a disaster that was felt severely during the War of Independence two years later.

Ezra Sherman remarked, "We were living on the kibbutz during Black Sabbath when the British surrounded the kibbutz and searched for weapons. We were in the dining room and put up some resistance. We threw chairs and whatever we had. We held them off for a couple of hours, but eventually they got in. They took us out, put us in a truck, and took us one and a half miles away to a military camp. After a day or so, they let us go back to the kibbutz. A lot of things had been broken, and they had dug all around and found a lot of weapons and taken them. We were a main cache for the storage of weapons. The mood was sad because we knew we needed the weapons to fight the Arabs later and because people were arrested and taken away."

"I was in a state of shock. I had a high fever, my stomach hurt. It was a painful experience, very traumatic," said Zakay.

Because so many of the kibbutz's members were imprisoned after Black Sabbath, volunteer workers streamed to Yagur from northern Palestine.

The Haganah had suspended action, but three weeks later, on July 22, Etzel used concealed weapons to demolish a section of the King David Hotel in Jerusalem that housed the British Criminal Investigation Division and other government offices. Ninety-one people were killed and forty-five injured in the attack. Britain retaliated. Curfews were established in Tel Aviv and Jerusalem, and Jewish homes on Ben Yehuda Street in Jerusalem were blown up, killing forty-eight civilians. In addition, British troops were banned from Jewish shops and homes.

Meanwhile, at Yagur, illegal military training by the Palmach continued with renewed vigor. According to Rubinstein, "Yagur was on a major road between Haifa and the Jordan Valley, and Jordanian soldiers who were there with the British used the road a lot going between Israel and Jordan. The teachers would take us out by the road, and we would hide by the sides of the road with our sticks — they taught us to defend ourselves with sticks — and pretend we had to attack the soldiers. It was scary and a good education." Some of the youths were already skilled in war. Ezra Sherman, for instance, said, "By January 1944, when I was thirteen or fourteen years old, the Russians returned to my area and a brigade commander took me in and 'adopted' me, so I learned how to use weapons and went with the brigade from the Ukraine to Berlin and finished the war with them."

The kibbutz divided the children, few of whom other than Aharon could speak Hebrew when they arrived, into two classes according to their math levels; some in the Dror group had not even learned to count to one hundred. Within a few weeks, they were communicating in Hebrew. Leon Rubinstein said, "We studied Hebrew for maybe four hours every day, as well as history and the Bible, from a cultural and historic approach, not a religious one. The kibbutz discouraged us from using other languages, and when you're young, you can learn languages easily." They studied basic math and the geography of Israel — the love of the land. Arie Medlinger, who was younger than the rest of the Dror group, was moved to a class with sabra children and became fluent in Hebrew within three months.

Aharon, already proficient in Hebrew, Yiddish, Polish, and

Ukrainian, became the letter-writer for the rest of the group. Whenever anyone wanted to write to relatives or the kibbutz administration, Aharon served as his scribe. In addition, said Medlinger, "he sang beautifully and was very well-liked. He was sociable...and had the most beautiful girl in the kibbutz as his girlfriend." Chana Haklay remembered, "Despite his handicap, he was very active and presented himself to us in a very delicate and proper way." According to Moshe Trosman, Aharon was always the "social" leader of the group, while Kalman Offir, who later became a commander in the Haganah, was the "physical" leader. "Aharon never lost his leadership in the group — and is still the leader, even today," said Trosman. Rubinstein said he was "always a little envious of Aharon because he worked in the office. Also, his room was on the first floor, and he always had books and was always reading. He was a likeable guy and everyone took to him, especially women." Trosman remarked, "Aharon never took advantage of his handicap. On the contrary, he got a driver's license and worked hard."

For others in the group, the kibbutz's socialism was uncomfortable. "Coming from my background, with my father owning his own business, kibbutz life didn't appeal to me," said Leon Rubinstein. He worked in the fields after classes, picking tomatoes or apples, or thinning out new corn and dropping rat poison in holes — it was backbreaking work, he said. He worked mostly with the sheep, however, milking them in the morning and taking them out to the field in the afternoon. The kibbutz made a delicious salty cheese from the sheep milk. The kibbutz also had a small apple orchard, grapefruit orchard, vineyard, and a herd of about one hundred cows. According to Rubinstein, Yagur was very wealthy by the time the Dror group arrived. "They tried to acclimate us to the country so that we would love it and love life on the kibbutz. They took us on outings to the mountains; as kids, we might have roamed the streets of our shtetls, but we had never taken hikes into the countryside. They taught us songs and dances — the Zionists were very dedicated at that time." But the secularism of Yagur bothered him, and he remembered walking four or five miles for Kol Nidre and other High Holiday services in 1946 and 1947 with some other youngsters. "The walk was dangerous, and the shul was so small we couldn't get inside, so we sat outside and listened," he said.

According to Zeev Dor in the *Yagur Book*, bandits from the Arab village of Balad El Sheikh (today Tel Hanan) commonly shot at Jews traveling between Yagur and Haifa. Between December 1947 and May 1948, attacks on Jews throughout Palestine continued unabated and were rarely investigated or prosecuted by the British. Jewish reprisals increased, although the Haganah continued to confine its activities to defending Jewish settlements and repulsing Arab attacks.[3] "The Arabs in the area," said Rubinstein, "harassed us and we harassed them. We were looking for a peaceful coexistence, but they would pick on the weakest people — they'd find someone on watch who was asleep and kill him. And we would retaliate. Nothing has changed. They initiate something, the Israelis retaliate, then they counterattack. Relations between the British and Palestinian Jews were rapidly deteriorating."

The Jewish Resistance was averaging seventeen anti-British operations a month. Although British losses in Palestine were insignificant compared to those in Europe, the fact that the enemies the Empire was facing down in Palestine were young Holocaust survivors was problematic for troop morale and its public image. In July 1947, not long after the arrival of the Dror children and the invasive searches of Black Sabbath, when the British hanged a group of Etzel leaders, Etzel struck back. They kidnapped and hanged two British officers and booby-trapped the area below the gallows, severely injuring the police who arrived to cut the officers down.

Some Jewish Palestinians serving in England's Jewish Brigade during the war fought anti-Jewish restrictions on immigration into

Mandate Palestine in a manner that is just now becoming known. They gave their identities to Displaced Persons and traded places with them so that they could enter Palestine. Brigade members then used false papers to travel and work with the DPs and redirected food, blankets, clothes, medicine, and entire trucks to their aid. In one such incident, they used thirty-four "borrowed" British Army trucks to carry a large number of Jewish refugees to safety.[4]

The 1947 United Nations Plan for Partition and Economic Union proposed the creation of a Jewish state, half of whose population would be Jewish and half Arab, and an Arab state that would be entirely Arab, linked in an economic union, with Jerusalem controlled by a United Nations Trusteeship Council. On the day of the partition vote, November 29, everyone at Yagur listened to the radio broadcasts from New York and kept count of its supporters and opponents. A majority of thirty-three countries supported the partition, with thirteen against and ten abstaining. The minute the deciding vote was announced on radio, they left the underground shelter where they had been listening and rushed into the dining room, dancing, singing, and celebrating.

Arab leaders immediately declared a protest strike and instigated prolonged rioting that claimed the lives of hundreds of Jews and Arabs. The area around Haifa was among the most dangerous. In the *Yagur Book*, Ze'ev Dor reported that Arabs attacked Jewish transport almost daily, and Jewish reprisals were intense. Yagur member Hanan Zelinger, who had grown up in Berlin and immigrated to Israel before the Holocaust, where she became a commander in the Haganah, was killed in a skirmish on the road to Haifa. In March of 1948, at least 20 Jews and 100 Arabs were killed in the Haifa area.

Rubinstein and Sherman recalled other conflicts in the vicinity at this time. Rubenstein said, "About 75 Jews and 150 Arabs worked at an oil refinery outside Haifa. A few months before the Declaration of the State of Israel [May 1948], Arabs from Balad El

Sheikh closed the gates of the refinery one day and slaughtered 40 or 50 of the Jewish workers. Then the Palmach, from Yagur, went into the village with bulldozers and wiped it out. I do not know how many people were killed."

Shoshana Ben Ari, a nineteen-year-old sabra from Yagur, was killed during an Arab ambush on a medical convoy bringing doctors and nurses to their shifts at the well-known Hadassah hospital on Mount Scopus. British soldiers did nothing to rescue the Jews. It later came to light that the British officer had made an agreement with Arab leader Mohammed Neggar to look the other way during the ambush, as long as the Arabs did not fire on British patrols.[5]

In April and May of 1948 there was another mass exodus of wealthy and middle class Arabs, especially officials, mayors, judges, doctors, businessmen, and other community leaders. The most dramatic flight occurred in Haifa, where seventy thousand Arabs lived. A steady stream had been deserting the city since the day of the UN Partition Plan vote. By the end of March, the flight of twenty-five thousand had already weakened the city considerably and left it bereft of moderate leaders.

For several weeks, rumors circulated that the Arab nations' air forces were going to destroy the Jews on Mount Carmel and Haifa; Arab religious leaders instructed their followers to vacate their homes temporarily so that the Arab forces could work freely; they would return soon to claim not only their old homes, but the homes and settlements of the soon-to-be massacred Jews. Twenty thousand more Arabs left Haifa, thinking they would soon return, but on April 23, the city was captured by the Haganah. Leading the action was Yagur member Moshe Carmel, the commander of the northern area.

Jewish leaders held impassioned meetings with their Arab counterparts, pleading with them to remain in the city, encourage their constituents to stay as well, and help establish peaceful relations.[6] Within thirty-six hours, however, most of the city's remaining thirty thousand Arabs fled, with Lebanon, Syria, and

Iraq as their main destinations. Fewer than five thousand stayed to rebuild the country. *The New York Times* reported that "tens of thousands of Arab men, women and children fled toward the eastern outskirts of the city in cars, trucks, carts, and afoot in a desperate attempt to reach Arab territory, until the Jews captured the Rushmiya Bridge toward Samaria and Northern Palestine and cut them off. Thousands rushed every available craft, even rowboats, along the waterfront, to escape by sea toward Acre (Akko)." *Time* magazine reported on May 3, 1948 that "the mass evacuation, prompted partly by fear, partly by orders of Arab leaders, left the Arab quarter of Haifa a ghost city.... By withdrawing Arab workers, their leaders hoped to paralyze Haifa."[7]

After Haifa and its approach roads had been secured, Yagur was considered a safe place. Indeed, it was not attacked during the war, and the nearest battlefield was six or seven miles away.

1. Howard M. Sachar, A History of Israel from the Rise of Zionism to Our Time, p. 270
2. Sachar, Ibid., p. 265
3. Martin Gilbert, Routledge Atlas of the Arab–Israeli Conflict, p. 38
4. Leah Abramowitz, Jewish Bulletin News (August 2002)
5. Larry Collins and Dominique Lapierre, O Jerusalem!, p. 285
6. Sachar, Ibid., p. 332
7. Sachar, Ibid., p. 333

The War of Independence

On May 14, 1948, the British withdrew from Palestine, and the pre-Israeli government, the People's Council, with representatives from the Zionist movement and the Jewish community in Palestine, proclaimed the new *Medinat Yisrael* (State of Israel). Here are some excerpts from the proclamation:

"The State of Israel will be open to the immigration of Jews from all countries of their dispersion; will promote the development of the country for the benefit of all its inhabitants; will be based on the principles of liberty, justice and peace as conceived by the Prophets of Israel; will uphold the full social and political equality of all its citizens, without distinction of religion, race, or sex; will guarantee freedom of religion, conscience, education and culture; will safeguard the Holy Places of all religions; and will loyally uphold the principles of the United Nations Charter....

"In the midst of wanton aggression, we yet call upon the Arab inhabitants of the State of Israel to preserve the ways of peace and play their part in the development of the State, on the basis of full and equal citizenship and due representation in all its bodies and institutions — provisional and permanent.

"We extend our hand in peace and neighborliness to all the neighboring states and their peoples, and invite them to cooperate with the independent Jewish nation for the common good of all. The State of Israel is prepared to make its contribution to the progress of the Middle East as a whole.

"Our call goes out to the Jewish people all over the world to rally to our side in the task of immigration and development, and to stand by us in the great struggle for the fulfillment of the dream of generations for the redemption of Israel...."

The next day, David Ben-Gurion broadcasted his first address to the nation saying, "Yesterday an event occurred in Israel, and only the next generations can fully estimate its historical meaning. On us, each and every one of us, the responsibility these days is to only build with love and belief, through Jewish brotherhood, the

Israeli State and to protect it with all our heart and soul as long as it is necessary. We are still facing a heavy double battle — a political battle and military battle."[1]

The first country to recognize Israel was the United States, followed in the next few days by the USSR, Poland, Czechoslovakia, and Guatemala.

The council elected Ben-Gurion, a Polish immigrant, the first prime minister of Israel. Born in Plonsk, Poland, in 1886, Ben-Gurion had been educated in a Hebrew school established by his Zionist father and had immigrated to Israel in 1906. There he helped create the first agricultural workers' commune and several trade unions in Israel, founded the Histadrut, and later served as its representative to the Zionist Organization (after 1960, World Zionist Organization) and the Jewish Agency. In 1935, he was elected chairman of both organizations.

One of Ben Gurion's first tasks was to unite the pre-State fighting forces into an official national army. Most of the officers of the Palmach were affiliated with kibbutzim and the Achdut HaAvodah political party, whereas Ben-Gurion's party was the Mapai. Both parties were part of the labor movement, but Ben-Gurion did not want the army to be under the influence of Achdut HaAvodah. Little by little, he started phasing out Achdut HaAvodah officers. There was considerable debate about whether or not he was jeopardizing the nation by removing the best officers. After much criticism, he let some Palmach officers stay, and they remained generals for many years.

The United States was the first country to recognize Israel and the Soviet Union was the second. The Russians felt Israel was helping break the British Empire apart and wanted to support it. Some people also felt that Russia was sympathetic to Israel because of Israel's strong labor movement, by means of which they thought they could gain a foothold in Israel. Regardless of their reasons, both the United States and the USSR recognized Israel quickly.

At the same time that the United States recognized Israel, it placed an embargo on all weapon sales to it, hindering the country's ability to defend itself. Russia had already begun to control what later became the Iron Curtain countries, and this helped Israel make a deal with Czechoslovakia's well-developed armament company, Skoda, world famous for the manufacture of quality weapons.

Immediately after the British withdrawal and the subsequent declaration of the State of Israel, well-equipped Arab forces from Jordan, Egypt, Iraq, Lebanon, Saudi Arabia, and Syria attacked from every direction. The Arab armies possessed arms and cannons, as well as combat aircraft and bombers. Israel had none of these and its arsenal was, in fact, pitiful. An Arab siege on the Old City of Jerusalem and its eighty-five thousand Jews was nearly disastrous. The supply line from Tel Aviv was blocked, and the Jews were nearly out of ammunition. The water pipeline from the coast was cut, and water became extremely scarce, as did food. Military priority was given to opening the roads to Jerusalem, especially near Latrun, an important Arab base. Between May 15 and early June, about two thousand homes in the city were destroyed and twelve hundred civilians killed. The Jews secretly enlarged a path, known as the Burma Road, to break the siege and bring food, water, and ammunition into Jerusalem. "Finally, by June 9, a primitive roadbed was cut through the Jerusalem mountains. The first trucks, loaded with cans of food and water, ventured out on the pitted makeshift highway. Several hours later they entered Jerusalem, where they were greeted rapturously by the awaiting Jewish population."[2]

On June 11, 1948, the UN Security Council mandated a four-week truce, which the Jews used for rebuilding and training troops, as well as for a reorganization into four separate fronts, in the north, east, center, and south. Ben-Gurion had already disarmed and then reunited the Haganah, Lechi, and Etzel under the banner of the Israeli Defense Force (IDF), but the move was not without challenges. The most difficult and controversial of these was the *Altalena* affair. The *Altalena* was a ship, carrying nine hundred volunteers and a tremendous quantity of arms to Israel, for Etzel. When the ship arrived, Ben-Gurion and Menachem Begin, the head of Etzel, came to an impasse. Begin would give no more than 80 percent of the weapons to the IDF. Ben-Gurion, insisting on Etzel submersion into the IDF, ordered an attack on the ship. In front of the Tel Aviv shoreline, a bloody clash erupted, during which at least sixteen died and ten were wounded; the ship caught fire after being hit and sank, taking all of the cargo with it.

A second truce followed on the heels of the first one. But in mid-September, while it was still in place, a group from Lechi murdered the UN mediator who was pushing for a new partition plan with less land for Jews, along with his assistant. The Israeli government arrested hundreds of former Lechi members, dissolved the former Etzel troops in the IDF, and on October 17, ordered that the Palmach disband.[3]

Enlisting with the IDF, the Dror group engaged in various battles in the War of Independence near Jerusalem, including Ma'ale HaHamisha, Abu-Ghosh (near what is now Beit Shemesh), and Beit Natif (which became kibbutz Nativ HaLamed Hay).

"The war began," recalled Behira Zakay, "and we who wanted to join [the army] started arguing." Some wanted to finish school while others were eager to join the army. After two older members of the Dror group, Kalman Offir and Eliezer [Leon] Rubinstein, volunteered, the rest of the young people enlisted together, even though most of them were younger than the required age of seventeen, Zakay said. At the time, she was anxious to join the war effort, but today she has mixed feelings about the recruitment of the Dror group. As orphans, they were not supposed to be allowed to fight, but the IDF recruited them anyway. Trosman left the kibbutz in which he had been living, Gan-Shmuel, and rejoined the group in May 1948 "when they decided to stop studying and to join the war effort," as he put it.

In a *Yagur Journal* article dated July 18, 1948, Aharon described the group's decision to fight. "Once the war broke out in the country," he wrote, "a visible change in our group's society and lives occurred. The first place this was felt was in our studies. Our thoughts were mainly directed to the military situation.... And as a result, some of the *chaverim* (members) stopped attending classes, and the desire to join the defense forces arose. A big argument started among us regarding enlisting immediately."

Aliyat HaNo'ar, the administration responsible for youth immigrants in Israel, told the Yagur group to continue studying for another six months. Some in the group agreed and felt that they were not ready to do otherwise, but "the pressure of those who wanted to enlist became stronger and stronger until in the end we found a compromise — we continued to study, but at the same time, we prepared ourselves seriously and vigorously for the day when we would depart," Aharon wrote.

After the disastrous first ten days of the War of Independence, when the poorly equipped new nation lost control of numerous settlements and entire regions, new recruits were desperately needed. Beni Marshak visited Yagur to enlist the Dror group in the IDF and found its members open to persuasion. Most of them were sent to a training camp in Kfar Yonah and became part of the Fourth Battalion of the Harel Brigade in Jerusalem; Aharon and several others stayed behind, forming a link between the group and the kibbutz, which sent packages of food and supplies. The first time that company commander Motti Efrati saw the Dror fighters, he tried to send them back because they were so young. As the group waited in a military bus, he and the brigade commander argued for hours until he was finally convinced to accept them because of Israel's desperate need for soldiers. Efrati's nickname henceforth was "Kindergarten Teacher."

Leon Rubinstein recalled, "As soon as they declared the State of Israel in 1948, the Egyptians, Saudis, and Jordanians attacked. The Jews started an army, and there was a hoopla and a need to defend the land. I was eighteen years old and joined the Palmach, with which we had already trained. Most of us were in the Seventh Division."

Ezra Sherman remembered, "After two years at the kibbutz, the War of Independence started. On May 15, 1948, after Israel was declared an independent state, there was a call for everyone eighteen and over to mobilize and enter the army. The real fighting had started back in November 1947 after the UN declaration, however. The Arabs had been attacking buses and villages, and we had trained as members of the Palmach. They took us to Tel Aviv to officially register, but most of us were sixteen or seventeen, and they didn't want to register us. We sat there for hours until the brigade commander, Beni Marshak, came over and started screaming. Finally, at four or five pm, they registered us."

Rubinstein said, "Kalman Offir and I, and a sabra from Yagur were the first to join the army. Kalman was the tallest and strongest of the group and was sent to officers' training school for paratroopers. He later became a high officer."

"Most of us were in the army together for nine or ten months, but a few went to different units," added Sherman. "I was in the Palmach's Harel Brigade under Joseph Tabenkin; this was part of the Storm Battalion, Battalion 4, which was under David Elazar or Dado. We sat up in the mountains, fighting Jordanians and local Arabs, to help open and secure the road to Jerusalem. Then we fought in the Negev and Sinai. We only had light weapons and three tanks constantly in need of repair, although at some point we got a few old French tanks left over from World War I."

"We didn't even have uniforms, just colorful patches sewn onto our clothes," said Rubinstein. "We were trying to cut off Egypt's army. General Nasser was brazen enough to come into Israel and got all the way to the outskirts of Tel Aviv. I was one of the first to go into Eilat, which is on the Red Sea on the Jordanian border, under the command of General Moshe Dayan. It took us two weeks to get there because there was no road, and when we arrived, the town had been abandoned. Today it is a beautiful city with luxury hotels. I stayed in the Israeli army for two years."

The group participated in Operation Hiram, under General Moshe Carmel, recapturing the Galilee and an area of Lebanon that was later returned during peace negotiations. It was also active in Operations Yoav and Horev in the Negev.

Seeking an approach into the Negev desert, which had been occupied by Egypt, Commander Yigael Yadin studied archaeological guides and discovered the existence of an ancient Roman road, the Ruheiba Trail. The Israelis restored it secretly to avoid discovery by the enemy, removing great quantities of sand and laying wire netting over weak sections. This opened the way from Jerusalem to the northern Negev. Subsequently, several battalions of Israelis under Yigal Allon drove the Egyptian army out and captured the Negev. During this phase, a member of the Dror group from Yagur took the silver pistol that King Farouk's cousin was carrying when he was wounded, and presented it to Elazar (Dado). The brigade then pressed on into the Sinai desert, where they shot down five British Spitfire airplanes. Sherman attested, "I was there. I saw the faces of the British pilots."

Yagur lost eleven people during the War of Independence and the commander of their unit, Motti Efrati, was killed. Kibbutz member Asaf Katz led a Bedouin Arab unit fighting on behalf of the Jews, but was killed by members of the unit during an argument, according to Sherman.

By the time a ceasefire ended the war, Israel had secured the territories allotted to it by the United Nations and more than half of the parcel that the Arabs had previously refused (21 percent more than in the original partition). Jordanian forces occupied the West Bank and Jerusalem, and Egyptian forces occupied the Gaza Strip. The area connecting them was won by Israel.

Israelis immediately began establishing governing institutions based on the existing Zionist institutions, elected the first Knesset, and wrote the nation's first laws. Domestic programs for housing projects, industrial enterprises, health services, educational networks, water systems, education, and a judiciary were organized and started.[4] Meanwhile, about 700,000 Palestinians had abandoned the country, anticipating a quick victory against the Jews, and they now began filtering back in.

Between 1949 and 1954, Arab saboteurs slipped into Israel and engaged in a program of destruction and murder, with ambushes, burning of fields, and bombings of the country's railroads, roads, and water lines. Israel filed complaints with the Mixed Armistice Commission, which was charged with monitoring the situation, but the commission did nothing. Finally, the IDF began to take retaliatory action across the borders.[5]

Israel suffered devastating losses of human life between November 1947 and January 1949. As demobilized soldiers struggled to reenter and build a new society, "statistics...cannot fully convey the pain and the sorrow of this war, by far the most difficult fought by the State of Israel and the only one in which it may have come close to defeat, if not physical extinction."[6]

1. Jehuda Wallach, Carta's Atlas of Palestine: From Zionism to Statehood
2. Howard M. Sachar, A History of Israel from the Rise of Zionism to Our Time, p. 327
3. Martin Van Creveld, The Sword and the Olive: A Critical History of the Israeli Defense Force, p. 89
4. Tom Segev, 1949: The First Israelis
5. Segev, Ibid.
6. Van Creveld, Ibid., p. 99

363

The Beginnings of a Normal Life

The Dror group was steadily preparing to establish a new settlement, and as soon as the war ended and the Palmach disbanded, they returned to Kibbutz Yagur and stepped up their preparations. They were now called Yagur Hachshara.

Usually, different groups merged to create a kibbutz, and the Dror group was no exception. "The main things that occupied us were unification of the group itself and unification with another group that would fit us," Aharon wrote in the July 18, 1948 *Yagur Journal* article. "The kibbutz secretary advised us to unite with Hevrat HaNo'ar of Kibbutz Beit Oren. A delegation went to Beit Oren to get to know the people and to study the situation. When they came back and gave a report, an argument erupted between those who were in favor of the unification and those who were against it."

Overcoming the cultural gaps between those from Yagur and those from Kibbutz Beit Oren was not easy. While the Yagur members were Holocaust survivors from Eastern Europe, their Beit Oren neighbors had fled Syria. "We were standing in front of our first crucial challenge," Aharon wrote, "but finally, what was in common overcame what separated us. We had one ideal, one goal, and one wish, and it overcame the differences of habits and character."

In November 1949, the Yagur and Beit Oren groups, joined by another group of young people from Kibbutz Ginnosar on the shore of Lake Kinneret, founded Mash'abei Sadeh. It was a barren place, deep in the Negev desert, with no houses or out-buildings and no reliable water supply. The week before they moved to the Negev, Aharon's roommate, Shimshon Klakstein, died.

Ezra Sherman said, "I went back to Yagur for a couple of months. By the end of 1949 or beginning of 1950, almost everyone in our group got together with another group and went to create Mash'abei Sadeh. We got there in winter, and we had nothing. At first, we lived in tents, then we put up a couple of shacks and built a dining room and kitchen. There was food rationing all over Israel, although there was no shortage of basic foods."

But they survived, with few conveniences — water and supplies had to be carted in from Be'er Sheva, an hour away — and minimal food, not even bread or salt. They immediately began a labor-intensive effort to cultivate soybeans and wheat on a 1,250-acre parcel of land forty miles north of the kibbutz. The land had formerly belonged to Arabs, according to Sherman, and had been allocated to the kibbutz after the war. Four to five people would travel to the farmland together and stay in an old house while they worked the land for a week or two, then return to the kibbutz. Sherman left after one year because he wanted to make his own decisions; he did not like the fact that the group made every decision together.

Leon Rubinstein said, "One time, when all they had was a few tents, Aharon wanted to see the kibbutz and Shimshon's place of burial. I was still in the military and was part of a military motor pool, so I had access to transportation — an open jeep. We drove there, looked at the grave, and spent about an hour at the kibbutz, then drove through the cold desert all night to my encampment — I had to be at work in the morning. Aharon got a ride from my encampment in a military truck, but I worried about the cold and chased after the truck and brought some blankets for him. Then I took a shortcut back to my tent and got stuck in the mud — that is how it was in Israel back then."

The new nation struggled to absorb the huge numbers of arriving refugees. A processing camp, *Sha'ar HaAliyah* (Gate of Immigration), was established on the site of a former British army camp. It was expected that refugees would stay there for three to seven days before starting their new lives in Israel. Immediately, however, the camp was overwhelmed. The stay of the refugees at Sha'ar HaAliyah stretched into weeks and months. Then they were taken to intermediate ma'abarot camps throughout Israel, sometimes for months.

Trying to build housing and infrastructure for the refugees,
Israel established new settlements at a rate of one every three
days, or one hundred a year, at high financial and social costs; during the Tzena between 1950 and 1952, the economy was severely
challenged by recession and an austerity period with strict rationing was instituted. At Yagur, members said, they ate "half an egg"
at a time. "People used to say the chickens had a razor blade in
their bottoms," Arie Medlinger said. Poultry was only available on
Passover, and dairy products, fruits, and vegetables were in meager supply.

Rubinstein said, "After I left the army, I moved to Haifa and
made plans to immigrate to the United States. I shared a tiny room,
about five feet by seven feet, with another young man. There was
no running water, no facilities, no telephone. He worked at night
and I worked during the day, so he slept in the bed during the day
and I slept in it at night. There was very little work in Israel then.
The company I worked for would give me an IOU slip because they
didn't have money to pay their workers. When I left Israel, I was
owed six months' pay."

Ideological questions wracked the country and in 1951, the
HaKibbutz HaMeuchad movement suffered a split, known as
HaPilug, between pro-Soviet and pro-Western foreign policy supporters, with Yagur favoring the West. "Only devoted Mapainiks
left the kibbutz," Medlinger commented, "and I think they regret it
until today." Like the *Altalena* affair, HaPilug is considered a painful
moment in Israeli history, although the factions reunited later.

Refugees continued to arrive, not only from Europe but from
Moslem countries in the Middle East. "Between 1948 and 1957, as
a consequence of government pressure, economic strangulation,
and physical pogroms, some 467,000 Jews would be compelled to
flee their ancestral homes in Moslem lands. The largest number of
them would find asylum in Israel.... Within a period of five years,
the Holocaust nearly doubled the Sephardi and Oriental component of world Jewry, and increased it to 45 percent of the reservoir

of likely immigrants to Israel."[1]

The Yemenites arrived first, with assistance from Israel in the form of Operation Magic Carpet. They were followed in quick succession by massive airlifts and other operations carrying Jews from Iraq (Operation Ali Baba), Libya, Syria, Egypt, Turkey, and Iran. "In the eighteen months following the Declaration of Independence, 340,000 Jews arrived in Israel.... During the Mandate, the rate of immigration had averaged 18,000 a year. During the first three years of statehood, the average reached 18,000 a month.... Between May 15, 1948, and June 30, 1953, the Jewish population of the country doubled."[2]

Immediately, of course, there was a housing and employment crisis. New refugees were provided with housing in abandoned Arab neighborhoods and in the few remaining British barracks, most of which had been systematically destroyed by the British before their departure, but this filled up quickly. Sha'ar HaAliyah was turned into a tent city and other tent cities were erected. Newcomers had no work, and there was little social continuity. Dispersing and integrating them into the country and finding work for them were huge challenges; only a small percentage of the new immigrants had professional training. Inflation hit the country hard, and there were severe shortages of staples; in response, the government instituted austerity measures, including the rationing of clothing and food, between 1949 and 1951. Despite the obstacles and the suffering, however, "by the end of its first decade, Israel was feeding itself in the key staples of dairy products, poultry, vegetables, and fruit."[3]

Today, some of the well-established kibbutzim have maintained their size and lifestyle. With about twelve hundred members, Yagur is still one of the largest kibbutzim in Israel. Its combination of agriculture, industry, and members' outside incomes has continued to be effective and has eased its transition into the twenty-first century. Yagur admits a new group of immigrants every four years, including many children who come to Israel without their families. Some children from troubled homes are also placed there. Two factories operate in Yagur: Lagin makes metal cans and Tuboplast, plastic tubes. One of the most famous nurseries in Israel is in Yagur, and its amusement park serves the entire area.

Mash'abei Sadeh, too, has maintained itself. Today, visitors say it looks like an oasis, with its tall palm trees visible from afar. Haklay, Peleg, and Zakay raised their children in this lively kibbutz.

1. Howard Sachar, A History of Israel from the Rise of Zionism to Our Time, p. 397
2. Sachar, Ibid., p. 395
3. Sachar, Ibid., pp. 404-409

Bibliography and Sources

Interviews

Golub, Aharon, interviews by Kitty Axelson-Berry, Bethpage, New York, June 2002, August 2002, January 2003

Edelman, Boris, telephone interviews by Kitty Axelson-Berry, Hallandale, Florida, January, February 2003

Furshpan, Moshe, telephone interview by Ben Golub, July 23, 2003

Gurfinkel, Itzak, telephone interview by Kitty Axelson-Berry, Ramat Gan, Israel, February 2003

Haklay, Hannah, interview by Hadas Ragolsky, Mash'abei Sadeh, Israel, August 2002

Katz, Arje (Leibel), telephone interview by Kitty Axelson-Berry, Brooklyn, New York, January 2003

Kleinman, Pesach, interview by Hadas Ragolsky, Ramat Gan, Israel, August 2002

Medlinger, Arie, interview by Hadas Ragolsky, Kibbutz Yagur, Israel, August 2002

Peleg, Shmuel, interview by Hadas Ragolsky, Mash'abei Sadeh, Israel, August 2002

Rubinstein, Leon, telephone interview by Kitty Axelson-Berry, Falmouth, Massachusetts, January 2003

Shafir, Shmuel, telephone interview by Kitty Axelson-Berry, Herzliya, Israel, February 2003

Shapira, Abraham, interview by Hadas Ragolsky, Israel, August 2002

Sherman, Ezra, telephone interviews by Kitty Axelson-Berry, Laurie Salame, Florida, January 2003

Trosman, Moshe, interview by Hadas Ragolsky, Ramat Gan, Israel,
    August 2002
Tuchman, Yona, interview by Hadas Ragolsky, Ramat Gan, Israel,
    August 2002
Zakay, Behira, interview by Hadas Ragolsky, Mash'abei Sadeh,
    Israel, August 2002

Maps
Ludvipol, originally by Baruch Guttman in Ludvipol's *Yizkor Book*,
    revised by Aharon Golub
Israel, redrawn from *National Geographic Atlas of the World*,
    Seventh Edition, Washington, D.C., 1999
Eastern Europe, redrawn from *National Geographic Atlas of the
    World*, Seventh Edition, Washington, D.C., 1999
Sosnovoye, Rivne, Ukraine. ©2003 Microsoft Corporaton.
    2000 Navigation Technologies. 2000 and Data B.V. 2000
    Compusearch
Micromarketing Data and System Ltd. 2000 Geographic Data
    Technology, Inc. (www.expedia.com)

Books
Aner, Zeev, editor. *Kibbutzim Stories*. Ministry of Defense
    Publishing House, 1998
Ascherson, Neal. *The Struggles for Poland*. New York: Random
    House, 1987
Butwin, Julius and Frances, translators, *Favorite Tales of Sholom
    Aleichem*, New York: Avenel Books, 1983
Collins, Larry, and Dominique Lapierre. *O Jerusalem!* New York:
    Simon and Schuster, 1972
Dinnerstein, Leonard. *America and the Survivors of the Holocaust*.
    New York: Columbia University Press, 1982
Encyclopedia Judaica. Cecil Roth, editor. Jerusalem: Keter
    Publishing House, Jerusalem Ltd., 1972
Gilbert, Martin. *The Holocaust: A History of the Jews of Europe*

During the Second World War. New York: Holt, Rinehart and Winston, 1985

Gilbert, Martin. *The Routledge Atlas of the Arab-Israeli Conflict*. New York: Routledge, Taylor and Francis Group, 2002

Gutman, Israel and Isreal Guttnamm, editors, *Encyclopedia of the Holocaust*, MacMillan Library Reference, 1995

Herzog, Chaim. *The Arab-Israel Wars: War and Peace in the Middle East, From the War of Independence Through Lebanon*. New York: Vintage Books (Random House), 1984

Hoffman, Eva. *Shtetl: The Life and Death of a Small Town and the World of Polish Jews*. New York: Mariner Books, Houghton Mifflin Company, 1997

Katz, Rabbi Arje, *Memorial Book for the Men, Women and Children from Ludvipol and Volynia*, Brooklyn, NY, translated from Hebrew by Aharon Golub), unpublished manuscript

Klagsbrun, Francine. *Jewish Days: A Book of Jewish Life and Culture Around the Year*. New York: Farrar Straus Giroux, 1996

Kumove, Shirley. *More Words, More Arrows: A Further Collection of Yiddish Folk Sayings*. Detroit: Wayne State University Press, 1999

Laqueur, Walter, editor. *The Israel–Arab Reader: A Documentary History of the Middle East Conflict*. New York: Bantam Books with B.L. Mazel, Inc., 1970.

Luke, H. C. and E. Keith-Roach. *The Handbook of Palestine and Transjordan*. Jerusalem, London: Macmillan, 1930

Prus, Boleslaw. *The Doll*

Rosensaft, Menachem Z., editor. *Life Reborn: Jewish Displaced Persons 1945–1951 (Conference Proceedings, Washington, D. C. January 14–17, 2000)*, a project of the United States Holocaust Memorial Museum and its Second Generation Advisory Group in association with the American Jewish Joint Distribution Committee, 2001

Rostein, Leo. *The Joys of Yiddish*. New York: Pocket Books, 1968

Rowley, Gwyn. *Israel into Palestine*. London: Mansell Publishing, 1984

Sachar, Howard M. *A History of Israel from the Rise of Zionism to Our Time*. New York: Alfred A. Knopf, 2002

Samuel, Maurice, translator. *Selected Poems, Chaim Nachman Bialik*, New York: The New Palestine, 1926

Segev, Tom. *1949: The First Israelis*. New York: The Free Press, Macmillan Inc., 1986

Spector, Shmuel. *The Holocaust of Volhynian Jews 1941–1944*. Jerusalem: Yad Vashem and the Federation of Volhynian Jews, 1990

Telushkin, Rabbi Joseph. *Jewish Literacy*. New York: William Morrow and Co., 2001

Van Creveld, Martin. *The Sword and the Olive: A Critical History of the Israeli Defense Force*. New York: Perseus Books, 1998

Wallach, Jehuda. *Carta's Atlas of Palestine: From Zionism to Statehood*. Jerusalem: Carta, Beit-Hadar, 1974

Wallach, Judah. *Not on a Silver Platter: A History of Israel 1900–2000*. Jerusalem: Carta, 2000

Weiner, Miriam. *Jewish Roots in Poland: Pages from the Past and Archival Inventories,* New York: YIVO Institute for Jewish Research, and the Miriam Weiner Routes to Roots Foundation, Inc., Secaucus, New Jersey, Jewish Genealogy Series, Secaucus, New Jersey, 1997

Weiner, Miriam. *Jewish Roots in Ukraine and Moldova: Pages from the Past and Archival Inventories.* New York: YIVO Institute for Jewish Research and the Miriam Weiner Routes to Roots Foundation, Inc., Secaucus, New Jersey, Jewish Genealogy Series, Secaucus, New Jersey, 1999

Yagur Book: Forty Years for Aliyah to the Soil. Kibbutz Yagur: HaKibbutz HaMeuchad, 1965

Yahil, Leni. *The Holocaust: The Fate of European Jewry*, translated from the Hebrew by Ina Friedman and Haya Galai. Oxford: Oxford University Press, 1990

Yizkor Book for Ludvipol Community/Selishtch Gadol, Nachum Ayalon, editor. Ludvipol Veterans Association, 1965

Zamoyski, Adam. *The Polish Way: A Thousand-Year History of the Poles and Their Culture.* New York: Franklin Watts, 1988

Articles
Abramowitz, Leah. "World War II refugees borrowed identities from Jewish Brigade." Jerusalem Post Service, Jewish Bulletin News, August 30, year unknown

Juchniewicz, Mieczyslaw. "Polacy w radzieckim ruchu podziemnym I partyzantskim 1941–1944." Publication unknown. Warsaw, 1973

Kovalchik, Pavlo. "Antisemitska diyalnist ukrainskikh nationalistiv." Publication unknown. Kiev, 1965

Samchuk, Ulas. "We Shall Conquer the Cities." Volhyn, September 1, 1941

Archives
American Joint Distribution Committee, 711 Third Avenue, New York City

Beth Hatefutsoth, Nahum Goldmann Museum of the Jewish Diaspora, Tel Aviv. University Campus, Klausner Street, Ramat Aviv, Tel Aviv

Jewish Historical Institute, Warsaw, Poland

Zentrale Stelle, Landesjustizverwaltungen, 714 Ludwigsburg, Germany

Simon Wiesenthal Center, Israel Office, 1 Mendele Street, Jerusalem

United States Holocaust Memorial Museum, 100 Raoul Wallenberg Place, SW, Washington, D.C.

Yad Vashem, The Martyrs' and Heroes' Remembrance Authority, Jerusalem

Websites
www.army.mil (U.S. Army)
www.es-conseil.fr/pramona (website of Philippe Ramona)

www.crif-marseilleprovence.com/histoire/juifsprovence.htm

http://fcit.coedu.usf.edu (Florida Center for Instructional Technology, College of Education, University of South Florida)

www.geocities.com/krszywonos (website of S. Ben-Arie, *A Tribute to Israeli Leaders*)

www.giga.co.il/hatavor/main.htm (Regional Council of Lower Galilee, website of HaKafat HaTavor, Israel's first running race)

www.historylearningsite.co.uk (History Learning Site of U.K. Association of Teachers' Websites)

www.history-of-the-holocaust.org/LIBARC/ARCHIVE/Chapters/Terror

www.jajz-ed.org.il/indexstam.html or www.jewishvirtuallibrary.org (Jewish Agency for Israel, Department for Jewish Zionist Education, Pedagogic Center)

www.jewishgen.org (website of Jewish Genealogy)

www.jewishsf.com (Jewish Bulletin of Northern California Online)

www.mapquest.com (MapQuest.com, Inc.)

www.mfa.gov.il (Israel Ministry of Foreign Affairs)

http://motlc.wiesenthal.org (Museum of Tolerance Online Multimedia Learning Center, Simon Wiesenthal Center)

www.pbs.org (Public Broadcasting Service)

www.press.uillinois.edu (University of Illinois Press)

www.ushmm.org (United States Holocaust Memorial Museum)

www.us-israel.org (Jewish Virtual Library, formerly JSOURCE, a division of American-Israeli Cooperative Enterprise)

www.yadvashem.org (Yad Vashem, Holocaust Martyrs' and Heroes' Remembrance Authority)

http://207.21.194.249/kvutsatyovel/netscape/history.htm (website of Kvutsat Yovel, current members of the Habonim Dror youth movement)